INVESTIGATING FORMATIVE ASSESSMENT
Teaching, learning and assessment
in the classroom

Harry Torrance and **John Pryor**

OPEN UNIVERSITY PRESS
Maidenhead · Philadelphia

Open University Press
McGraw-Hill House
Shoppenhangers Road
Maidenhead
Berkshire
England
SL6 2QL

email: enquiries@openup.co.uk
world wide web: www.openup.co.uk

and
325 Chestnut Street
Philadelphia, PA 19106, USA

First Published 1998
Reprinted 2002

A catalogue record of this book is available from the British Library

ISBN   0335 19734 5 (pb)   0335 19735 3 (hb)

Library of Congress Cataloging-in-Publication Data
Torrance, Harry.
    Investigating formative assessment: teaching, learning and assessment in the classroom / Harry Torrance and John Pryor.
        p.   cm.
    Includes bibliographical references and index.
    ISBN 0-335-19735-3. - ISBN 0-335-19734-5 (pbk.)

    1. Educational tests and measurements -Great Britain.
2. Educational evaluation – Great Britain. 3. Effective teaching -Great Britain.
4. Interaction analysis in education. 5. Learning. 6. Educational psychology.
I. Pryor, John, 1954-   .   II. Title.
LB3056.G7T67   1998
371.26'0941-dc21   98-7255
                                                        CIP

Typeset by Type Study, Scarborough
Printed in Great Britain by Marston Lindsay Ross International Ltd, Oxford

Contents

Foreword

I am pleased to have been asked to write a foreword for this thoughtful and constructively challenging book. Based on empirical work with classes of 4 to 7-year-olds in English primary schools, it provides an analysis of how classroom assessment occurs within routine teacher–pupil interaction. The lessons of the research have significance for practices of formative assessment with any age group, for the key innovative element of the study is the application of what Torrance and Pryor call a 'micro-sociological' perspective. This significantly broadens the frame of reference and the conceptual tools which are brought to bear on routine classroom events. Thus, beyond the conventional instructional and cognitive purposes of assessment activity, attention is drawn to the ways in which teachers' assessment actions also influence pupil behaviour, and to the ways in which issues of power are embedded and played out through consequential interaction.

In the UK, USA and elsewhere across the globe, a constructivist challenge to conventional testing has been gathering momentum for some years. Classroom-based formative assessment has been seen as a means of getting close to children's thinking and as a way of providing direct support and 'scaffolding' for their development. Formative assessment has thus been directly linked to Vygotskian arguments giving teachers a key role in extending understanding as it develops. However, Torrance and Pryor's application of the micro-sociological perspective generates a number of empirically-based challenges to educationalist assumptions about the unalloyed benefits of such formative assessment. Indeed, beyond a teacher's intention to openly facilitate pupil learning, there are likely to be implications for classroom relationships which may not have been considered. At their most challenging, Torrance and Pryor suggest that the constructivist rationale may break down to reveal a behaviourist or mastery-based reality in which direct reinforcement is better seen as part of a teacher-controlled instructional process. In this regard, it is interesting to note how, in English education during the 1990s, commitment to formative 'teacher assessment' has largely been transformed into acceptance of new national requirements for 'Teacher Assessment'. In so doing, teacher concern to engage with the emergent understanding of pupils has been colonized by government agencies requiring 'consistent judgements' to be made about the National Curriculum 'levels' which pupils have reached. Such judgements are reflected in reports to parents and, increasingly, in the 'setting' of pupils for differentiated teaching programmes. Clearly there are also macro-sociological issues at play here.

This book clearly demonstrates that assessment is an inevitable element in the tangled web of teacher–pupil interaction and relationships. Further, given the particular classroom roles of teachers and pupils, the processes by which teachers form judgements and respond to pupil performance cannot be separated from issues of power. However, the analysis is fundamentally supportive of teachers, recognizing the practical difficulties of their work and realistically facing the challenges which develop between aspiration and application. This process occurs reflexively, and any critique is applied as much to educationalist advocates of formative assessment as a self-evident benefit to learning as to teachers. At the culmination of the book a 'conceptual framework' on convergent and divergent forms of formative assessment is offered, in which practical and theoretical implications are made explicit. This should be a useful analytic tool in clarifying assessment issues as they emerge in classroom practice and in the development of professional judgement and reflection.

A significant characteristic of this book is that it is positioned at the interface of psychology and sociology. Whilst there are benefits from disciplinary specialization, there are also weaknesses, and one of these is to undermine claims to holistic validity. Consequential problems may then arise in convincing research 'users' of the relevance of the work. A core strength of the present book is that it takes psychological, pedagogic and sociological insights and considers them together. More specifically, the analysis draws on sociological studies of classroom interaction and power relations, and on psychological work on learning, motivation and attribution. Stepping across such disciplinary boundaries may be academically risky but is soundly justified, if it yields a more valid analysis which practitioners can understand and apply.

This report stands as an example of high quality research. It measures its claims carefully and maintains awareness of both theory and practice in an exemplary way. It combines academic rigour with the humility which is appropriate for most forms of social science. Published at a time when educational research in the UK faces substantial attack and critique, it is good to have such work in the public domain.

Andrew Pollard, University of Bristol

Acknowledgements

The research on which this book is based was funded by the Economic and Social Research Council (Grant No. R000234668).

We are grateful for the agreement of editors and publishers to use extracts of the following previously published articles deriving from the research: parts of Chapters 2 and 3 first appeared as 'Investigating Teacher Assessment in Infant Classrooms: methodological problems and emerging issues', *Assessment in Education*, 2(3): 305–20 (Carfax Publishing); parts of Chapter 6 first appeared as 'Teacher-pupil interaction in formative assessment: assessing the work or protecting the child? *The Curriculum Journal*, 7(2): 205–26 (Routledge and The Curriculum Association) and as 'Formative assessment in the classroom: where psychological theory meets social practice', *Social Psychology of Education*, 2: 1–25, 1998 (with kind permission from Kluwer Academic Publishers).

We would like to acknowledge the advice of Barry Cooper, whose perceptive comments at various times during the project have helped us to clarify a number of issues, and who commented on drafts of some of the chapters. Thanks also to Andrew Pollard for agreeing to write the foreword, Maggie MacLure for suggesting some helpful references and to Shona Mullen for her patient support in getting the book from initial idea to published product. We should also like to thank the transcribers who have worked with us: Julia Martin-Woodbridge, Anahì Mincioni, Sarah Higginson, Hayley Kirby, Penny Searles, Margaret Ralph, Pat Bone and Beryl Clough. They produced excellent first drafts of often very taxing audio and video recordings from which we then created the transcripts used in this book. We are also grateful to David and his teacher for use of the cartoon on the front cover.

Above all we must thank the teachers and the children who have not only allowed us to observe them at work but have also contributed a great deal of time to interviews and discussions and always made us feel very welcome in their classrooms.

List of abbreviations

AT	attainment target: part of the nomenclature of the National Curriculum; attainment targets can be broadly defined as curriculum goals, statements of attainment (SoA) as objectives.
BERA	British Educational Research Association
GCSE	General Certificate of Secondary Education
HMI(s)	Her Majesty's Inspector(s) of Schools
IRF	Initiation, Response, Follow-up/Feedback
LEA(s)	local education authority(ies)
R	reception class (age 4, pre-Year 1, see below)
RoA	record(s) of achievement
SAT(s)	Standard Assessment Task(s)
SCAA	School Curriculum and Assessment Authority
SEAC	School Examinations and Assessment Council (subsequently known as School Curriculum and Assessment Authority, SCAA, see above, and now known as the Qualifications and Curriculum Authority, QCA).
SEN	special educational needs
TA	Teacher Assessment
TASK	Teacher Assessment at Key Stage 1 Research Project
TGAT	Task Group on Assessment and Testing
Y1, Y2, etc.	Year 1, Year 2 etc. of the National Curriculum (Years R/Y1–Y11; ages 4/5–16)
ZPD	zone of proximal development

1

Introduction

The changing role of assessment

Research in assessment has traditionally been concerned with studies of the validity and reliability of externally designed and administered tests and examinations. This book, by contrast, is based on a research study which investigated classroom assessment and its impact on pupil learning. Reviews of the role and development of assessment have varied in the precise number of purposes identified for assessment, but the range has traditionally revolved around issues of selection, guidance and the prediction of future performance within what has been called a measurement-oriented or psychometric paradigm (cf. Murphy and Torrance 1988; Gipps 1994). More recently attention has focused on three broad purposes – those of the certification of student achievement (with attendant implications for selection); the accountability of schools and the education system as a whole through the publication and comparison of results; and the promotion of learning through the provision of helpful feedback (Black 1993). It is this third purpose – the interrelation of assessment and learning – with which this book is particularly concerned.

The shift in emphasis from selection to certification, accountability and learning, seems to have come about as a result of concerns over educational standards. Thus assessment is being seen not just in terms of the individual life chances of students – whether or not they pass particular tests and examinations, and with what consequences – but also in terms of the education system *as a system*. Policy makers and assessment researchers alike are focusing on the role that assessment can play in monitoring and raising educational standards across the system as a whole. This goal tends to be approached from very different perspectives, however. For policy makers the issue seems to be how to design an assessment system which embodies high standards and monitors performance through testing programmes – i.e. focusing on the *procedures and products* of assessment. For educators and assessment researchers the issue is more to do with how the *processes* of assessment might assist learning in the classroom.

These concerns are being played out in different ways in different contexts. In the United States, for example, much has been made of the way in which new forms of testing could and should embody higher order skills and thus present students with more demanding and 'authentic' tasks (Wiggins 1989). Initially James Popham (1987) argued that educators should recognize that teachers and students alike attend to test preparation because of the consequences that test results carry. Therefore we should design 'measurement-driven instruction' systems to raise educational standards by constructing tests which embody the key objectives which we want students to learn. Much debate ensued about whether or not tests could achieve this, or whether in fact tests *per se* actually contributed to *lowering* educational standards by encouraging teachers and students to focus on too narrow a range of educational objectives (cf. Bracey 1987, Shepard 1991a). However, the idea of developing better assessments, more demanding assessments, to contribute to raising educational standards, has been a very powerful one in the UK as well as in the United States, and indeed in other countries as well (Torrance 1995, 1997). As Resnick and Resnick (1992:59) have put it: 'if we put debates, discussions, essays and problem solving into the testing system, children will spend time practising those activities'.

In the UK such arguments have been manifest in the debate over both the curricular content and the methods of assessment associated with the introduction of the General Certificate of Secondary Education (GCSE) in the mid 1980s, and the implementation of the National Curriculum in the 1990s. Writers of curriculum documents and designers of assessment have attempted to put more demanding tasks of investigation, problem solving, report writing and so forth into the curriculum and, in turn, have had to think of more flexible ways of assessing such activities than traditional paper-and-pencil tests. Thus a key part of the argument surrounding the introduction of new forms of assessment is that higher educational standards require more demanding tasks to be undertaken in schools. In turn, those more demanding tasks must be underpinned by more sophisticated forms of assessment. We need to move beyond paper-and-pencil tests of the recall (memorization) of knowledge, towards more extended and open-ended forms of assessment – assignments, projects and practical activities – in order both validly to assess new curricular goals and to reinforce the pursuit of those goals.

Alongside such thinking, however, sometimes running in parallel, sometimes overlapping, have been discussions which are more concerned with the process of assessment at classroom level and its potential impact on the process of learning. While debates about 'measurement-driven instruction' and its more educationally friendly variant 'authentic assessment' have been essentially concerned with the development of more valid ways to measure more complex educational goals, discussions of 'teacher assessment' or 'formative assessment' have accentuated the teacher role in day-to-day classroom assessment and the positive formative impact which good quality teacher feedback to students can have on student learning. The argument is that teachers are in the best position both to collect good quality data about students over an extended period of time and to make best use of it in their feedback. Thus new methods of assessment can be used to *promote* learning as well as measure the outcomes of learning more validly. Such arguments have probably been most fully articulated in policy contexts in Europe and the UK (cf. Weston 1990; Nisbet 1993). In the USA, by contrast, they have received extended attention from cognitive scientists, who were originally interested in developing more accurate ways of measuring the results of experimental interventions, rather than in classroom assessment as such. Thus psychologists interested in social constructivist and particularly Vygotskian approaches to learning began to investigate ways of measuring the 'zone of proximal development' in order better to structure learning activities for the benefit of students (e.g. Brown and Ferrara 1985). This was done on a very small scale, however, in experimental settings. More recently such work has involved designing interventions for use in ordinary classrooms (Newman *et al.* 1989) and has been drawn on to under-pin theoretical arguments for more flexible and demanding approaches to test design (Brown *et al.* 1992), but overall this work has tended to be addressed to a research audience interested in how learning takes place in social contexts, rather than to a policy audience interested in school reform. We shall review these developments at more length in Chapter 2. For the moment the point to note is that interest in the interrelation of classroom assessment with teaching and learning derives from a number of different research and policy perspectives, and one might be tempted to suggest that while the debate in the USA has perhaps been over-theoretical, in the UK it has been too focused on practice, too little informed by theory.

About this book

This book has been written in an attempt to bridge this gap and bring together various perspectives from the fields of assessment policy development, theories of learning, and the sociology of the classroom. The book derives from our interests in what one might call the 'micro-sociology' of classroom assessment and classroom learning. We are interested in *how* the assessment of young children is carried out in classrooms, and with what possible consequences for their understanding of schooling and the development of their learning in particular subject areas. Theoretically, the book draws on and attempts to integrate insights from three distinct fields of study: first, class-room interaction studies, particularly those focusing on the structure of teacher–pupil linguistic interaction and the way in which pupils understand and respond to teacher questioning; secondly, cognitive science and particularly social constructivist theories of learning, i.e. the way in which knowledge is apprehended and learned in social contexts and through social interaction; thirdly, more straightforwardly psychological studies of motivation and attribution, i.e. the factors to which pupils attribute their success and failure. The book also considers issues of classroom power and pupil empowerment, exploring the ways in which some pupils can exploit assessment 'incidents' to their advantage, seizing the opportunities which teachers provide in ways which other pupils cannot. In some respects our interest in combining social interactionist perspectives on the realization of classroom life with social constructivist perspectives on learning, parallels that of recent work by Andrew

Pollard and colleagues (Pollard with Filer 1996). However, our focus is much more fine grained, with our unit of analysis being the interactive 'assessment event' or 'assessment incident', which might last between 1 minute and 20 minutes, rather than the pupil as case study subject, tracked over a period of years. Nevertheless we would agree with Pollard that such a combination of theoretical insights is long overdue.

Empirically, the research on which the book is based derives from the policy context provided by the introduction of National Curriculum Assessment in the UK. The research was designed to investigate some of the more grandiose claims which were, and indeed still are, being made for the role of 'teacher assessment' in National Assessment at Key Stage 1 of the National Curriculum (ages 4+ to 7). In 1988 the UK government introduced a National Curriculum coupled with a programme of National Assessment designed to measure how much children were learning and how effective schools were in implementing the National Curriculum. National Assessment was to be carried out by a combination of externally designed and marked 'Standard Assessment Tasks' (SATs) and 'Teacher Assessment' (TA), i.e. judgements by teachers of pupils' classwork. Much debate ensued as to whether Teacher Assessment should only be used to produce 'summative' judgements for reporting to third parties in the context of National Assessment results, or whether the opportunity provided by the formal requirement for teachers to assess their pupils could be used to develop the teacher's classroom assessment role so that it might become 'formative', i.e. providing feedback to pupils on their achievements, strengths and weaknesses in order to aid learning. This debate is reviewed in more detail in Chapter 2. Many claims were being made about the efficacy of formative assessment, but with very little discussion of the theories of learning which might underpin different approaches to formative assessment, and with very little empirical evidence of what it actually looked like and whether or not it was effective in practice (see Torrance 1993 and our further discussion in Chapter 2).

It was in order to investigate these issues that Harry Torrance submitted a research proposal to the Economic and Social Research Council. The resulting project – 'Teacher Assessment at Key Stage 1: Accomplishing Assessment in the Classroom' (TASK) – was funded from 1993 to 1996 and provides the empirical data on which this book is based. Harry Torrance directed the project, John Pryor was the Research Fellow. However, the book is not simply, or even largely, a straightforward empirical research report. Rather it explores and develops an argument concerning the 'social construction' of classroom assessment and classroom learning. Our contention is that claims for the positive effects of formative assessment on learning, are both overstated in terms of empirical evidence and undertheorized in terms of how learning actually takes place in social contexts – particularly early years classrooms. Teacher questions and pupil responses are in no sense a straightforward and transparent medium whereby information about pupil progress is transmitted unproblematically to teachers, and back again to pupils. Linguistic interaction in the classroom is much more complex, communicating through its pattern and structure implicit messages beyond the immediate spoken word, and thus realizing in action both the social relationships of schooling and the social construction of knowledge. On the other hand, the assessment tasks that children undertake and the assessment 'conversations' which they have with teachers and with other pupils can provide rich contexts in which learning is 'scaffolded' through focused questioning and spoken articulations of perceptions and emergent understandings. These are the issues which the book explores – initially identifying and describing the complexity of assessment 'incidents' before going on to analyse the problems and possibilities inherent in classroom assessment practices.

As noted above, arguments about the positive role that new forms of assessment could play in promoting learning are not confined to the UK. Extensive debate has ensued in the United States in particular, with respect to the implications for teaching, and especially for assessment, of new understandings about the way in which learning occurs. In many respects the particular policy discussions which have surrounded the introduction of National Curriculum Assessment have been rather parochial, and while they provided the initial setting for the original research study, our intention has been to produce a book which will also contribute to wider debates about the way in which learning can be scaffolded through the *process* of classroom assessment, rather than restricting ourselves to the procedural specificities of a particular policy context. Similarly, although early years (infant) classrooms provided the context for the study, the analysis is equally significant for other age groups.

Research design and methods

Overall, the TASK project sought to:

1 identify and describe how teacher assessment was being interpreted and implemented in infant classrooms (i.e. by teachers of children aged 4+ to 7); and
2 focus on particular assessment 'events' or 'incidents', explore to what extent teachers and pupils shared a common understanding of the nature and purpose of such events, and consider to what extent such events might be said to constitute 'formative' assessment.

A key theoretical interest was to explore the social construction of assessment and learning *in action*, in ordinary classroom settings. In addition, the theoretical conceptualization of assessment and learning as socially situated acts, led to a focus on the interactive 'assessment incident' as the unit of analysis – the interpsychological 'space' or 'moment' wherein learning is collaboratively constructed (cf. Newman *et al.* 1989). Thus data was gathered by a combination of interview (of teachers and pupils) and, particularly, extensive classroom observation, recorded on audio and video tape. Initially the research adopted the approach of multi-site case study (Stenhouse 1982) in order to identify a reasonable range of practice while allowing for fairly detailed investigation in each case. As the research developed, a much more focused programme of observation was mounted in a small number of classrooms. Nine schools have been involved in fieldwork from two different Local Education Authorities (LEAs – i.e. school districts). The interview data presented in this book derive from unstructured tape-recorded interviews with teachers in all schools involved and with advisory staff from both LEAs (Chapter 3). The transcribed observational data derive from over 100 hours of video tape-recordings made in the infant classrooms of a small village primary school, an inner city primary school and two suburban primary schools. Those interested in a more detailed description of, and rationale for, the research methodology and design should refer to the project's final report (Torrance and Pryor 1996).

The focus of the classroom observation and its subsequent analysis was the interaction between teacher and pupil, and sometimes, in small group situations, between pupil and pupil, during which an assessment was being conducted by the teacher and feedback provided. Transcripts of the interaction were produced featuring both the words of the actors and a description of the classroom context and the actors' behaviour (the 'stage directions'). An analytic commentary was then added to the transcription to provide an interpretative account of what was happening, why, and with what possible consequences. Extracts from such transcripts and the associated commentaries are used in the book as the basis for our description and analysis of classroom assessment (pseudonyms are used throughout; a key to the transcript conventions is included in Appendix 1). The transcription and commentary are presented as parallel columns – allowing the reader to follow the action and our interpretation. The left column contains the transcription, along with the 'stage directions' in italics; the column on the right shows the authors' commentary. This technique has the advantage of enabling us to present relatively long extracts from transcripts, which is essential to any fine grained analysis, and yet also to highlight incidents of interest as they occur. We are not claiming complete objectivity for either left or right hand text – both are to a greater or lesser extent our own constructions – but the simultaneous provision of both may facilitate the reader's own understandings of the data, with the gap between the two texts permitting alternative interpretations to ours.

We should also acknowledge that some of the incidents featured may in some respects appear to be unfair to the teachers concerned and, certainly, a 'fair' evaluation of any particular teacher's practice would require a different research design. However, it was not and is not our intention to evaluate, but rather to use the incidents to illuminate key tensions and important opportunities in the assessment process. In order to explore the data further and validate our interpretations we also replayed and discussed the incidents with the teachers concerned, employing the technique of 'stimulated video recall' (Cowan 1994). Data from these interviews is also presented where relevant to our analysis.

The outline of the book

The book therefore identifies the complexity of routine classroom assessment as exemplified initially by teacher questioning strategies and the way in which pupils respond to them; it moves on to explore the way in which classroom assessment can be used to communicate messages about appropriate pupil behaviour as well as cognitive development and academic achievement. We then discuss the impact of different sorts of teacher feedback on learning and motivation; and finally we review the positive possibilities of different approaches to classroom assessment and their implications for the promotion of learning.

Chapter 2 reviews the theoretical background to the research study and to the book in more detail, in particular focusing on the complexities of teacher–pupil interaction in the classroom and the different (in many respects implicit and unarticulated) theories of learning which underpin claims for formative assessment. Chapter 3 reports teachers' understanding of their role in 'teacher assessment' and their perspectives on the relationship between ordinary, routine classroom assessment, teaching and learning. Chapter 4 describes and analyses the complexity of classroom assessment in terms of the structure of teacher–pupil linguistic interaction and the ways in which teachers routinely 'cue' pupils' responses to their questions in order to accomplish the lesson and pursue a particular teaching agenda, rather than eliciting informative responses from individual children. Chapter 5 develops this 'micro-sociological analysis' further with respect to the way in which assessment incidents can be used to control children and communicate implicit messages about appropriate behaviour. However, Chapter 5 also illustrates that power is not exercised unproblematically by teachers and without resistance from pupils. Power can be seen as a resource which is struggled over and which some pupils have more access to, and can make better use of, than others. This theme is taken up in subsequent chapters as we explore the social construction of learning in action. Chapter 6 reviews more specifically psychological theories of motivation and attribution, before analysing data which demonstrates the ways in which teacher feedback can impact on pupil motivation and approaches to learning.

Chapter 7 presents examples of different forms of teacher questioning and reviews the possibilities for promoting learning inherent in assessment incidents which involve a genuine discussion about criteria and strategy rather than a ritualistic cueing of 'right answers'. Chapter 8 develops this positive agenda further by reviewing in detail a 'focus group' assessment incident in which the teacher's observational role, combined with principled, sequenced questioning, provides the pedagogical context in which the group of children themselves begin to 'scaffold' their own learning. They articulate understandings and appropriate each other's words in a dynamic process which both demonstrates their individual comprehension of the task and collaboratively extends it to produce new learning through pursuit of the task. Finally, Chapter 9 reviews the problems and possibilities inherent in classroom assessment and presents a heuristic model of formative assessment which suggests its development should be based on an understanding of its possibilities in context, rather than, as at present, a potentially very mechanistic set of disseminable procedures.

2

Defining and investigating formative assessment

Introduction

Distinctions are now routinely drawn between formative and summative assessment, with definitions of the two usually revolving around differences in both function and timing. Summative assessment is generally considered to be undertaken at the end of a course or programme of study in order to measure and communicate pupil performance for purposes of certification and (latterly) accountability. Formative assessment is generally defined as taking place during a course with the express purpose of improving pupil learning. However, there is still considerable disagreement over the roles of teachers and pupils in this process. Thus the process of formative assessment could be largely teacher controlled, with teachers providing feedback to pupils on how well they have achieved particular objectives at a particular point in time, and what else they might need to do in order to improve. On the other hand, it can be argued that formative assessment should be essentially focused on the pupil experience; that it must inevitably involve pupils reflecting on what they have achieved and how they have achieved it. These possibilities are not mutually exclusive, of course, and we might characterize them as opposite ends of a continuum. Our own view tends very much to the latter end of the continuum – focusing on pupil understanding of and reflection on the process. However, even this might come to be realized in practice as a potentially mechanistic and rather truncated set of procedures and, as this chapter and the remainder of the book intend to demonstrate, the process is much more complex still.

The development of approaches to formative assessment in the UK

Debates about the formative potential of assessment have a long history, but came particularly to the fore in the UK over the course of the 1980s, initially with respect to secondary education, and in tandem with the introduction of the General Certificate of Secondary Education (GCSE) and Records of Achievement (RoA). With GCSE the argument revolved around the possibilities inherent in teacher-assessed coursework, with pupils' own class teachers being in a position to provide feedback on practical activities and drafts of work so that the final product could be improved (Torrance 1986). A parallel development, which in some cases became directly linked to particular examination syllabuses, was that of 'graded assessment'. Here, short modules of coursework, linked to hierarchically organized tests, allowed pupils to progress through a syllabus at their own pace, taking the tests when they were ready (Pennycuick and Murphy 1988). The danger with this, and indeed with coursework more generally, is that teaching and learning can become overly focused on the grade-awarding process and thus become rather too narrow and instrumental. Pupils therefore approach the task of gaining higher grades through incremental improvement on limited and circumscribed tasks, rather than through the development of improved general understanding and capability; in effect jumping through a series of hoops rather than learning much that is useful and/or long-lasting.

Records of Achievement engaged with similar ideas about feedback on progress but additionally brought the pupil role much more to the fore. On the one hand, teacher–pupil dialogue about strengths and weaknesses, and negotiation of targets and outcomes, were encouraged with regard to what one might call the 'academic curriculum'. On the other, pupils were invited to suggest other non-academic 'achievements', accomplished in and out of school, for inclusion in their record, thus broadening what would count as an 'achievement' and thereby giving more credence and recognition to pupils' sense of themselves (Broadfoot et al. 1988; Torrance 1991; Pole 1993).

More recently it is the implementation of the National Curriculum and National Assessment which have crystallized policy debates about the role and purpose of formative assessment, and indeed the balance to be struck, or tensions to be resolved, between formative and summative assessment. Initially the National Curriculum Task Group on Assessment and Testing (TGAT) claimed that a properly designed system of National Assessment could produce both formative and summative assessment data – at the level of the individual pupil and at the level of the school and national system for accountability purposes (TGAT 1988). Subsequently, some commentators have argued that formative procedures and data must be kept separate from summative, precisely because they address quite different purposes: to use the former to supplement the latter would inevitably involve distorting the process of formative assessment (e.g. Harlen et al. 1992). Others have argued the reverse – that two separate sets of procedures would produce an intolerable burden on teachers and that, in any case, in such circumstances the summative would always overshadow the formative because of the demands of accountability. Thus for formative assessment to survive at all it must be developed in tandem with, and linked to, summative assessment (Black 1995; Wiliam and Black 1996).

Our purpose here is not so much to try to settle the argument as to unravel its complexities. One of the problems seems to be the implicit assumption in much of the debate that formative assessment is a 'good thing', but a 'good thing' that might be squeezed out of the system by not being properly recognized and supported. Our own position is that formative assessment is an 'inevitable thing', i.e. *all assessment practices will have an impact on pupil learning*, but whether or not it is a 'good thing', and if it is, how this is actually accomplished in practice, is an empirical question. Thus, although it is helpful to distinguish in principle between formative assessment and routine classroom assessment – with the distinguishing feature being that formative assessment is *intended* to have a specific and positive impact on learning, whereas routine classroom assessment may be as much to do with modifying behaviour as improving understanding – in practice it is very hard to maintain such a distinction. Moreover, even the use of phrases such as 'good thing' or 'inevitable thing' belies the complexity of the processes at issue. Formative assessment is not a 'thing'; rather it is a construct, a name that is given to what should more accurately be characterized as a social interaction between teacher and pupil which is intended to have a positive impact on pupil learning, but may not.

Policy on formative assessment

These problems of lack of agreement over the definition and practical realization of formative assessment derive in part from the policy debate being driven by political concerns for accountability, rather than by educational concerns for learning, and also in part from the fact that no comprehensive overview and analysis of the purposes and practices of formative assessment has previously been attempted. So, with respect to the policy debate, while there was a good deal of practical experience to draw on (GCSE, graded tests, etc. outlined above), there was little in the way of fully explicated theory. It seems to be the case that educationists, charged with the responsibility of producing a workable system of national testing, sought also to incorporate elements of formative assessment within it under the auspices of 'teacher assessment'. Thus the TGAT Report made an explicit link between assessment and learning before going on to outline the way in which the teacher role could be developed within the national system:

> Promoting children's learning is a principal aim of schools. Assessment lies at the heart of this process. It can provide a framework in which educational objectives may be set, and pupils' progress charted and expressed. It can yield a basis for planning the next educational steps in response to children's needs ... it should be an integral part of the educational process, continually providing both 'feedback' and 'feedforward'. It therefore needs to be incorporated systematically into teaching strategies and practices at all levels.
>
> ((TGAT 1988, paras 3–4)

The basic argument of the report was that assessment would provide information on children's strengths and weaknesses, in relation to their progression through the National Curriculum as a whole, which teachers could use in planning what to do next. Additionally the report argued that this formative rationale for National Assessment would be best realized through extensive use of teacher assessment (TA) with externally devised Standard Assessment Tasks (SATs) used sparingly to moderate TA for reporting purposes and ensure some degree of comparability in the system. TGAT also recommended that TA and SATs should involve 'a wide range . . . of modes of presentation, operation and response' (para 48), emphasizing in effect the variety of ways in which teachers routinely make judgements about achievement and the fact that this variety should be preserved and indeed enhanced in any national system.

It is clear that the assumption of the report is that teachers should be in control of the process (i.e. the GCSE/graded test model, rather than the RoA model), and moreover that it is a process which perhaps should more accurately be construed as a set of procedures – conduct assessment, derive information about individual pupils from the assessment, decide what to do next on the basis of what the pupil can/cannot do. Furthermore, as has become apparent with implementation, teacher assessment is by no means synonymous with formative assessment. The need to produce reliable judgements for National Curriculum levels, has greatly influenced developments at school level, resulting in teacher assessment being as much, if not more, to do with summative assessment as with formative assessment (Pollard *et al.* 1994; Gipps *et al.* 1995; see also our data from teacher interviews reviewed in Chapter 3).

Now of course there has been considerable political interference with the developing national system (Black 1994), but the basic argument about the positive educational role of formative assessment has been widely accepted within what we might term 'mainstream' educational circles. Also, official and quasi-official reports aiming to promote the development of teacher assessment have tended to assume that teacher assessment is indeed synonymous with formative assessment, and have taken a very positive and uncritical stance, assuming the veracity of TGAT's claims to be proven and taking for granted the continued integration of teaching and assessment. Thus HMI's reports on National Assessment have laid particular emphasis on teachers conducting assessment in the context of ongoing classroom interaction:

> Good assessment practice involved a carefully balanced combination of . . . observation, questioning, discussion and marking . . . for example practical work gave the opportunity for questioning and discussion . . . perceptive questioning helped children to learn and their responses provided evidence of the depth and quality of that learning.
>
> (HMI 1991:13)

Similarly the report by Alexander *et al.* on primary teaching methods suggests that 'Teachers should . . . create . . . the time and opportunity for assessment and diagnosis to take place, using both observation and interaction . . . [and] combine assessment of work completed with assessment of work in progress so as to understand the pupil's thinking as it happens' (Alexander *et al.* 1992: 39).

Theories of formative assessment

These are highly ambitious claims and prescriptions which raise important questions about their theoretical justification and empirical realization, but they have nevertheless been largely endorsed by assessment theorists. Such discussion as there has been about the impact of assessment on learning, and the specific potential of formative assessment, has tended to assume or even explicitly prescribe this level of teacher control and direct one-to-one involvement with individual pupils. Thus for example the British Educational Research Association (BERA) Policy Task Group on Assessment defines formative assessment in terms of 'monitoring learning and informing teaching decisions on a day-to-day basis' (Harlen *et al.* 1992:219). Tunstall and Gipps (1996a:389) suggest that:

> Formative assessment . . . means teachers using their judgements of children's knowledge or understanding to feedback into the teaching process and to determine for individual children whether to re-explain the task/concept, to give further practice on it, or move on to the next stage.

Black (1993, 1995) takes a very similar view while also suggesting that very little of such activity actually takes place in classrooms, at least within the context of coursework assessment or teacher assessment. Rather, once the teacher/assessor role becomes formalized, the demands of reliable grading quickly outweigh the potential for providing helpful feedback.

Harlen and James (1996) are more specific still, suggesting in their discussion of the potentially positive impact of assessment on learning that they are 'working towards a conception of formative assessment which . . . involves helping teachers use *information* about pupils which they have gathered in the course of their teaching' (p. 1, original emphasis); and 'knowing about pupils' existing ideas and skills, and recognising the point reached in development and the necessary next steps to take, constitutes what we understand to be *formative assessment*' (p. 4, original emphasis). The emphasis on 'using information' clearly places control of the process in the hands of the teacher and suggests a procedure directly akin to that implied by the TGAT report: assess, derive information, plan next steps. Yet for us, this is a process more akin to *curriculum evaluation* than *formative assessment*. It is as if the pupil has no role at all, and indeed as if assessment can be carried out without having an impact on the pupil – the assessment procedure produces results (information) but has no impact on the learning process in and of itself. Harlen and James (1996: 6) even go so far as to assert that 'It is not necessary to be over-concerned with reliability . . . since . . . there is always quick feedback for the teachers and any misjudged intervention can be corrected'. In other words, the pupil 'stands still' until the teacher intervenes again, with a 'misjudged intervention' having no impact on learning whatsoever. Thus despite the rhetoric of facilitating learning, formative assessment is seen as located in the teaching process, and only indirectly concerned with learning.

To be fair, Harlen *et al.*, Black, and Harlen and James all do at various points identify a role for the pupil and assert the importance of the pupil playing an active part in the process, but this is far less articulated than the teacher role and tends again to be construed in terms of the pupil also understanding and acting upon the 'information' produced by the assessment rather than actively engaging with, or being affected by (positively or negatively), the process itself. As Harlen (1996:130) has put it: 'Formative assessment is essentially feedback to the teacher and to the pupil about present understanding and skill development in order to determine the way forward . . . so that the appropriate next steps can be considered.'

Tunstall and Gipps (1996a,b) go further, analysing the variety of feedback that teachers can and do give – descriptive and evaluative, positive and negative – and investigating young children's understanding of this feedback. These are two of the very few papers that move beyond exhortatory rhetoric to begin to investigate the empirical reality of formative assessment. But even Tunstall and Gipps's analysis operates at the level of broad description of 'types' of feedback, self-reports from teachers about what they (think they) do, and interviews with young children (5- to 6-year-olds) about how they perceive teacher feedback (smiley faces put on 'good work' and so forth). The actual interactive process is not directly investigated, and thus exactly what classroom assessment looks like, what formative impact different types of feedback might have, and if so, how, remain unexplicated.

Beyond the UK, and at a more general theoretical level, Crooks's influential review of the literature on classroom assessment also sees the process as one in which the skilled teacher controls the agenda and makes positive use of the opportunities for feedback:

> In order to obtain full benefit from classroom questioning . . . questions should be directed to as many students as possible (to encourage all towards active learning) . . . teachers need to practice phrasing questions in ways that communicate the task clearly . . . the difficulty level should be such that the majority of questions receive satisfactory responses, and the responses to other than simple factual questions tend to be fuller and more appropriate if several seconds are allowed between question and response . . . Feedback should include knowledge of results, but should only make limited use of praise (e.g. praise might be used mainly for correct responses from anxious or less capable students) and very little use of criticism.
>
> (Crooks 1988:454)

However, as Sadler has observed, even good quality teacher feedback isn't necessarily enough. He noted:

> . . . the common but puzzling observation that even when teachers provide students with valid and reliable judgements about the quality of their work, improvement does not necessarily follow. Students often show little or no . . . development despite regular, accurate feedback.
>
> (Sadler 1989:119)

Having recognized this, Sadler goes on to present a very detailed excavation and exposition of the logical implications of formative assessment, putting the communication of standards and strategies for improvement at the heart of the process so that pupils might eventually become self-monitoring:

... for students to be able to improve, they must develop the capacity to monitor the quality of their own work during actual production. This in turn requires that students possess an appreciation of what high quality work is, that they have the evaluative skill necessary for them to compare with some objectivity the quality of what they are producing in relation to the higher standard, and that they develop a store of tactics or moves which can be drawn upon to modify their own work.

(Sadler 1989: 119)

This conception of formative assessment affords the active engagement of the learner a much more central role in the model, and derives from Sadler's interest in the complexity of learning tasks and outcomes. He argues that most previous work on learning has been 'based on stimulus–response . . . theories . . . While . . . student development is multidimensional rather than sequential, and prerequisite learnings cannot be conceptualised as neatly packaged units of skills or knowledge' (p. 123). However, even here we are focusing on intentions and procedures which seem remote from the pace and complexity of school classrooms.

Formative assessment and theories of learning

Part of the problem seems to be that, in the UK at least, commentators have been so concerned to establish the distinction between formative and summative assessment, that most attention has been paid to the role of the teacher, with respect to valuing routine classroom observation, questioning and the like, rather than to the role of the learner. Formative assessment *per se*, as opposed to formative assessment distinguished from summative assessment, has received relatively little attention. Further than this, there has been very little theoretical discussion of the different models of learning which might underpin different perspectives on the roles of teacher and learner; and very little attention paid to the classroom context in which formative assessment must be realized. This is particularly surprising, since if we are invoking classroom processes as a key element in formative assessment we also need to investigate those processes in order to establish whether or not our assumptions are justified. The assertion is that formative assessment, formative feedback, can and will aid learning. But can it? What theories of learning give us grounds for believing this? And if they seem plausible, what does it look like in practice: what does the interactive process involve and how might it work?

With respect to theories of learning, Sadler's distinction offers some clues here. He identifies two very different perspectives on formative assessment which certainly seem to have had an implicit impact on UK policy and practice, even if they are rarely acknowledged explicitly. Developments in the UK have taken place on a fairly ad hoc and pragmatic basis. However, two underlying perspectives can be discerned. One remains essentially behaviourist in the mastery learning tradition (Bloom 1971 cited in Shepard 1991b; Popham 1978, 1987) – define your objectives and teach to them quite specifically, making sure that teachers and pupils alike know what behaviour is required of them, i.e. what counts as achieving the objective. Such an approach to teaching and learning has been massively influential over many years. The assumption is that complex knowledge can be broken down into its constituent parts, with hierarchies of learning being established and learners encountering and mastering 'simple' facts and concepts before moving on to learn more complicated material. The corollary of such an approach is that 'unit tests' can then be developed to establish what the pupil knows at a particular point in time and provide accurate feedback on this:

> We have ... [analysed] each unit into its constituent elements. These ranged from specific terms or facts to more complex and abstract ideas, such as concepts and principles . . . We have considered these elements as forming a hierarchy of learning tasks . . . we have then constructed brief diagnostic-progress tests to determine which of the unit's tasks the student has or has not mastered and what he or she must do to complete his unit learning.
>
> (Bloom 1971:58, quoted in Shepard 1991b)

This sort of model has an obvious affinity with the graded test approach outlined above and certainly appears to underpin the policy makers' view of the incremental organization of the National Curriculum into ten levels of achievement through which pupils should progress during their period of compulsory schooling (ages 5–16 years). However, this model is also now rather discredited, with cognitive scientists seeing learning as a much more interactive process: pupils do not simply encounter and learn material, moving from the simple to the complex; they actively engage with and attempt to make sense of what they encounter, and incorporate it into their developing schematic understandings (Wertsch 1985; Shepard 1991a; Berlak *et al.* 1992; Gifford and O'Connor 1992).

This alerts us to a second and rather more ambitious model of formative assessment, deriving from the social constructivist perspective in cognitive psychology; ambitious in that it does indeed take account of the role of teacher–pupil interaction in the learning process. Here, teacher–learner interaction goes beyond the communication of test results, teacher judgements of progress and the provision of additional instruction, to include a role for the teacher in assisting the pupil to comprehend and engage with new ideas and problems. The *process* of assessment itself is seen as having an impact on the pupil, as well as the product, the result. The argument, deriving from Vygotsky (1978, 1986), is that it is important to identify not just what pupils have achieved, but what they *might* achieve, what they are now ready to achieve with the help of an adult or in some circumstances a collaborating peer in the 'zone of proximal development' (ZPD) (Vygotsky 1978:86). Thus learning should be 'scaffolded' (Bruner 1985) by children being set appropriate tasks and being provided with appropriate support, with the purpose and focus of assessment being to identify what children could achieve next (cf. also Brown *et al.* 1992). Thus, as Wood (1987:242) has argued in a wider discussion of what an educational as opposed to a psychological approach to assessment might look like, formative assessment should identify: 'the level of task that a child is ready to undertake on the basis of what he can already do, *as long as he receives the best possible help from an adult'* (original emphasis). What we have here, then, is a notion of assessment which looks forward rather than backwards and which envisages teacher–pupil interaction as part of the assessment process itself. As Wood goes on to note, one of the implications of such an approach would be 'that the teacher/tester and pupil *collaborate* actively to produce a best performance' (p. 242; original emphasis).

Such an interpretation of formative assessment takes us into much more dynamic and challenging territory, and has the merit of identifying an integrated role for assessment in the learning process itself. Yet exactly what the differences between a behaviourist and a constructivist approach to formative assessment might look like *in practice* is by no means clear. As noted above, while some examples of Records of Achievement certainly involved more teacher–pupil dialogue than many graded test schemes (see also Torrance (1989, 1991) for further discussion), equally, many different UK assessment developments of the mid to late 1980s shared a very similar basic structure of short-term goals combined with fairly brief feedback to pupils. This is the sort of 'public model' of formative assessment which has been available to teachers becoming newly involved with TA in National Curriculum Assessment, and indeed which seems to have informed many initial discussions of the distinction between formative and summative assessment.

It must also be recognized that while there is an extensive literature on constructivist approaches to teaching and learning, there is relatively little on the relationship between teaching, learning and *assessment*, and what there is tends to derive from very particular studies and settings. Thus while publications such as Gifford and O'Connor (1992) have argued for new approaches to assessment based on constructivist theories of learning, such empirical evidence as exists on constructivist approaches to learning and assessment derives from very small-scale studies, often of non-formal educational settings. For example, Cole (1985), reviewing the concept of the zone of proximal development with respect to the relationship between material context and individual cognition, notes that it makes most explanatory sense in studies of mother–child interaction or relatively informal educational situations such as apprenticeships, since the implied level of adult/tutor support exceeds that which one could reasonably expect to find in ordinary classrooms. Forman and Cazden (1985) likewise note the detailed level of teacher–pupil interaction implicit in the idea of 'scaffolding', and explore peer collaboration as a way of overcoming some of the logistical problems of the traditional classroom. Brown and Ferrara (1985) report on an explicit attempt to develop instruments to measure the zone of proximal development, precisely in order to use assessment formatively, but they were working in experimental settings with individual children. Their concern was to develop a more sensitive and meaningful instrument than the traditional intelligence test.

Newman *et al.*'s (1989) exploration of the social context and indeed the social construction of individual cognition, raises further issues. They draw attention to the differences between what they characterize as research-oriented 'dynamic assessment' (similar to Brown and Ferrara cited above) and the 'assessment while teaching' which teachers routinely engage in and which necessarily, because of the imperatives of classroom life, subordinates assessment to instruction and particularly to the periodic reinforcement of learning irrespective of whether individual pupils require such reinforcement (pp. 80–7). Their work also raises some interesting questions with respect to teachers identifying evidence of *individual* achievement and capacity to achieve more, when their attention is usually geared towards groups of pupils, if not the whole class, and when 'cognitive change is . . . as much a social as an individual process' (p. 76).

Classroom interaction and the language of teaching

This focus on the social context and process of cognition is one to which we will return below. Equally important for a well-founded understanding of the problems and possibilities of classroom assessment, and particularly formative assessment, is how the social context of classroom life is constructed and maintained in itself. Here we can turn to the extensive literature on teacher–pupil interaction in the classroom and the role of language in constructing and realizing the teaching and learning process in action. Claims for formative assessment, particularly as manifested in the practice of teacher assessment advocated by HMI and Alexander *et al.* quoted above, seem to assume that the assessment process is entirely transparent, with teachers being able to elicit clear responses from individual pupils in an unambiguous manner. A good deal of research suggests that this is not the case, especially with respect to younger children. Considerable work has been done investigating how and why young children can make apparently simple 'errors' when being questioned, with the role of context and language being shown to be particularly important in children's perceptions of the task. Thus it is not necessarily the case that they didn't 'know the answer' or could not 'answer the question', but that they thought they were being asked something else, or thought they had to answer the *implicit* question deriving from the context of questioning, rather than the explicit question, and so forth (e.g. Donaldson 1978; Beveridge 1982). Similarly, studies such as that of Cicourel *et al.* (1974) have demonstrated how even apparently straightforward standardized test questions can be interpreted by pupils in different ways and produce misleading results. More recent work by Cooper (1992, 1994) has shown that even when test items attempt to introduce elements of contextualization, scope for misinterpretation remains and in some respects is increased, as pupils struggle to come to terms with new forms of task presentation.

Perhaps more important still, however, with respect to routine classroom assessment, is research evidence demonstrating that teachers' questions and pupils' responses carry meaning about the structure of classroom interaction as well as its content. A number of studies have demonstrated the role that teacher questioning plays in establishing and continually confirming teachers' control of the classroom environment and in constructing and sequencing the very definition of a 'lesson' (Mehan 1979; Edwards and Furlong 1978; Edwards and Westgate 1987); i.e. teachers' questions are as much to do with accomplishing the lesson – making it happen as a piece of social interaction – as they are to do with eliciting particular information from particular pupils.

Teacher–pupil interaction has been shown to incorporate a basic three-part sequence of Initiation (by the teacher), Response (by the pupil) and Feedback/Evaluation (by the teacher) (IRF; Sinclair and Coulthard 1975). This sequence can be extended if the Response is not considered appropriate by the teacher. Thus:

> . . . each initiation act compels a certain type of reply. Once an initiation act has begun, interaction continues until symmetry between initiation and reply acts is established. If the reply called for by the initiation act appears in the very next turn of talk, the result is a three part teacher-student sequence. If the reply called for by the initiation act does not immediately appear, the initiator 'works' (prompts, repeats elicitations, simplifies initiations) until this symmetry is established. As soon as the students provide the reply that completes this symmetry, the teacher marks the completion of the extended sequence in the same way that she would mark the completion of a three part sequence. She positively evaluates the content of these replies with such terms as 'good for you' or 'that's right,' often while repeating the substance of students' replies. The result is an extended sequence of interaction.
>
> (Mehan 1979:62)

However, the appropriateness of the Response is often defined in relation to classroom management – 'keeping the lesson moving along' – rather than a narrowly construed notion of a 'correct' answer. Thus, for example, Mehan (1979) and more recently Edwards and Mercer (1987) have investigated how teachers use pupils' responses, even when they are quite partial or tangential to the matter at hand, as a 'resource' to be appropriated and utilized in the teaching process – with a 'reinterpreted' and 'reconstructed' version of 'what has just been said' or 'what has just happened' being fed back into the teaching and learning encounter. Edwards and Mercer (1987) identified some of the misunderstandings which could occur as pupils struggled to comprehend the questioning process and as both teachers and pupils accumulated and carried forward a mental context of 'common knowledge' to which they had recourse in order to make sense of what was happening but which was not necessarily entirely shared. Given the almost universal endorsement of teacher questioning as a key strategy in formative assessment, it is salutary to note their observation that, in the context of routine teacher–pupil interaction, 'repeated questions [by the teacher] imply wrong answers' (p. 45). Thus, exactly what is being recommended for gathering in-depth 'information' about pupil achievements, could actually interfere with pupils' taken-for-granted assumptions about the teaching process and thus interrupt the learning process. In fact Edwards and Mercer's statement derives from observations of teacher–pupil interaction in the context of an individual lesson rather than, for example, repeated questioning over a sequence of lessons. Nevertheless it is interesting to speculate on whether or not teachers' felt need to explore, confirm and reconfirm that pupils do indeed 'know' or 'understand' something, will be interpreted by pupils as *not* knowing it.

Appropriation for learning

However, appropriateness and the concept of appropriation, can also be seen from the perspective of constructivist psychology, and as such can be seen to take on a more positive role in the learning process, as well as in the process of classroom management. While Piaget saw the individual learner actively constructing his or her learning through interaction with the environment, this was nevertheless construed in terms of accommodation and assimilation. However, a *social* constructivist position, articulated by Vygotsky and particularly his colleague Leont'ev (1981), sees this process in terms of two-way appropriation: '. . . the objects in the child's world have a social history and functions that are not discovered through the child's unaided explorations' (Newman *et al.* 1989:62).

Thus, to take Vygotsky's simple example, a child does not 'discover' what is the usual function of a hammer; rather, he or she is shown it and thus both comes to an understanding of its particular mechanical uses *and, at one and the same time*, appropriates the cultural meanings embedded within its use. Thus artefacts are both material and ideal (Cole 1996) and:

> The child's appropriation of culturally devised 'tools' comes through involvement in culturally organised activities in which the tool plays a role. Some tools are quite different . . . like the mother tongue a child is exposed to . . . but the basic principle remains . . . children . . . cannot and need not reinvent . . . artifacts . . . The child has only to come to an understanding that is adequate for using the culturally elaborated object in the novel life circumstances he encounters . . . [and] . . . The appropriation process is always two-way. The tool may also be transformed, as it is used by a new member of the culture.
>
> (Newman *et al.* 1989:63)

In this respect, then, 'appropriation' takes on a much more positive aspect, since we can construe the teacher 'appropriating' the child's response to a question in terms of *both* the 'mechanical' task of keeping the lesson 'on track' and the cultural task of communicating embedded meanings through re-interpretation and re-presentation. The child is simultaneously engaged in the same process, albeit with different levels of comprehension and motivation:

> . . . the teacher reciprocally applies the process of appropriation in the instructional interactions. In constructing a ZPD for a particular task, the teacher incorporates children's actions into her own system of activity . . . *Just as the children do not have to know the full cultural analysis of a tool to begin using it, the teacher does not have to have a complete analysis of the children's understanding of the situation to start using their actions in the larger system.* The children's actions can function within two different understandings of the significance of the task: the child's and the teacher's . . . The fact that any action can always have more than one analysis [i.e. interpretation] makes cognitive change possible.
>
> (Newman *et al.* 1989:63, original emphasis)

It is in this juxtaposition of insights deriving from social constructivist psychology and classroom interaction studies, that the real theoretical justification for, and potential of, formative assessment can be apprehended. Ultimately an approach which is grounded, however implicitly or intuitively, in a behaviourist perspective, and which seeks to place teacher knowledge of the child at the heart of the process, cannot explain *how* the child will learn from feedback, however detailed; nor indeed would it be logistically feasible to operationalize a very detailed behaviourist feedback model in a busy classroom. A social constructivist perspective can theoretically accommodate both of these problems, though whether it can in practice will be explored in subsequent chapters. The key issue in practice is that both forms of appropriation must be accomplished simultaneously – the teacher must appropriate the child's response in order to realize the social construction of the lesson and in order to scaffold the social construction of cognition. The children must appropriate the cultural tools being presented to them, into their developing understanding of the subject matter at hand and the social processes of schooling. This in turn begs questions about the children's interest and motivation and the impact that assessment interactions might have on them.

Summary

These are the issues which the rest of the book will explore. This chapter has reviewed some of the key claims for formative assessment, particularly with respect to the positive intentions of formative feedback, which in principle distinguish formative assessment from routine classroom assessment. However, such claims rest on unexplicated theories of learning and, in practice, the distinction is likely to break down since routine classroom assessment could have a positive impact on learning without being directly intended to; and, vice-versa, feedback which is intended to be positive may not be perceived as such by pupils. A key theoretical supposition of the book is that classroom assessment is a social construction, accomplished by teachers and pupils through social and pedagogic interaction. Thus neither its processes nor its outcomes are straightforward or transparent, but neither are they without positive possibilities and consequences. The very complexity and indeterminacy of classroom assessment, as a set of social practices, also renders it a site of immense significance with respect to how teachers interact with pupils and how children learn about themselves and about the processes of schooling. These issues will be explored chapter by chapter, as we identify, describe and analyse the problems of accomplishing classroom assessment (Chapters 3–6) before moving on to review some of the more positive possibilities inherent in the classroom incidents which we have observed (Chapters 7–9).

3

Teachers' perceptions of 'teacher assessment'

Introduction

This chapter draws upon data from semi-structured tape-recorded interviews of between 20 and 90 minutes with 40 teachers in nine schools and five advisory staff in two local education authorities. These interviews were carried out in the first phase of the TASK project, during which we were seeking to ascertain teachers' perceptions of what they thought was implied by the term 'teacher assessment' and how they were attempting to put it into practice in their classrooms. We were also interested in their understanding of the relationship between teaching, learning and assessment more generally. Our intention then, and indeed within this chapter, was not only to construct a broad account of the range of practices and attitudes towards teacher assessment that were emerging, but also to use the data to raise further questions about perceptions of formative classroom assessment for more detailed analysis.

While the chapter presents an overview of perceptions and practices, and necessarily therefore condenses nuanced accounts into categories and summary statements, it is important to stress the notion of range. There were differences in perception and attitude between the teachers we worked with (both within and across schools), and indeed individual teachers often expressed contradictory views within the same interview. Some of this complexity – ensconced within the fine grain of classroom interaction and individual assessment 'incidents' – will be presented in subsequent chapters. Our purpose here is to provide the backcloth to that more detailed description and analysis.

This first phase of fieldwork took place at a time of great stress and great flux for schools and teachers. There had been frequent changes to the design and content of the National Curriculum, particularly fundamental revisions to the mathematics and science programmes of study, and yearly changes to the Key Stage 1 testing arrangements and the requirements for reporting of teacher assessments. The Dearing Report (1994), recommending slimming down much of the detail of the National Curriculum and testing arrangements, had just been published when interviewing began, bringing with it the promise of relief but also the threat of yet further change – at least in the short term. As a result, one of the most persistent themes in the interviews was that teachers were pretty much at the end of their tether, and in this respect our data very much accords with that of other surveys and evaluations conducted during the early to mid 1990s (e.g. Pollard *et al.* 1994; Evans *et al.* 1994):

> I think we've all reached saturation point and we just think, well we're not going to do any more. We're just putting our feet in the mud and staying there.
>
> (Reception (R) teacher)

> The changes in the National Curriculum have been destroying, has nearly killed staff because it's taken away your confidence and you're just getting to grips with it and it all changes. The recording system caused chaos . . . and assessment has just been the final straw.
>
> (Year 2 (Y2) teacher)

> They've changed what they want so many times that everybody is I think somewhat confused as to quite what is required and what isn't. I do what is required, most of it is I hope useful, but I'm not always sure that all of it is.
>
> (Special Educational Needs (SEN) teacher)

Thus perceptions and practices were by no means settled, nor indeed particularly well thought through, let alone implemented, though they did vary with school context. While individual teachers differed in their understanding of and commitment to the changes being imposed by government, responses also owed something to current practice and leadership within their schools. So, for example, in one of the two small village primary schools we visited, the teachers seemed particularly demoralized, having little belief in the direction of change and not much more in their own routine practices; confidence in their own abilities had been undermined without anything of substance replacing it. In the other village school, the emphasis was still on implementing the National Curriculum itself – on whole school curriculum planning – rather than on teacher assessment; but still, at least there was an emphasis on something. At a larger suburban primary school and a similar school serving a large council-built estate, we found considerable self-belief and well-articulated accounts of classroom assessment practices, combined with closely-argued criticism of government policy. At two larger primary schools in inner London, individual teachers could describe and justify their practice in some detail, but without it necessarily being part of a coherent and supported school policy. One point which was consistently noticeable, however, was that teachers largely focused on what we might characterize as the 'formalities' of Teacher Assessment (capital 'T', capital 'A'), rather than on the routine practices of classroom assessment, at least until prompted to go beyond the formalities.

In an earlier study of teacher assessment, Gipps *et al.* (1995) reported that teachers found it very difficult to describe their practice spontaneously. Gipps *et al.* therefore developed an activity whereby teachers were asked to summarize their own practice by identifying with descriptive quotations derived from initial interviews. This resulted in the formulation of three 'models' or ideal types of teacher assessment: 'intuitives' who resisted National Assessment, either on the grounds of its conflicting with children's needs or because they had 'tried and tested' methods of teaching and assessment which they were not prepared to alter; 'evidence gatherers' who coped with the demands for National Assessment by collecting evidence of attainment for later analysis and evaluation in such a way that it did not interfere with their teaching; and 'systematic planners' who, as the name implies, planned assessment opportunities as part of the teaching process.

Our experience was rather different. Unsurprisingly, perhaps, in view of the further implementation of the National Curriculum, we found that all the teachers interviewed could make some description of their teacher assessment practices; usually, as noted above, by focusing on the formal requirements of recording and reporting attainment. It seems that in the intervening years, with pressures to produce Teacher Assessment evidence coming from the external moderation and audit of results, coupled with local and national systems of school inspections, the 'public face' of teacher assessment had become very much a formal one, sometimes to the extent that some of our respondents confessed to 'not doing it yet'. An expectation of such excessive formality had been communicated to schools, that teachers with what appeared to be perfectly reasonable practices felt they were hardly doing the job at all, let alone doing it well. It was also apparent that the ideal types identified by Gipps *et al.* had shifted and become less clear cut. While we certainly encountered practices which could have been categorized as 'intuitive', 'evidence gathering' and, especially, 'systematic planning', we also found there was a tendency for such types to overlap, with what would be conflicting attitudes and practices occurring within the same people. Thus, while some might act largely intuitively, they often felt insecure about this and felt the need for guidance from their headteacher and/or the LEA advisory service; others had well worked out plans for conducting assessments in the context of particular topic work, but often felt uneasy about this and yearned for more flexibility and spontaneity in the way they could respond to individual children.

Perceptions of teacher assessment

Overwhelmingly, then, assessment was perceived as a formal activity oriented to producing valid and reliable summative measures of performance, and teacher assessment was assumed to be part of this process. The model which seemed to spring to mind in the first instance was one of external examining, combined with the need for teachers to produce evidence of their judgements which would stand up to scrutiny within what one might call this 'measurement paradigm':

> I can see why they want the formal paper and pencil test because every child will do it. You will mark, it will be right or wrong, there will be a

score at the end. With teacher assessment you still have this open to interpretation

(R/Y1 teacher)

Within this general orientation, however, considerable disparity was then revealed between what teachers perceived as the government's intentions, and their own routine practices. Time and again we were told that, of course, 'teachers have always known how their children are performing in their class', but that this had never been formalized, recorded or reported in the way that was now perceived as necessary:

We've always done that, but now it's got to be put in writing.

(Y2 teacher)

Teachers have always assessed . . . you can't teach unless you assess . . . It's this change between knowing in your mind where a child is and actually committing it to paper.

(Y2 teacher)

On occasions, such a perception was expressed in very disparaging terms, with one teacher referring to parent helpers in the classroom 'baby minding while I stood around with a clipboard'; but nevertheless he felt 'obliged to do it'.

This focus on putting it 'in writing' derived in large part from teachers' perceptions of the purpose of the exercise being that of increased accountability. Teachers were no longer being trusted to work with children over a period of time and offer general observations about progress; detailed evidence, collected in relation to National Curriculum statements of attainment, was now required:

What I understand about teacher assessment is that it is what I was doing before . . . but now I have to relate it to the National Curriculum programmes of study, attainment targets, and for want of a better word, putting the children into categories . . . on this ten-level scale we now have.

(R/Y1 teacher)

Teachers have always assessed and monitored in their own mind . . . now we have to have evidence for it . . . now we've got the planning sheet that shows what we have focused in on . . . I can put a tick by all the children in my class saying that they have done a topic on dinosaurs . . . I can pick out certain attainment targets . . . then I can also tick those at the end of the topic when I've talked to the children and seen what they've produced.

(R/Y1 teacher)

Such views were particularly expressed by headteachers,[1] who often characterized their task as being that of bringing rigour to existing practice:

Good teachers have always been making assessments of children's performance, what we haven't been doing is formalizing it.

(headteacher)

I think in common with all schools there certainly is a lot of teacher assessment going on . . . [but] . . . it's not really being formalised . . . I just don't think at the moment it's rigorous enough in this school.

(headteacher)

These concerns were frequently expressed through a focus on recording and reporting which effectively conflated and confused the process of assessment with that of recording and reporting:

Yes, we've got a policy . . . we debated . . . how we would go about it, how we actually go through the routines of actually recording our assessment etc. so we have National Curriculum grids that we use, we have little forms that we fill in to attach to children's work so that their portfolios contain evidence of achievement and attainment.

(headteacher)

More positively, however, some teachers also acknowledged that a more formal approach to assessment could bring benefits in terms of equity: deliberately making sure that children had the opportunity to display their achievements was recognized as important, rather than making assumptions about what they could or couldn't do:

It's really important that we assess all the children and we don't leave out the ones that need it or the ones who are not good enough so they couldn't possibly do what we're assessing. All of them are assessed. We don't make any assumptions and even if children are absent, then we catch up when they come back to school.

(Y1 teacher)

I always think with children, it's very important to actually find out what they already know and you, you do make assumptions . . . Now we're assuming that that's the average child, will need those sort of things, but, sometimes, children surprise you and they know an awful lot more about what you're doing than, you, you would have given them credit for, so in that case, yes it is like an audit.

(R teacher)

Interestingly enough, this second teacher relates the need for careful review to her own teaching, rather than rendering accounts to others; and indeed with further probing, teachers did begin to talk at more length about their everyday assessment interactions with children, often then contrasting the process, as well as the formal recording and reporting of it, with what they perceived as government policy:

I feel . . . National Curriculum [Assessment] is something completely separate from the type of assessment you're talking about . . . it's very much a tick on the sheet, we've covered that work, and then move on to the next thing. It's not really tied in to how the child is doing in themselves, what their interests are, how they could go forward, or what their particular needs are.

(Y1 teacher)

There is discussion amongst the staff to try and get an idea of what the levels are . . . to get an idea of where they should be for the National Curriculum . . . but . . . you've got your own assessment of the child . . . how's the child getting on in reading for example . . . are they able to read a sentence . . . or is it disjointed, are they having to build up every word, and you can determine from that where the child is with the teacher and how to go forward.

(Y2/3 teacher)

Here, then, we catch a glimpse of routine classroom assessment with a much more diagnostic and formative orientation. We shall return to this below, but what is of interest for the moment is that it is characterized as *not* the sort of teacher assessment with which the government is concerned and, interestingly given the discussion in Chapter 2, is conceptualized in terms of teacher-controlled data gathering about the pupil, rather than as an interactive process which affects the pupil.

Planning

Given that the broad perception of teacher assessment was that of a formal activity, how did this manifest itself in practice? First and foremost teachers talked about planning – whole school and year group planning of the curriculum, coupled with detailed weekly or fortnightly teaching plans into which, in turn, assessment opportunities were planned, or were meant to be planned. Thus the first priority (and in some of the schools we visited this was a continuing priority) was that of organizing teaching programmes, resource availability and so forth, into the stepped progression of the National Curriculum programmes of study. In some subject areas such as English and maths this was largely a task of reorganization and rationalization, but in other subject areas such as science, technology and history, it often meant virtually starting from scratch – with new materials to be acquired and in-service courses to be attended. Certainly, just getting to grips with covering the content of some new programmes of study, and recording that the correct content had indeed been covered, was demanding enough for many of the teachers interviewed, let alone assessing it accurately and with positive formative impact.

Within this overall context of planning, individual teachers sometimes then planned their assessment activities individually, in relation to the particular topic they were teaching and the way in which the topic developed. They addressed the issue of reporting comparable levels of achievement *post hoc*, through in-school moderation of the products of assessment. However, others worked as year groups from the start, planning activities which would yield common assessment opportunities, and even agreeing common worksheets to be used and common questions to be pursued:

In our weekly planning meetings for the year group, we decide how to assess and what to assess, so we decide whether individuals should answer questions and what sort of questions they should be.

(Y1 teacher)

> What we would do in our planning meeting beforehand, we would say
> okay we're doing this learning intention, or these learning intentions this
> week. What are we going to do? How are we going to check that the chil-
> dren know, or have learnt something?
>
> (R teacher)

> We have weekly planning meetings and in those meetings we define the
> area of assessment which had already been defined by the topic anyway
> and we formally decide what we are going to do for that assessment . . . if
> we decide to use questions we have a specific question, if we're going to
> do worksheets then one person makes the worksheet and it's given to
> every teacher.
>
> (Y1 teacher)

On occasions such planning also included thinking about a range of attainment targets across several subject areas such that an extended topic-based
task was used to assess many more than one statement of attainment. Indeed,
one school had a specific policy of designing 'quality tasks' for assessing multiple outcomes:

> We are making postcards which is covering each of the attainment targets
> in design technology at level 3. Two of them at level 2 and also there is a
> measuring one for maths and 2 English ones, so that's all in one task. So
> there is an awful lot there.
>
> (Y1 teacher)

Headteachers and others such as subject coordinators with overall responsibility for reviewing teachers' individual planning expected to see details of
what formal assessment would be accomplished during the week or fortnight
in question when reviewing planning sheets and files. Thus teachers were
accountable formally for the planning of teaching and assessment and increasingly, it seemed, they were accountable informally to each other through joint
planning. In smaller schools, teachers of adjacent classes got together on an ad
hoc basis to compare notes, but in the larger ones where there were parallel
classes, as noted above, joint planning took place on a regular basis. However,
many teachers also acknowledged that much opportunistic assessment still
took place, often with a sort of intermediate status – they were planned in the
sense that the teachers were aware of the criteria for each activity, but not in
the sense that a particular task was designed or time was put aside to
accomplish specific observations:

> I'll set up for example a maths activity then I will be looking for specific
> things within that activity and noting them down, so from the beginning
> I'll have quite a clearly defined criteria for what I'm looking for in each
> child and I'll be noting that down. With every activity I carry out with my
> children I am looking for things and I'm noting them, I'm observing.
>
> (Y1 teacher)

Furthermore some teachers were still very much going their own way, reviewing their teaching and the achievements of pupils retrospectively:

> I'm much more um, do it retrospectively, look at what I've done . . .

you've planned out which attainment targets are meant to be covered so really I suppose that is really what you're assessing as well . . . I'll be sitting in the next week or so with last term's topic books and looking through them and doing my assessment from those. Other than that it's generally what I remember.

(Y2/3 teacher)

Ironically, given the Dearing Report's emphasis on teachers making more use of holistic judgements, this teacher's practice is likely to prove most 'cost effective' in terms of producing summative levels of achievement, even if it does not attend to the impact which different classroom processes might have on learning.

Organizing and conducting assessment

Moving on to the level of classroom organization and the actual conduct of teacher assessment, most assessments seemed to take place in 'focus groups', largely because infant teaching is organized around small group work. This involved new work being introduced to the whole class and then children pursuing particular tasks as individuals and/or collaboratively in small groups (as with the postcard activity cited above). In some schools children would have a list of activities, which they knew they had to get on with, and would move from one to another when each particular task was complete. The perceived necessity to organize formal opportunities for assessment seems to have given an extra 'spin' to this enduring form of classroom organization:

I tend to work very much in groups . . . and have a focus to a group which gives me a good opportunity to talk to each child each day.

(Y1 teacher)

. . . a group of children sitting round a table with a set of solid shapes, wooden shapes . . . me asking children to name the shapes and tell me how many faces the shapes had and how many sides and see if they could do that.

(Y2 teacher)

Teachers also remarked, however, that organizing groups to make sure every child was seen and heard was not necessarily straightforward, indicating some change in their routine taken-for-granted grouping practices:

The first thing is you've got to try and manage the group so everybody gets a turn at what they know, or don't know.

(R teacher)

If you want to assess a group you will choose the children to go into that group . . . if there were three children that were really quiet that you knew never really contributed much to group activity . . . another two that absolutely are going to take over and these three children you won't be able to assess because they aren't going to get a word in . . . it took a while to get used to actually grouping the children how you wanted them.

(R/Y1 teacher)

Thus teachers reported, and indeed we subsequently observed, that they would often sit or stand with a selected group (their 'focus' group for teaching *and* assessment purposes) while the rest of the class got on with other work. The word 'focus' referred both to the group of children under scrutiny, and to the content of the interaction – teachers were focusing on the children and on the particular National Curriculum attainment targets embedded in the task which had been set. The assessment methods they used with these groups primarily involved looking, listening and questioning the children:

Assessment for me is, first of all watching the children observing the children and how they do it, and listening to the children. The way that they talk to each other and the way they talk to adults.

(R teacher)

I'll keep my eyes open . . . I ask questions and then I can see how they are doing.

(Y2 teacher)

However, while the purpose of the exercise was ostensibly to observe and question, often the opportunity arose to intervene and extend or 'scaffold' the group's learning. Thus the task which was provided for the class as a whole might or might not have been the same, across groups, but the pedagogical approach to the focus group seemed to differ from that used with the others. In focus groups the teacher often appeared to be using a Vygotskian guided discovery approach to learning, designing a flexible task with reference to National Curriculum attainment targets, observing and questioning the group as they worked, but also intervening to support learning when appropriate (see Chapter 8 for an extended example). In the non-focus groups learning seemed to be predicated much more on what might be characterized as a Piagetian model, overlain with elements of behaviourism (reinforcement). Work was provided by reference to National Curriculum attainment targets at what the teacher thought was an appropriate level of difficulty for the children's stage of development. However, there was much less positive intervention, and feedback was often of a 'classroom management' variety – offering clarification or further instruction on how to proceed, rather than engaging in extended dialogue about the learning intentions underlying the task. The success (or otherwise) of the pupils in these groups was thus held to depend on the creation of a good learning environment: if tasks, activities and lessons were well designed, it was assumed that the children would learn what was appropriate to their developmental stage, provided motivation was maintained and what the teacher regarded as key learning achievements were appropriately reinforced.

Some teachers also made use of classroom tests for teacher assessment. In most cases these were very quick and routine activities such as short spelling tests. However, in a small number of cases more formal tests were set to gather evidence under more controlled conditions than normal classroom inter-action:

> The work is very difficult to do because, the observations, you're meant to be teaching the class and sitting with a group and writing at the same time . . . which is incredibly difficult to do, most of the time you find you have to sort of watch, hope you remember and write up what you've remem-bered which is not really how you are meant to be doing . . . I will actu-ally give them a test because I think that's about the only way I can, they need to be in absolute silence they get very, very easily disrupted.
>
> (Y1 teacher)

Furthermore, it was increasingly being seen as important to give children experience of test-taking situations because of the formality of the Standard Tests which replaced Standard Assessment Tasks at the end of Year 2. Some-times 'last years SATs'[2] were used in ordinary classroom situations, but some-times they were administered as tests, or used as models for tests which the teachers designed and administered themselves:

> I will test the whole group . . . and I will be doing a formal assessment to see are they a level 2 or not.
>
> (R/Y1 teacher)

> I don't do it for reception but for level 1 I have to start doing that. Because I am aware that in a year's time they are going to be tested at SAT and there are things that I obviously want them to attain.
>
> (R/Y1 teacher)

> A lot of . . . assessment is from observation of their practical work rather than their written work but . . . in about two weeks – before Easter, in about two weeks' time . . . I will actually give them a test.
>
> (Y1 teacher)

Recording assessment and retaining evidence

Having conducted assessments, keeping a detailed record of what transpired was perceived as necessary. Indeed, the recording of assessment data was the topic which received most attention from our interviewees and attracted most adverse criticism – the 'putting it in writing' mentioned earlier. Various meth-ods and formats for active record keeping were mentioned including note-books, sticky label 'post-its', tick lists of attainment targets, dictaphones, and files with a page devoted to each child for unstructured note-making. Additionally, whatever form of record keeping teachers used 'on the hoof', all of the schools maintained either their own detailed National Curriculum grid, listing by subject, attainment target, level and letter all 222 statements of attainment that pertained for Key Stage 1 at that time,[3] or used a grid provided by their LEA or purchased commercially (e.g. 'Modbury Books' – Modbury School 1990). Filling in this composite 'checklist' usually involved marking each statement of attainment as 'covered' (i.e. taught) and then subsequently as 'attained' (i.e. learned, or not as the case may be). This was accomplished by some combination of colour coding, or an oblique line inserted first (covered) followed by the line being crossed (attained). In some cases a further category of 'assimilated' or 'applied' was added (i.e. the pupil had subsequently demonstrated the achievement in other circumstances). Small wonder that such practices were regarded as 'ridiculous', 'a complete pig's ear', and 'a minefield of paperwork'.

Quite why this level of detail was perceived as necessary is not clear. It might be linked to some of the in-service materials which the School Examinations and Assessment Council (SEAC) produced in the early 1990s (e.g. packs A, B, and C, SEAC 1990) which stressed the need to focus on each statement of attainment. For example, one of the packs insisted that:

> There are six steps in using Statements of Attainment (SoA) to make formative assessments:
>
> 1 Identify the SoA your lesson plans will promote.
> 2 Note carefully opportunities for the child to demonstrate achievement.
> 3 Focus on the performance, looking for evidence of achievement.
> 4 Offer the child a chance to discuss what the activity was for and what was achieved.
> 5 Record what you have identified as noteworthy.
> 6 Modify your teaching plan for the child, if necessary, to manage the next stage of learning.
>
> You may find it helpful to remember these steps by the word **INFORM**, since Teacher Assessment is designed to inform your decisions on the way forward for your children.
>
> (SEAC 1990:2)

In fact schools were under such pressure at the time these materials were produced, that in many schools they were either never opened by headteachers or, if they were, they were never used, since heads felt they would simply enrage and demoralize staff still further. However, it might be argued that such materials would communicate a general sense of 'official expectation' about what was to count as 'good practice', even if they didn't cross the desk of every teacher. More particularly they will have influenced the expectations which LEAs had, and schools certainly felt they were being urged to adopt very detailed recording practices for teacher assessment by their LEAs, even though they were given very little direct help with how to do so. Local authority advisory staff said that they felt under a strong obligation from the government to promote a detailed approach to tick lists, since this seemed to be the only way that teacher assessment was able to be adequately recorded according to the law. Advisers claimed that they had never actually urged schools to adopt checklists at this level of detail, and indeed their published guidelines bear this out, but it seems plausible to suggest that their desire not to jeopardize their position by acting against perceived government policy led to an ambiguity about the level of recording required such that teachers felt insecure and unsupported. In addition, the general climate of public opinion fed by what Ball (1990) has termed a political 'discourse of derision' may have further contributed to teachers' feelings, noted above, that they were no longer trusted to carry out their duties in a professional manner. In such circumstances the tendency would have been to 'over-record' – to 'cover your back' just in case.

The teachers we interviewed were also very concerned to collect and retain evidence of the children's performance – to 'prove' their records were correct. At the same time schools were developing policies around the compilation and retention of 'portfolios' of work. Sometimes portfolios were entirely described and justified in terms of the benefits for the pupils: '. . . to keep an individual portfolio, it's a very valuable thing to do for the child's sake . . . they can think about themselves developing and look back at work they've done' (LEA advisory teacher for Assessment). But more often portfolios were linked to the perceived pressures of LEAs auditing teacher assessment levels, thus offering a good way to combine feedback to the children (and their parents) on progress with rendering accounts to other interested third parties. In this respect the 'Record of Achievement' movement manifest in secondary schools in the 1980s offered a model for primary schools in the 1990s:

> They bring it and show it to me, then I'll tick it and I'll put the date on . . . that helps me when I'm writing my report, or I want to take that as an example to put into a portfolio.
>
> (R teacher)

> We have little forms that we fill in to attach to children's work so that their portfolios contain evidence of achievement and attainment.
>
> (headteacher)

> If you're going to have Records of Achievement you've got to kill two birds with one stone . . . what a child would see as 'these are the pieces of work that I've selected to represent me, my work' will also be pieces of work that will have been annotated for National Curriculum purposes.
>
> (headteacher)

Thus, when retained for audit purposes, samples of work often had appended to them notes describing context, statement of attainment and level, usually in a prescribed format. In some cases there was also a justification of the level awarded by the assessing teacher. Such editing processes clearly rendered them somewhat different artefacts from those to which a 7-year-old could easily relate.

Time and again, therefore, the underlying assumption which was constantly returned to during interviews, be it with respect to planning, conducting, recording or reporting 'teacher assessment', was that the purpose of the enterprise was to produce periodic, cumulative evidence that National Curriculum attainment targets had (or had not) been achieved. Often this was seen as separate from, and even in opposition to, a more routine monitoring of progress, which also involved responding to children's problems or achievements as they were encountered. Occasionally the staccato formalities of producing levels were seen as running counter to the espoused purpose of making use of teachers' long-term judgements, raising issues of the validity of the whole endeavour:

One of the things that nobody ever seems to mention is that these recordings that we do, they are a one-off, now my understanding of observation of a child working would not be to look at it one time in a formal activity but to review that child performing that same activity in similar circumstances several times to see if there's a pattern.

(R teacher)

Nevertheless the thrust towards formality was largely taken for granted, and the reliability and comparability of teacher assessments were much more often a concern than their validity. As such the orientation was towards producing summative assessments for third parties rather than formative assessments to support learning.

Classroom assessment and formative assessment

Considerable detail on routine classroom assessment was also revealed by the interviews, however, particularly when teachers talked about their 'own assessments', as opposed to those which they carried out for the purposes of 'Teacher Assessment'; it is these which provided the focus for the second phase of the project and for the substance of this book. Furthermore, elements of formative assessment practice were described or alluded to, though the implicit model was one of teacher-controlled monitoring of progress rather than reflection on the impact of assessment on learning; i.e. it seemed to be assumed that when assessment was to be used formatively, this would involve teacher judgements about achievement feeding forward into the teaching process, rather than classroom assessment processes and teacher feedback having a direct impact on the pupils to promote learning:

Working out where they are and where they're at . . . talking and listening to the children, observing them . . . they are actually doing something and you can assess whether they have understood it . . . you just think, oh, they've grasped that and they're using it.

(R teacher)

There is no point in you doing this with a child and the child doesn't know, who's sitting there sort of looking up in the air, probably doesn't understand what you're giving to them, what you're delivering to them. Children have got to know . . . and understand what they're doing . . . because how can you go forward if the child hasn't understood what they've had before. Therefore the teacher assessment is there to see whether the children actually do know what they're meant to be doing . . . You've got to know that the child is understanding and able to do so. Your assessment is by seeing so the child can progress.

(Y2/3 teacher)

Feedback was mentioned, though usually in terms of short-term rewards rather than detailed analysis of problems and suggestions for improvement, a point to which we will return below. Overall, however, it was almost as if much that might be effective with respect to the way teachers use informal assessment at classroom level, had come to be regarded by them as a rather 'low-level' intuitive activity, which they were unable to organize into a coherent theoretical alternative to the incremental evidence gathering which they thought was required for TA. Thus the constant monitoring of progress was often referred to as 'part and parcel of teaching', even if not recognized as an equally legitimate constituent of reportable assessment:

> I think assessment is very valuable, we all assess whether we know we are doing it or not, we do, it's part and parcel of teaching by talking to the children, working with them. You do assess them in order to help them to move on.
>
> (Y1 teacher)

> It goes on all the time, because obviously you won't know where they've reached or where they're going to go next. It's a spiral process, continuous.
>
> (Y2 teacher)

When articulated in a little more detail there are obvious connections with Vygotskian notions of scaffolding learning reviewed in Chapter 2:

> You're listening to their responses to see if they've actually understood the concept that you're trying to put across and if they haven't then you have to reword it . . . and try again and you've, you've got to watch them the whole time, because you may *think* that they've understood but then when they try and put something on paper, it becomes obvious that they haven't or there's something they've forgotten or something they've got confused, at which point you intervene again, . . . if necessary modify what you're wanting them to do so that they're more able to cope with it.
>
> (SEN support teacher, original emphasis)

Interestingly enough, however, this constant reconnaissance 'to see if *they've* actually understood' and the claim of helping '*them* to move on' (our emphasis) was not often articulated with respect to individual children, or if it was, it was couched in terms of almost instantaneous help and advice in the context of an instructional interaction. Extensive reflection on the detailed progress of each individual pupil was not considered feasible – there are just too many children in the classroom. Rather, the focus of attention and prospective planning tended to be the class, or perhaps the small group, rather than the individual child – are *they* ready to move on, rather than is he or she?

> Not each child but a lot of children on each activity they'd been doing, how they got on, how I thought they should have got on . . . I've got 32 very active children wanting my attention a lot of the time and it's quite difficult to sit back and make an accurate assessment.
>
> (Y1 teacher)

This level of 'group' assessment, rather than individual assessment, could also be influenced by the collaborative planning practices which we mentioned above, and team-teaching situations which were often encountered in integrated Reception and Year 1 'classrooms', i.e. open plan spaces in a defined part of the school:

When we've done an assessment the outcome of that will have an effect on what the children do next. So for instance one major topic that we are dealing with at the moment is DT [design technology] – building a house or shelter for 'Teddy'. What we have learnt from the children's experience of that will help us when the next time they come to do technology, we'll be able to build on the skills that they've already learned, hopefully.

(R teacher)

Such 'group level' assessing and planning was also manifest and exemplified in the many examples of 'ability' groupings which we encountered. Many times teachers talked of organizing their class and their work in terms of high, middle and low ability groups, though more accurately their organization might be said to reflect each child's current achievements and general orientation to schooling rather than ability. Once more, however, the key issue was 'are *they* ready to move on?' Sometimes this was reported in terms of monitoring the progress of the class overall but only focusing in detail on those whose performance was causing concern:

If you've got 30 children . . . you will have a top sort of flying group, you will have this big bulge in the middle and then these little ones at the end that need, you know, all the support they can get.

(R teacher)

You know the children who are possibly worrying you because you think they should be on the move more than they are. Why aren't they? What is the reason, let's find out and give them a bit extra.

(Y2/3 teacher)

This form of what we might characterize as 'naturalistic' teacher assessment – monitoring the performance of the class as a whole, being broadly satisfied that particular groups and individuals are moving at the pace one would expect, only focusing on individuals in detail if they are causing real concern – begs some interesting questions with respect to the definitions and expectations of formative assessment discussed in Chapter 2. It would appear that teachers monitor the impact of their teaching at an overall level, much more than they monitor the progress of each individual pupil in detail. Now it may be argued that they *should* monitor the progress of individual pupils in detail, but this still raises the issue of feasibility, as well as whether or not such a focus fits with the 'ecological balance' of the classroom. Our own view is that the issue of how and in what ways assessment does and should impact on learning, is much more to do with the quality of teacher–pupil interaction and the feedback provided by teachers during the course of such interactions, than it is to do with the incremental use of assessment data. We will return to such issues in more detail in subsequent chapters. For the moment, however, we can also note that teachers did indeed focus on individuals, and saw the benefit of doing so, in certain circumstances, but that this could not be sustained at such a level of detail over a significant period of time.

Thus, for example, one teacher recalled a particular incident which revealed that a pupil had misheard and misunderstood the number sequences he was working with:

> For instance, the other day I had a little boy [doing] tens and units work
> . . . when he was counting he got muddled in his counting and he'd
> counted 10, 20, 30, 40, 15, 16, 17, in his mind 40 had become 14, which
> said to me he doesn't really understand, I thought he did but it made me
> rethink totally . . . We talked about it quite a bit . . . and we worked on it,
> and it's something I've written down that I must come back to and look
> at him again.
>
> (Y2 teacher)

Others talked of making similar discoveries and of the almost instant decisions
which have to be made about intervention, support, or possibly just leaving
the problem to one side and returning to it some days or even weeks later
when the child might be more ready to respond:

> I think I usually try to be as positive as possible . . . and . . . if they hadn't
> understood it, I wouldn't say they hadn't . . . I might say something like
> perhaps we'll have another try at that another day . . . I might intervene
> and actually help them to do the task . . . it would overcome their feeling
> that they can't do it.
>
> (R teacher)

> I had an example yesterday. I had somebody who I thought could actually
> start some formal handwriting and [she] didn't actually do anything
> because I think the challenge was too much, I'd gone up too many steps
> . . . and she needed to go back to some sand play or some writing in sand.
>
> (R teacher)

Such decisions are clearly grounded in a kind of latent formative assessment,
but are hardly based on incremental evidence about whether or not a child can
progress to a new level in the National Curriculum. Rather than the reference
point for judgement being an externally determined curricular sequence, it
was the teachers' experience and knowledge of the child in context. And with
this we encounter another enduring and widespread facet of routine classroom assessment – that knowledge of the 'whole child' is deemed important
in interpreting performance and achievement. Sometimes this concern was
expressed in relation to knowledge of the child's home background and what
difference this might make to more formal teacher assessments:

> I don't think it makes it more difficult for me to be objective although it
> does influence my assessment. Let me think. [long silence] I suppose
> maybe it does affect my objectivity, maybe it does 'cos what I give you an
> example, I've got a child at the moment who's got a lot of problems at
> home and so I will plan an activity for that child and if that child can't see
> themselves to the end of the activity I record what they have achieved but
> I suppose I'm giving them the benefit of the doubt and thinking they
> could have achieved more if they hadn't been going through all these
> emotional turmoils at home. So maybe I'm not being objective, I don't
> know.
>
> (Y1 teacher)

But more often concern for the 'whole child' was noted with respect to making ipsative judgements about progress in the classroom – what they had done before, whether what they were doing now represented real progress – irrespective of whether or not it met a criterion for a particular level of achievement:

> They go backwards and forwards to consolidate but it's really the knowledge that you build up with the children and what they can achieve and what they have done and what they've found difficult.
>
> (Y1 teacher)

In turn, such concerns sometimes shaded back into reflection on the validity of judgements made over a period of time, and how such judgements of progress related to explanations and possible interventions:

> It could be that you think 'Crikey, that's really bad today', perhaps some people wouldn't go into 'why is it like that today?' Some people could just take it face value couldn't they?
>
> (Y2/3 teacher)

Reflecting on why a child has not accomplished a task as expected or, perhaps, has exceeded expectations, and in so doing, taking account of previous effort and achievement in this process of reflection, seems a legitimate and indeed laudable use for teachers' previous knowledge of a child. However, as the following incident demonstrates, making allowances for one child may carry implications for others who wouldn't necessarily understand the basis for the teacher's differential judgement and behaviour.

A classroom incident

The incident occurred at a large primary school on an urban council estate. In the school there was a policy of teaching language in cross-class sets determined by children's word recognition skills at the beginning of the year and then amended as deemed necessary. It was the summer term and the end of Key Stage 1 National Assessment was in its later stages. The incident was part of ordinary classroom work but the teacher had indicated that most of her work at this stage of the year was influenced by the need to produce formal TA grades. Pseudonyms are used throughout.

The children had been asked to do some book research. This involved choosing a 'minibeast' from those that had been discovered in the school grounds, drawing it, reading about it in the books and then writing about it. The teacher had made it clear to them that she was most concerned with the finding out – indeed this was the only aspect that she had written on the blackboard as a reminder for pupils of what they were to do. She also said that she did not want copying from the book.

Craig had chosen to write about snakes (not discovered in the school grounds) and produced a piece where he had chosen two small pieces of text from the book and copied them down almost word for word. His writing did not make a great deal of sense, partly because he had ignored the punctuation which he and the teacher then added, but also because the second of his extracts about how snakes move was originally the caption to one of a series of linked diagrams. Craig received public praise for his work and was given a good work sticker. The teacher's comment to the researcher at the time was that précis was a difficult skill and he had done well.

Claire had chosen to write about a butterfly. Her writing was much less scientific in style but when compared with her source it could be seen to be original. For example, in her book she had read that the creature liked dark places and it was pictured by the entrance to a cave; she had written that it lived in 'creepy caves'. When she brought her work up to the teacher she was not given positive feedback, but had spelling errors pointed out to her and was sent away to correct them. At this point she was asked by the researcher what the teacher had thought of her work; she said: 'Not very good', and added that the reason she knew this was that she had been asked to do something more to it. She put right her mistakes and went to show her work again to the teacher. Unfortunately she had missed one rogue capital letter and the teacher sent her back again to put it right. Claire went back to her place and started to cry. When the teacher's attention was drawn to this she asked her why she was crying. Claire replied, 'Because I can't do it.' At this point the teacher took her onto her lap and reassured her that she had produced a lovely piece of work and that her crying was unnecessary. She was asked to get the sticker box, although the force of this was rather diminished because the teacher then gave a sticker to every pupil because they had worked so well during the session.

After the children had gone, the teacher told the researcher that she had been focusing on National Curriculum 'English', Attainment Target 2, level 3(f), which requires children to 'devise a clear set of questions that will enable them to select and use appropriate information sources and reference books from the class and school library'. She said that both children had shown that they were able to use information books and that they were now ready to go to the school library and devise their set of questions so that they could demonstrate their achievement of the statement of attainment.

The incident is a fascinating one since it demonstrates the way in which ostensibly similar feedback with respect to ostensibly the same statement of attainment has actually been provided in different ways and with different impact for the two children involved. Claire produced a piece of work which demonstrated understanding of the task and a capacity to carry it out. It met the teacher's expectations and so she suggested further improvement could be made by focusing on spelling and presentation. Claire, however, interpreted this not as improving on something that had already been done well, but rather as 'I can't do it'. Craig, by contrast, received very public praise and a public reward, even though it might be argued that his effort barely met the statement of attainment, if at all, and the strength of the positive feedback he received reflected more about what the teacher *thought* he needed, rather than what he actually achieved. We shall return to investigate such issues in more depth in Chapters 6 and 8.

Feedback to pupils

We might speculate that this teacher's feedback was generated in the context of her 'teaching agenda' rather than thinking through its ramifications for learning. She intended to have a positive impact on Craig, but also had an unintended negative impact on Claire. Thus, reflecting on why children have or have not made progress still remains 'part and parcel' of teaching rather than learning. Getting children to reflect on progress themselves, to climb to the 'high ground' from which they can survey their own knowledge and process of learning (Bruner 1986), might be said to be one of the most ambitious purposes for teacher assessment, and one which would involve detailed feedback to pupils on both what they had achieved and how they had achieved it. In turn the nature of such encounters should impact directly on the learning process as the assessment 'conversation' scaffolds learning. Some teachers were beginning to struggle with more complex interpretations of feedback – and recognizing the conceptual complexity and logistical demands of such an endeavour:

> Children will not work independently and will not sustain any task if they don't have (a) input, (b) don't have feedback on their progress and (c) there isn't someone to nudge them a bit further. Part and parcel of achieving quality is that you've someone there who is questioning you on what you've done so far and how much further you could go . . . we're trying to move towards something that we found quite difficult, teachers giving much more feedback.
>
> (headteacher)

For the most part, however, feedback was almost wholly characterized in terms of short-term rewards – praise and/or team points, 'smiley face' stickers etc. – rather than detailed comment on how to develop an idea further or help with particular problems:

> Praise is something I use a lot. I give them stickers . . . and . . . they love ticks.
>
> (Y1 teacher)

> Initially it's giving them verbal praise and verbal reward for doing well . . . that's the whole basis of this classroom is built on praise and encouragement . . . you get praise from me and you get a team point and ultimately they take it to the Head if it's a really good piece of work.
>
> (Y1 teacher)

> The 'special mention' is that . . . teachers are encouraged to say 'that's a lovely piece of work, I'm very pleased with you, go and show Mrs. So-and-so next door.
>
> (headteacher)

> We praise them and if a person has really done something good I'll point it out and ask them to read what they have recorded or written.
>
> (R teacher)

Often, constant encouragement was also articulated as a classroom strategy for keeping all children 'on task', rather than a 'reward' saved for particularly good work:

> You have to keep putting activities in front of them that repeat certain skills over and over again because you've got to be continuously looking to see for little bits of development or changes or sudden moves forward, and you've got to be aware of them when they happen, praise them like crazy when they happen, so that they can all feel thrilled to bits and do loads more of it.
>
> (R teacher)

Here, then, we see a whole constellation of strategies – private praise in the classroom, public praise in the classroom, public praise elsewhere, individual stickers, team points – each or all of which could be part of a whole-school policy or not. Whether or not a blanket policy, and particularly one involving public praise, would always be effective in every case is a moot point, however. We have already noted the problems which ipsatively referenced praise might cause for other children in the classroom; some teachers also noted that praise itself had to be apportioned with great care with respect to the individual child concerned:

> Some children don't like being praised in public, don't like to be drawn to the centre of attention, so you've really got to know your children very well . . . I'm beginning to sort of realize who wants, who *needs* the praise . . . the ones that really just wouldn't cope without that.
>
> (R teacher, original emphasis)

Exactly why school policies and practice on feedback in the classroom have focused on rewards, rather than extended dialogue about the quality of the work produced, is an interesting issue. It seems to derive in part from school policies which take for granted the efficacy of behaviourist reinforcement systems, particularly with regard to so-called 'assertive discipline':

> I think the assertive discipline has helped . . . the principle is that children have a right to learn and teachers have a right to teach and therefore children shouldn't disrupt . . . but if you are going to tell a child off you should try and think of two positive things before you say a negative.
>
> (headteacher)

> Part and parcel of an assertive discipline policy is that you've got your rewards and sanctions in place . . . it's part and parcel of our policy that teachers know we will reward children for their achievements at all levels.
>
> (headteacher)

However, teachers also had to struggle with the ritualistic perceptions of and responses to schooling by very young children: being asked to 'evaluate' their work, to 'do more' to it, could be interpreted by the children as an indication of teacher disapproval rather than a source of helpful advice (cf. the example of Claire cited above). However, in some respects teacher behaviour itself, at least as manifest in the taken-for-granted norms of classroom management, seemed to play a significant role in setting up such expectations, as the following observed interaction and brief interview with the pupil (Jane) makes clear:

Teacher: Very good, very good. I liked that. Now what I really like is, a full stop there. Very good . . . And you've put lots of capital letters, but you haven't always got full stops. Let's put in the full stops. And look, you've got 'played'. You've spelt that just right there. You're getting really good. Have you got 'played' spelt right everywhere?

Jane: Ummm.

Teacher: Because if I look at that one, what's happened to that one?

Jane: Cos I forgot the 'y' [almost laughing].

Teacher: You forgot the 'y'. Can you put it in the right place? . . . Do you think you could look through and find some more full stops and capital letters? Do you think you can do that Jane?

Jane: Yeah . . .

(audiotaped)

The researcher then asked Jane whether she thought she had done good work:

Jane: All right.

Researcher: Do you think Mrs White [the teacher] thought you had done good work?

Jane: All right.

Researcher: How can you tell if she thinks you've done good work?

Jane: When it's good she tells you to get on with the next thing.

I noted this idea, that the ultimate conferral of the teacher's approval was to be told to get on to something else, in three other cases during the session . . . It was summed up finally by another child, who, when asked what Mrs White said when you showed her some very good work said: She usually says 'It's very good, now do something else.'

(fieldnotes)

Here the ordinary routines of classroom assessment, management and responses to children seem to be outweighing the positive 'formative' feedback which the teacher is trying to communicate. Being told 'to get on with the next thing' is a more trustworthy indicator of teacher approval than specific positive feedback. Again, we will return to this issue of how formative feedback is inevitably embedded within and contributes to the taken-for-granted routines of classroom interaction in later chapters.

Tension and anxiety in teaching and assessing

This brief overview of teacher perspectives on teacher assessment has had to ignore many other issues that emerged from the interviews. However, before moving on it is important to recognize the emotional turmoil that seemed to come through in many teachers' accounts of their current practice. There is a danger that any brief summary may identify misunderstandings and problems of workload and support, but without fully reflecting the intense anxiety expressed by some of the teachers in the study. Strongly held beliefs were being disparaged in the course of the concurrent political debate, and long-standing practices challenged – no more so than in the policy imperative of bringing in formal assessment for very young children. Thus there seemed to be in the teachers' accounts two discourses running simultaneously – one about child-centred schooling and the teachers' motivation to listen to, get to know, and teach young children, and a second concerned with measurement, categorization and accountability where the focus is on assessing, recording, and reporting progression. Reconciling these two accounts of the purpose and practice of 'teacher assessment' was proving extremely difficult. This may in part account for the complexity which we noted at the beginning of the chapter in individuals' ideas of teacher assessment, and for the seeming contradictions in some of the interviews.

The idea that teachers, particularly primary teachers, in the developed English-speaking world, carry a great burden of guilt has been advanced by a number of writers (e.g. Nias 1989; Broadfoot and Osborn 1993). A particularly interesting and detailed perspective on this has been articulated by Hargreaves (1994), who draws on the work of Davies (1989). He distinguishes between persecutory guilt, which results from 'doing something that is forbidden or from failing to do something which is expected by one or more external authorities' (Hargreaves 1994:143), and depressive guilt, which arises when 'individuals feel they have ignored, betrayed or failed to protect the people or values' that they hold dear (Davies 1989:59). Feelings of this sort were certainly apparent in some of the interviews we conducted.

However, the teachers we interviewed also saw the introduction of National Curriculum and Assessment as bringing with it an increase both in the accountability and in the intensification of the work they had to do. According to Hargreaves's analysis, 'accountability and intensification provide a potent cocktail for inducing feelings of persecutory guilt' (Hargreaves 1994: 149). The position is further complicated by the differing orientations towards TA and the type of pedagogy needed to implement it: where a teacher feels they are failing satisfactorily to do the assessment required by the new system, but as a result of this activity do not have time for the activities that they value, they are potentially victims to a complex nexus of guilt. Interestingly, the word 'guilt' was not mentioned during our interviews; but teachers did frequently refer to feeling 'anxious' or 'worried', 'not coping', 'being destroyed', and even to 'almost dying'. They also stated that they did not really like the idea of assessment (cf. also Harlen and Qualter 1991), though they were often lost for words when struggling for another term to describe their interaction with children in the classroom: 'I don't like the word . . . I don't know what the word, another word you could use really' (R teacher). One LEA adviser commented that 'for teachers it has become a dirty word because of the connotations with comparing children, schools and authorities'.

Thus many of the teachers we interviewed felt they were being asked to act in ways which were antithetical to their values and their theories of teaching and learning. They were concerned about whether children were happy or not, an aspect of their interest in the 'whole child', and several justified their position by stating that this, rather than educational attainment, was what parents were interested in at the infant stage – 'has he or she settled in alright – are they making friends?' Whether or not teachers felt guilty about assessing children is a moot point, but many expressed a concern that in some sense they felt they had to protect the children from the harshness of being judged too soon, against criteria which weren't really appropriate. 'Protecting' children in this way is by no means an unproblematic activity, and we shall interrogate some of the complexities in Chapter 6 in particular. For the moment, however, the point to note is the tensions aroused by the process.

Summary

Overall, then, the teachers we interviewed seemed to regard 'assessment' as a distinct activity from 'teaching' and one, furthermore, which they were being asked to conduct in order to gather data for third parties – for purposes of accountability – rather than to benefit themselves and/or their pupils. With further probing, informal classroom assessment was acknowledged as an important activity, particularly with respect to questioning and observing pupils, but one which was now considered rather too intuitive to merit a great deal of attention. Moreover it was an activity which was still likely to be perceived as having potentially negative, rather than positive, consequences for pupils, with its impact on motivation and learning having to be extensively mediated through praise and rewards. As we shall see in subsequent chapters, however, claims for the benefits of teacher questioning are much more problematic than most discussions admit; but at the same time, fears about the negative impact of assessment on motivation and learning may also be misplaced, or at least betray misunderstandings about the nature of the teacher–pupil relationship and the learning that can be constructed through assessment interactions.

Notes

1 Interestingly, in several of our case study schools heads had recently been promoted to new positions because of their experience with Year 2 SATs and/or LEA audit work. In the late 1980s and early 1990s, experience of assessment seemed to have replaced experience of curriculum development as the key indicator of ambition and competence.
2 Despite the change in official nomenclature, our respondents still routinely referred to externally designed 'Standard Tests' as 'SATs', short for 'Standard Assessment Tasks'.
3 E.g. English 3:2a – produce independently pieces of writing using complete sentences, some of them demarcated with capital letters and full stops or question marks; science 1:2f – record findings in charts, drawings and other appropriate forms; etc., etc.

Classroom assessment and the language of teaching

Introduction

We have already noted that a tendency of those discussing the relationship of assessment to teaching and learning is to under-problematize theoretical issues and over-simplify practical difficulties. One of the most important reasons for the complexity of classroom assessment is that it does not occur in isolation; it is accomplished within a social and educational context where a great number of apparently straightforward transactions are influenced not just by the circumstances of the moment, but by expectations and under-standings deriving from much longer established and taken-for-granted prac-tices. This chapter begins our detailed exploration of classroom assessment by considering the language in which it is accomplished and how it relates to the micro-sociology of the classroom. Here we demonstrate the complex dynam-ics of routine classroom assessment, in whole-class and small-group settings, before going on in subsequent chapters to interrogate the relationship of class-room assessment to the socialization of pupils, and the impact of assessment on learning.

We have also already noted that classroom talk can be seen to be structured differently from other speech, incorporating a basic three-part sequence of Initiation (by the teacher), Response (by the pupil) and Follow-up – feedback or evaluation (by the teacher) (Sinclair and Coulthard 1975). This structure allows the teacher to control the discourse, as not only do they initiate the exchange by asking the question, but also the third move enables them to extend the sequence if the Response is not considered appropriate. Sinclair and Coulthard concentrated on the language of teachers rather than pupils, since pupils 'have only very restricted opportunities to participate in the lan-guage of the classroom' (Sinclair 1982:6) and since what pupils did say was controlled and structured by the teacher's moves. Sinclair and Coulthard's intentions derived from their interest as linguists in the structure of talk *per se*. However, their work was quickly developed by educational researchers, and how pupils understand classroom processes has come to be a key focus for studies of classroom interaction (e.g. Mehan 1979; Edwards and Mercer 1987). Studies of language in the classroom from many different points of departure have raised a number of different issues, but seem to agree that once the pupil's perspective is taken into consideration, a picture of great complexity emerges. In particular, the assumptions of those currently determining policy on assessment, that teachers can easily interpret pupil behaviour and ask clear questions that elicit clear and discrete answers, are not well founded, as our data will demonstrate.

The central problem of classroom language is that it embodies both the form and the content of classroom life – what Bruner (1986:131) describes as 'the "two-faced" nature of language'. Teachers and (especially) pupils have to achieve competence in both. Thus, the participants in classroom life have to understand their roles in relation to each other (who is allowed to speak, where and when) and the function that language plays in continually creating and re-creating these rules and expectations, as well as decoding and responding to the specific content of any particular question and answer sequence. And as our review of previous research in Chapter 2 demonstrates, the possibilities for misinterpretation are many and varied.

Assessing in the context of whole-class teaching

Our data confirm the extent of this complexity and the opportunity for misunderstanding in even the most apparently straightforward of classroom assessment contexts. In the following transcript of a Year 2 (whole-class) maths lesson, for example, the teacher is revising work on 'tens and units' before going on to extend the work by introducing the concept of 'rounding up' to the nearest appropriate number. The extract demonstrates the way in which questions are routinely asked of individuals, but in the context of 'teaching' the class; i.e. questions are not simply and solely directed at the individual concerned, but serve other purposes with respect to keeping the class on task and moving the lesson along. Towards the end of the extract it also demonstrates how a very simple misinterpretation of linguistic meaning can lead to a misjudgement of pupil understanding. In the extract the children are seated on the floor in a fairly tight group in one corner of the classroom, in front of a whiteboard on which the teacher is writing numbers. As noted in the Introduction, the transcript is presented in two columns: the left-hand column includes a description of the interaction (italicized) and the speech of the teacher and children, the right-hand column includes our commentary on the action – a first level of analysis. Pseudonyms are used throughout this and subsequent chapters.

T picks up pen and begins to write the numbers 20, 40, 60, 80 spaced out across the top of the whiteboard.
T   here now these are -
About a third of the children raise their hands. T turns to face the class.

T	what I want to know is - if you know what all those <u>four</u> numbers are - so put your hand up if you can tell me what all <u>four</u> of those numbers are -

11:41

At this point most of the children have their hands up.

T	OK - I want to know who knows all four of them - Becky	T wants to confirm that 'the class' knows the numbers and to establish a basis for the rest of the lesson. T chooses a weaker pupil; if she gets it right T can be almost certain that the rest of the class also understand, so that the lesson can 'move on'.
Becky	twenty / forty /sixty /eighty	
T	OK - good - put your hands down we've had the answer - next question is - I want to know how many tens there are - in all of those numbers -	'OK – good': the first IRF sequence is safely completed; T draws a verbal line under the first interaction, the base is established.

About half the class raise their hands.

T now moves on to the first 'real' topic – tens and units.

T	Martin -

Martin turns to face T.

T	I want <u>all</u> of them

Some of the children with their hands up let them droop, most children keep them up.

T appears to have chosen Martin because he thought he was not paying attention. In addition, Martin is more of a barometer for the class than Becky – if Martin gets it right T can move on with confidence that most children are following with understanding; if not, some instruction will be in order.

Martin	TWO
T	which number
M	all of them - two / two / two

By this stage only a few hands are still raised.

The Response is not satisfactory so T extends the sequence.

T	No - so you're saying there's two tens there

T half turns to the whiteboard and points to the figure 20. Children are gradually raising their hands so that around a half of them are now bidding.

Why does Martin say two? Does he really not understand tens and units? Has he been panicked by being picked unexpectedly and wants to please – any answer is better than no answer? He has been reminded that a correct answer will refer to all four numbers, but for whatever reason this does not provide sufficient scaffolding; so T takes him through the task number by number.

M	mm

Martin nods.

T	and two tens in that number

T points to 40.

M	mmm

Martin puts his head on one side

This is said with falling intonation, suggesting that Martin has little confidence in his answer.

T	how many in that number Martin - how many > tens <
M	> four < =
T	= right how many tens make sixty =

Nevertheless, focusing the question helps scaffold Martin's answer and he now seems to understand T's expectations.

'right' – sequence complete, move on to the next IRF sequence.

T points to 60

M	= six
T	how many tens make ~

T points to 80.

M	eight =

Having established a rhythm, from which T assumes the child now understands the nature of the task and the correct Response, the Feedback doesn't have to be explicit; simply moving

Although the hands of the other children have been drooping during this exchange it is only when this point is reached that a significant number take them down completely. The children's faces remain fixed on the board and the T.

T	= have you noticed - when you said eight - eight's there

T points to the 8 in 80

T	and when you said six there's a six there -

T points to the 6 in 60

T	did you notice when you said four - there's a four there -

T points to the 4 in 40

Martin	yeah > (**) < =

. . . *[inaudible, a few seconds]* . . .

T	> the first number < tells you how many tens there are - so I'll put a little tee for tens -

T turns back to whiteboard and writes the letter T above the 8 in 80. He turns back to the class. All hands are now down except for Hannah's.

T	eighty has ~ > eight tens <
Cs	> eight tens <

T turns back to white board and writes the letter T above the 6 in 60.

T	sixty has > six tens <
Cs	> six tens <

T writes the letter T above the 4 in 40

Cs	forty has four tens =

T turns back to class

T	=shhh - right then - how many units - are there -

Faye raises her hand and is rapidly followed by several other children. T turns half round and points to the 20.

T	in <u>this</u> number - how many units are there Faye =
F	= none

Most of the hands go down but some remain up

T	= none - there's no units - Alice
C	> none <
A	> none <

on to the next question (Initiation) is sufficient to confirm the correct answer when used in conjunction with suitable gesture and intonation.

However, T seems concerned that Martin (and/or other members of the class) may only be recalling the numbers – six 10s are 60, eight 10s are 80 – rather than discerning the answer from what is written on the board and making the connection between tens and units, so he explicitly reiterates the point.

Further scaffolding is provided for the whole class – the column is now to be headed 'T'.

T cues class as he writes.

'right then' – a 'framing move' – closure on the first part of the topic – another verbal line is drawn.

IRF begins again with 'how many units are there in this number?' The question is then focused on a specific individual but as part of the whole-class teaching strategy.

The Response is straightforward and correct. However, since we have moved on to a new part of the topic, T explicitly confirms the Response with definitive Feedback ('none – there's no units') before checking with another child.

This first extract of transcript, then, demonstrates very clearly the way in which individual children are selected to answer questions for reasons which go beyond simply gathering data on whether or not they 'know' the answer. The answers are utilized as part of the whole-class teaching strategy, both to continually establish and re-establish the teacher's control of the discourse – asking questions always puts the questioner in a powerful position – and to move the lesson towards the substantive goal which the teacher has in mind. The teacher then moves on to the next topic of 'rounding up':

T   OK that's the first question - now I'm just going to write some different numbers now and I just want you to watch - I'm going to write some different numbers - now - on here - OK

'OK' – once again closure is announced, but closure does not lead immediately to moving on since T has to write more numbers on the whiteboard before announcing the next topic.

T turns away from the class and begins to write random two-digit numbers spread haphazardly across the whiteboard. As he does so he hums. Children start to put their hands up.

'OK' – enunciated as a question, but of course T is not asking for the children's agreement, this is an instruction to be quiet.

C   (*I've got a)

This comment is whispered. T looks over his shoulder at the class . . .[ ] . . .

11:43

T   - shhh - just watch please OK - (**) to get a few more on -

Again, 'OK' is enunciated as a question, but actually marks the instruction.

Cs remain quiet

. . . [T continues to write] . . .

T turns back to face class

T   OK now - we're going to do some - <u>rounding up</u> - I'm going to write that on the - whiteboard for you - we're going to do some - <u>rounding up</u>

'OK now' – another marker – now the topic can be introduced.

T writes words 'rounding up' in capitals above the random numbers. He turns back to the class.

11:44

T   I'll explain - <u>rounding up</u> - you've got four numbers here - twenty - forty, sixty, eighty -

T is half turned to the whiteboard drawing circles round the numbers at the top of the board.

T   I'm going to choose one of these numbers - I'll choose this number here

T points to the number 37 which is situated at the top right-hand side of the whiteboard about 5 cm from the number 80. He turns back to the class.

T   that number's got three tens and seven units right - thirty seven - which number - is this nearest to -

A few hands go up.

T   look at thirty seven - is it nearest to <u>twenty</u> or is it nearest to <u>forty</u> - is it nearest to <u>sixty</u> or is it nearest to <u>eighty</u> - which one of those four numbers is this nearest to - Ellen

By this stage most children in the class have raised their hands; many lower them when Ellen is nominated.

E   erm eighty

T   so you think that thirty-seven is nearest to eighty - OK - what do you think Alice

Ellen screws up her face.

A   erm forty

More children begin to raise their hands.

T   forty - what do you think Rachel

R   twenty

T   you think it's nearest to twenty - what do you think Charles

Ch   forty

T   forty - what do you think Tim

Th   forty

T   forty - what do you think Kate

K   sixty

T   sixty - what do you think Elspeth

E   forty

T   forty - what do you think Christina

Ca   sixty

T   sixty - what do you think Miles

M   forty

Ellen seems to have interpreted 'nearest' in terms of physical proximity to the next number written on the board, rather than in terms of the maths task at hand, rounding up. T misses this (though recognizes it when reviewing the videotape later). Instead T notes the answer neutrally ('OK') but by immediately repeating the question to another child implies it is not correct.

T gets a satisfactory Response but does not close the sequence; his repetition of the question implies that yet another answer may be required. Rachel may or may not think 20 is correct, but she seems to have been persuaded that 40 is wrong.

By continuing to repeat the question T seems to want to establish by consensus what the correct answer is, rather than just telling Ellen she is wrong. Is T trying to be kind to Ellen? Or has T been so 'knocked off balance' by such an 'obviously' wrong answer that a wide survey of class opinion is required?

Whatever T's intentions, the repeated question seems to be starting to confuse the children. Several children have answered 'forty' yet T is still asking the question - so perhaps 'forty' is wrong, let's try 'sixty'. Thus it may be that Kate and Christina, as with Rachel before them, think 'forty' is correct but are giving an alternative because 'forty' hasn't been confirmed.

The teacher goes on to 'survey' class opinion on the matter by asking children to 'vote' (by putting up their hands) on which number is 'nearest' to 37; the teacher then tries to settle the issue by employing a large tape measure (the class 'metre monster') and asking children to count the spaces from 20 to 37, 37 to 40, and so forth. At this point physical proximity of the numbers along the tape does come into play, implicitly, as the concepts of nearest appropriate number and nearest physical proximity are conflated. However, the origin of Ellen's misunderstanding is not uncovered or addressed. Overall the two extracts provide plenty of evidence of the continuous process of individual questioning which goes to make up so-called 'whole-class' teaching. Both teachers and pupils (and assessment policy makers) have to be able to recognize that such question and answer sessions are as concerned with accomplishing the lesson as with assessing individuals. There is no sense in which teachers could treat such questions as 'items' in the sense of examination questions, and explicitly monitor and record the responses to them. At the same time, however, it is inevitable that teachers will come to cumulative judgements about who is making appropriate progress and who is not; who can be relied upon to give the correct answer when required, and who will be cooperative even when they are struggling to give the correct answer. This is the reality of day-to-day 'teacher assessment'. It is also the case that in such whole-class teaching situations, misinterpretations such as those of Ellen cannot be explored in detail, as to spend time focusing on one child's responses would risk losing the attention of the majority of the class (cf. Wong 1995). This may lead to significant misjudgements about pupil understanding and achievement.

Ambiguous questioning in a small group

In fact, of course, detailed assessment of individual pupils is much more likely to be planned for, and to occur, in the context of small group work. However, the size of the group does not escape the issue of linguistic structure and expectation, nor the problem of linguistic uncertainty and the possibilities for misinterpretation. In the following extract the teacher's intuitive employment of the phrase 'this one' introduces an element of ambiguity into a 'focus group' teaching and assessing session on number recognition with three reception class pupils. The teacher has initially used the story of the 'Three Bears' along with three toy teddy bears to introduce the topic of counting and number recognition, and now is distributing large tiles with the numbers 1, 2 and 3 written on them.

T	what number what number's that -	T grasps tile whilst still talking about the story of the three bears and, without a pause, starts to ask a question about the number on the tile (number one). The question seems to be addressed to the group in general and is now about recognizing the symbol for one rather than counting the three bears.
T holds up large tile with figure 1 written on it.		
Cs	one	
T	now you have the one	There is no explicit acknowledgement of the correct answer, but distributing 'the one' seems to confirm it and constitute Feedback.
Hands tile to Jimmy revealing the number two tile.		
. . . [a few seconds mumbling] . . .		
T brings forward the number two tile and		

looks at Seb.

T   what number's >that one<

Simon   >umm<

T is looking at Seb and puts her finger to her mouth when Simon says 'umm'.

T   >do you (*know what that is)<

Simon   um - three

T   it's a three you think -

T looks back at Seb

T   what number do you think it is Seb

Seb   um - two

T   two -

T looks back directly at Simon

T   it's a two -

T looks back at Seb

T   so you have the two

T gives the number two tile to Seb; number three tile is revealed. T closes Three Bears Book and places it behind her on the floor. T turns to face Simon directly across the table.

T   what number's that one Simon

Simon   er - (*four)

T   it's a - three

Simon   three =

T   = that one's a three

T hands the tile to Simon.

Jimmy   you don't know all your numbers

T   sorry - Jimmy- could you say that again - I didn't quite hear

Jimmy   he dun't know about (*all of) his numbers

T   he doesn't know about all the numbers - well we can help him can't we . . . [ ] . . .

We have already had number '1', T now introduces the word 'one' to denote something other than the number '1'.

An answer is clearly expected and Simon gives one, either not recognizing, or ignoring, T's injunction not to speak. It is not correct but has he been influenced by the original task focusing on the three bears story book; would he expect to be shown the number three? Can we make a judgement about his capacity to count and recognize numbers? Whatever is the case, T repeats the question, and much more explicitly, so long as 'it' is correctly interpreted.

She is correcting Simon's mistake, presumably assuming that he cannot recognize the numbers two and three.

'the two' – not two bears, nor two tiles, but the tile with the '2' printed on it. What might Seb and Simon make of this phrase – two what?

Some sort of symbolic closure is taking place here. This is no longer a language activity – the book has been replaced by the number tiles.

T again uses the word 'one' in her question, this time while holding up the symbol for three.

T seems to be certain that Simon has said a wrong number, perhaps because he got it wrong last time, although it is not clear from the recording.

The confusion of one and three is compounded.

Two errors are generalized to 'all your numbers' (note personalizing possessive). This comment does not seem to be kindly meant by Jimmy, and highlights the public context of much classroom assessment, even when exposure is only within a small group. And why does T apparently compound the problem by asking Jimmy to repeat his comment? Did T really not hear, or is this an example of a question whose locutionary force is different from its ostensible purpose; designed to give T the opportunity to draw the group together to 'help' Simon – always presuming he needs help. This could be seen as a sympathetic gesture in the context of providing scaffolding for Simon, but does he think he is now the recipient of the group's pedagogical condescension?

Much later in the interaction, a noise disturbs the group and they look round to see the rest of the class being taken out of the classroom by the nursery teaching assistant. At this point Simon demonstrates that whether or not he has recognized the numbers on the tiles correctly, he certainly can count (in a more informal or 'authentic' situation) though it is not clear if the teacher picks up on this:

T writes down. The door squeaks again –
Seb, Jimmy and T look round.

Simon   (*) how many've we got
              there - one two three four
              five - that's all

Simon turns around and looks at the rest of
the classroom. He points to each person in
the classroom in turn.

Someone has left the room. Simon notices that there are only five people in the classroom (the fifth is the researcher). In a real context he has been able to demonstrate his knowledge and understanding of number up to five. Moreover, he has a notion of that being a relatively small number in the context of the whole class.

So, opportunities for misapprehension and ambiguity are legion in infant school classrooms (and indeed many others). Possibilities for opportunistic 'authentic' assessment also exist, as with the example of Simon above, but making the most of them would require immense perspicacity from teachers and an orientation to the divergent possibilities of the infant classroom which a focus on National Curriculum attainment targets and statements of attainment, or even level descriptors, is unlikely to encourage. Our point is not that we wish to criticize these individual teachers – quite the reverse, when reviewing such extracts we can visualize ourselves making similar moves, they are the very stuff of routine teaching – but such ambiguous encounters are likely to carry consequences for individual children's learning, and they certainly demonstrate the need for caution when discussing the problems and possibilities of classroom assessment.

Thus, to reiterate, teachers' questions and pupils' responses will always be serving a number of different purposes and accomplishing a number of different functions at one and the same time. In particular, pupils constantly strive to interpret teachers' questions and 'make sense' of what is being asked of them in the context of this interactive process, over and above what might be taken to be the 'obvious' meaning of a particular question. Now this does not mean that all attempts at formative classroom assessment will necessarily founder, but it does mean that the process of accomplishing formative assessment is likely to be a good deal more complicated than presently acknowledged.

A guessing game

In order to investigate this further and analyse these issues in more depth we shall look at an example from our data at more length. A crucial complicating factor in the following incident is the teacher's concern explicitly to 'assess' the children's level of understanding and competence, rather than to 'teach' them something. This seems to derive partly from her understanding of the formal status of 'teacher assessment' and partly from her commitment to 'discovery learning'. Whatever the reason, it prevents her from engaging in direct instruction when perhaps she should. Rather, she attempts to cue and elicit correct responses through a convoluted series of questions and mimes. From the teacher's perspective this can be seen as giving the children every possible opportunity to demonstrate what they know. However, the result is almost a caricature of non-interventive 'child-centred' learning, with the teacher engaging in an ever more complicated 'guessing game' with the children, the rules of which are never made explicit.

Avis Green teaches a mixed Y1/2 class. She has been teaching in the same small school for a number of years – so small in fact that classes are organized in 'vertical' mixed age groups. The transcript extract derives from a small-group science activity involving the teacher and three children – two girls and a boy. The activity involves conducting a 'scientific' test to investigate the different ways that two identical pieces of paper fall when one is left as a sheet and the other is screwed up into a ball. How and why do the pieces of paper come down in different ways at different speeds?

> I was interested in getting over the idea of change of variables, AT1 . . . The activity was really about finding out for themselves, AT1. To get them to describe movements and the effect of change of shape and how this gives different movements . . . The main thing about this activity was that I'd introduced the idea of a fair and an unfair test.[1]

For this exercise the children have been sorted into 'ability groups'. Avis considers that this gives her a more accurate and reliable assessment as each child is 'able to give a truer account of their level of understanding' since 'the more able tend to do all the talking in mixed ability groups'. Avis has already taken most of the children through the task in small groups. The group of children featured in the following transcript is the one that Avis considers to be least able. As a result of her estimate of this group's level of understanding Avis does not expect that these children will be able to achieve much; however, she has decided to proceed since she wishes to give every child an opportunity to complete the task, as it will form part of her National Curriculum Teacher Assessment for science. In passing we can also note that Avis is not particularly confident about teaching aspects of the new National Curriculum programmes of study, and has enrolled on an in-service course on teaching primary science to improve her knowledge and skills in this area.

The rest of the class has been set work to do in the classroom, and a parent helper has been assigned to solve any difficulties. Avis has taken the small 'focus' group into the practical activities area adjacent to the classroom. There is a mezzanine floor above this area (up 'the stairs').

T is sitting on a chair facing the children. She has a number of sheets of yellow A4 paper on her lap which she is counting. She has already given two sheets each to Carrie and Robert. The three children are sitting cross-legged on the floor looking up at T.

10:22

T   I'm just going to ask you whether you can tell me anything about the pieces of paper -

This appears to be an open question, which could elicit a number of descriptions of these pieces of paper, were the pupils sufficiently 'primed' to the teacher's agenda. However they seem rather nonplussed by the question – what can you say about a piece of paper, other than that it's a piece of paper.

T hands two sheets of paper to Gillie. Carrie and Robert are shuffling through theirs.

T   have a look - touch them - look at them what they're like in your hands -

T has picked up a piece of paper in her right hand and is slowly moving it up and down.

T   what are those pieces of paper like?

T now holds a piece of paper in each hand and is moving both of them alternately up and down so that the left hand is down as the right is up and vice versa. Carrie is imitating the alternate movement, Robert and Gillie are looking at the papers and moving them about in their hands.

Carrie   soft

T   they're soft are they? how would you describe the pieces of paper Robert -

Everyone is momentarily holding the paper still and looking at Robert.

Robert   um (*)

T   **look** at them - how would you describe the paper?

10:23

Robert snatches one sheet from his right to his left hand

Robert   throw them down the stairs

Robert holds one sheet up in his left hand

T   throw it down the stairs but > what < does it look like the paper?

Robert   > yeah<

Robert turns to look at something behind him

T   Robert - the paper -

T leans forward nearer to Robert. He looks back at her. T still has one sheet in each hand which she brings forward in front of her knees. Carrie is now balancing a sheet in each hand again, Gillie is scratching her ear.

T   what do you think of this paper - is it tissue - paper - is it paper that you use for drawing on =

Carrie   = yes =

Carrie gives an exaggerated nod as she says this

T   = what does it feel like?

Carrie   paper what you draw on

Although her words suggest that the question is still open, the bodily action appears to be cueing a specific response: the alternate motion is that used conventionally when miming a pair of scales, implying that the weight of the two pieces of paper should be compared.

Carrie immediately shows herself as most receptive or possibly attentive by modelling T's action.

Carrie also shows her engagement by being the first to make a response. It is accepted relatively neutrally but the immediate repetition of the question to Robert suggests that this was the 'wrong' answer, at least in the sense that it is not the response that T is looking for.

T instructs Robert to carry out an important scientific procedure – i.e. observation – but the context and tone of her utterance does not indicate that she is helping him to understand it as a scientific procedure, and conduct it as such, but rather that this is an issue of classroom control – appropriate classroom behaviour.

Robert knows what happened from watching the other groups and wants to get on with the action!

Once again the repetition of the statement appears to be intended to suggest that the response is not exactly wrong, but is not what T is seeking.

By 'naming' Robert, T is attracting his attention and bringing him back on task. This is the first of many occasions when she does this.

Until now it has appeared that T has had a particular answer in mind – that the sheets of paper are the same size, shape and weight – an answer that she is cueing by her action. However, simply asking (pseudo) open questions (Barnes 1976) has not elicited this. T now moves to more of a multiple choice format, though presumably she hopes that through a process of comparison a reference to 'sameness' will emerge.

T now uses an explicit 'reformulator' (French and MacLure, 1983) which is usually used to cue the

T   it's paper you draw on is it -
T looks briefly at Carrie. Robert and Gillie
are still looking at T and handling their
paper. T looks over to Gillie.

'correct' answer. However in this case this attribute is not 'the answer' so much as a staging post towards the answer that T requires.

T   would you say that's the sort
          of paper it is Gillie? -
Gillie   - mmmm

T seems now to be interested in getting Gillie to say something.

Gillie appears unwilling to respond, but then she is not given much time in which to do so.

T   what sort of paper would you
          say it is - can you tell me any-
          thing about the paper whether
          the paper's -
T is now repeating the alternate paper
movement.
T   what it's like?
T looks back towards Carrie, still waving
the paper up and down.

T   do you think both pieces -
          how do they feel -
Carrie   soft
Carrie nods as she says this. Robert has put
his paper down on his left and slightly
behind him.

T has introduced the word 'both'. For the first time she is indicating that there might be some element of comparison. However, the children do not pick up this nuance. Carrie returns to her original idea.

T   they feel you still think they
          feel soft?
T now looks back at Gillie. T appears to
throw the paper very slightly up in the air
and now has her hand underneath each
sheet waving them slightly up and down
this time simultaneously.

The word 'still' seems to indicate that this is not an acceptable answer.

Is she suggesting light weight, floating?

T   what about - is there anything
          you can tell me - about the
          paper anything other than it
          being soft?
T is looking now towards Robert who has
picked up his paper again.

This confirms that 'soft' is not correct.

Gillie   erm -
Robert   I know
T   what's that?
Carrie   bouncy
Carrie pushes both pieces of paper upwards
and forwards.
T   it's bouncy
Robert   bouncy > bouncy <
. . . [*brief interruption by another child*] . . .
10:24

The first of several occasions when Robert says he knows, but where we are unable to find out what he knows because Carrie immediately intercedes before he can continue. Is this deliberate on Carrie's part?

This might be an interpretation of T's cueing.

Another neutral evaluation – 'OK but not what I'm after.'

T   now - I want you to look at
          one piece of paper and look at
          the other one
T is now doing the alternate motion again.
Carrie puts her paper down and picks it up

'now' – re-establishing the group back on task. T makes the notion of comparison more explicit. However, she is determined to lead the children to this through returning to her pattern of pseudo-open questions (Barnes 1976); her role as teacher-assessor compounds her tacit adherence to a model

again so that she is holding it like T with her hands underneath. Robert looks back in the direction of T.

T   right now close your eyes still hold them in the same hands

All three children are moving the papers about in their hands

T   - both hands - right - that's it hold the paper in your hands - close your eyes

R is turning papers round in his hands

Robert   wait a minute

Robert adjusts his papers so that he has one in each hand. The children all giggle and T smiles.

T   right - close your eyes - what can you tell me about the weight of the paper? - does the paper feel

Carrie has dropped one of her sheets of paper. She picks it up and holds both sheets between her two hands, running them over the surface, then puts them back, one in each hand. T is doing the simultaneous movement again.

T   - do they both feel -

T goes back to the alternate movement this time emphasizing it with her shoulders.

T   does one feel <u>different</u> from the other - or are they both the same

Carrie   both the same

Carrie looks up at T and pushes her sheets forward again.

T   you think they're both the same?

Carrie nods

Robert   **yeah**

T   how could we find out if they were both the same - what could we do - what could we do to find out if they were both the same?

A piece of paper slips off T's lap onto the floor

Robert   you've dropped your paper

Robert points to the paper

T   I know I've dropped a piece of paper

Carrie reaches over to pick up the piece of

of guided discovery learning where a question such as 'How are these pieces of paper the same?' would be considered too directive. In fact her cueing would suggest that although ostensibly more open, the locutionary force of the questions she is actually posing is considerably narrower.

T admits defeat. She has now told them that she is interested in the weight of the sheets of paper. In fact the children do not respond to this telling any more directly than they have to the miming. Is this because they do not understand what she means by weight, or is it that they are already confused and find the pseudo-open form of her question difficult to engage with? Or is it both?

Carrie seems to have picked up on the word 'feel', but related to her earlier response of 'soft' (i.e. touch) rather than weight.

Had this been the starting point, the children might well have been less confused. They might also have been more likely to focus on the scientific principle at stake rather than on the effort of determining what T was after.

Finally we reach the 'real' topic of concern for T: AT1 and the construction of a fair test.

Robert seems to be more concerned with the extraneous events which punctuate the lesson, than with the substance.
T is annoyed; just when she appears to be getting somewhere; the falling paper distracts the children.

paper. T raises her foot slightly, putting it between Carrie and the paper.

T   it's all right where it is thank you Carrie

Carrie sits back without touching the paper.

T   - how could we find out if they were both the same what would you do -

Robert and Gillie both look round away from T, Carrie is looking at T. T now looks exclusively at Carrie.

T   if these were two bags of sugar how would we find out if they were both the same?

10:25

Robert and Gillie look back briefly in the direction of T, then turn round again.

Carrie   hard

T   pardon?

Carrie   hard

T   hard -

Carrie nods her head. The other two children are now looking at their paper.

T   it's very hard to do that is it? - how would you do it - how does mummy do it to find out if there's something when she's doing her cooking -

T, who is still holding a piece of paper in each hand performs two sequences of the simultaneous movement followed by the alternate movement. She is still looking exclusively at Carrie.

T   what does she use mummy for her cooking to find out wha\ about things (*) - they're the same -

T's hands are now at rest on her lap.

T   does mummy ever use anything?

Carrie nods. Robert, who is pushing his paper up in the air and catching it, loses a sheet behind him. He turns round and picks it up.

T   what does she use in her cooking to find out a\ how much things are?

Carrie   carrots

T is fishing for the idea of weighing the two sheets to confirm that their mass is similar. However, although comparison has been established, the idea of weight has not. In order to establish that the two pieces of paper weigh the same, T needs to go through a particular question and answer sequence. She has identified Carrie as the child most likely to provide the right answer and now ignores the other two.

Comparing bags of sugar obviously suggests a weight relationship to T, but this is not made explicit to the children.

T appeals to the children's experience of home. In the context of school mathematics this can cause more difficulties than it solves (cf. Cooper 1992, 1994). However, in this case it seems particularly ill-judged, as it is appealing to an image of a mother doing her cooking which seems grounded in the 1950s rather than the 1990s.

T is appealing to a stereotypical image of mother and daughter cooking together. Carrie may never have had such an experience; if she has had, it is unlikely that it would stress the importance of weighing and measuring. In reality, of course, it is far more likely that 'mummy' buys things ready-made at the supermarket or uses packaged cake mixes.

T is obviously desperate for an answer and Carrie is very keen to provide one. It has obviously got something to do with food, so Carrie guesses 'carrots'.

Carrie waving her paper up and down slightly.

T   she uses carrots does she? but what does she find out with her carrots -

T performs the alternate movement followed by the simultaneous movement. Robert goes back to pushing the paper in the air and catching it. Carrie and Gillie are looking at T.

T   when she's making a cake what does she do to see whether they're both the same weight -

The paper on T's right hand falls off. T moves forward and catches it again. Robert looks at T.

T   what does she use - what does mummy use - when you do your cooking when you make mince pies and the bread what do we find what do we use to find out how much flour we've got? -

T looks at Gillie

10:26

T   what do we use Gillie - when we've got

Carrie   (*flour)

T looks back at Carrie

T   pardon - what do we

T glances over at Gillie

Carrie   (* > * <)

Robert   > I I (*know) <

As he says this Robert puts his hand up. T, Gillie and Carrie all look at him. Carrie flapping the paper in her right hand briefly.

T   what do you - what is it called -

Robert brings his left hand down onto his head and puts his right hand in his mouth

T   we put the we put the flour into a pan

T makes a pouring movement with her right hand followed by a circular motion. Robert has put his left hand up straight again but then soon lets it drop again.

T   the\ the special white pan don't we -

T performs a placing mime.

Does T really believe that Carrie's mother uses carrots as weights?

T again gives up and reintroduces the word 'weight' that she had previously been trying to elicit; however, her form of words conflates 'mummy making cakes' at home (the act of weighing) with the comparison task in school – 'the same weight'.

'you do your cooking' now appears to be a reference to cooking at school.

T's faith in Carrie was obviously misplaced. She returns reluctantly to the other two children. This is the first time she has looked in their direction since Robert pointed out that she had dropped her paper. Carrie is stung into response by T's addressing of the question to Gillie.

The use of the accompanying mime is redundant in terms of the children's understanding of the words. Is the teacher miming because she hopes it will make her weighing motion more understandable to the children?

T has now used 'we' several times – appealing to what she hopes is shared 'common knowledge' of cooking at school.

Robert   > and it (*) <
T   > and then we put it < on
          something - what is that thing
          called =
Robert raises his hand.   Despite his use of the confident phrase 'I know', 'a
Robert   = I know - a pot   pot' is said with a rising intonation as if he is unsure.
*T shakes her head and leans forward
towards Robert. Carrie and Gillie are look-
ing at him.*
T   no - what do we put the flour
          before we put it into the bowl =
Carrie turns her head towards T.
Carrie   (*)
*T still leaning forward, looks now at
Carrie. The other two children are now
looking at T.*
T   so that we - know we've got
          enough flour - to use -
T   what do we use - how do we
          weigh something - what do we
          use to weigh - what do we call
          it when we're weighing some-
          thing - a pair of sca\   These four clues are rather confusing – the first
Carrie   (*)   would suggest a noun, the second an adverb, the
T   pardon you said it - a pair of -   third a noun and the fourth a verb.
          scal\
Gillie   a pair of -
Carrie   (*)
T   yes that's right scales
T nods her head and leans back again.   This movement is the visible sign of a relaxing of
T   - a pair of scales - we could use   tension. The guessing game has lasted almost two
          some scales   minutes. Did T actually tell them or did she not?
*T drops one piece of paper and places the   Does it really matter?
other on top of it.*
T   I'm just going to go and - can
          you go and get the balance -   Having worked so hard to elicit the word 'scales', T
                                          now refers to a balance!

We have included only the opening section of a much longer small-group session (Avis worked with these three children on this activity for 23 minutes).
As the activity developed, Avis 'changed tack' and became less ambitious with
respect to her original agenda. Broadly speaking she was satisfied with the
encounter and what she learned from it:

> I was surprised that we got so much out of it as we did . . . Carrie will be
> able to use a balance now . . . For that group the most important thing was
> talking about balancing. It was an unintended outcome. When I realized
> that they didn't really understand about weight I got the balance, I
> changed tack to concentrate on the balance . . . I'm introducing the
> vocabulary. Carrie didn't know heavier and lighter so I was able to

introduce the scales . . . I decided to home in on Carrie. I feel that Carrie's self esteem is low and so it's nice to get her to talk about things and succeeding. Had I tried to get something out of Robert and Gillie, Carrie would have been lost. She tends to look round and gets easily bored . . . I'll follow it up next week because even though it's not in my plan it came out of the work so I'll just put it in . . . It gave me the information that lots of work on balances is needed when we do measures in maths.

Thus Avis modified the statements of attainment that she was trying to assess, in response to the way in which the children reacted to the task. In a sense, therefore, one could argue that this represents a successful example of teacher assessment. In a complex interaction where many factors need to be considered, Avis established that these children did not understand the scientific principles at stake and were unable to respond even when given many clues with respect to developing and designing a 'fair test'. She then used this information to change direction and succeeded in diagnosing an important problem area on which to do further work. She also felt that she had been able to make an important intervention, with potentially favourable effects on at least one pupil's motivation. From a session that seemed to be heading nowhere she can be said to have gained important assessment data.

And yet, to reiterate, this assessment lasted for 23 minutes virtually uninterrupted; in the context of the complexities of the classroom and the difficulty that teachers often express in finding time for focusing on individuals and small groups, this assessment would have to yield something quite significant to justify the amount of time spent. Also, the exercise had already been repeated several times to cover the whole class. The outcome, however, only seemed to confirm what the teacher thought she knew to be the case in the first place. It is hardly likely that it would be otherwise, given the level at which she had previously assessed the children. Is there any point in setting this sort of task for children whom Avis herself considered to be the 'least able' in her class of 6- to 7-year-olds? Differentiation is as crucial an issue for assessment as it is for curriculum planning. Indeed, there is some irony in that an important aim of formative assessment is supposed to be to provide work 'matched' to pupils' levels of attainment, so that they do not flounder around with material which is obviously beyond their range of understanding; but here, assessment is the instrument by which this actually occurs. What appears to be at issue more than anything else is that Avis has identified this activity as an assessment exercise for the purposes of her recorded National Curriculum Teacher Assessment and is determined to go through with it, not so much for its value in informing the future learning of the children, but to obtain the data which she can record on the children's records.

However, the main question that we wish to engage with here is that which concerns the structure of the language through which this assessment takes place and the relationship between the language of teaching and the conduct of assessment. Edwards and Mercer (1987) identified a teaching culture prevalent in primary schools which they summarized as:

1 Setting up conditions which they believed would allow children to discover things for themselves . . .

2 Planning their teaching to include activities which would give children direct, concrete experience, and which would require them to act, not just to listen, read or write . . .

3 Attempting to refer to children's wider, out of school experience when explaining curriculum topics (in the sense of 'general knowledge' but hardly ever by reference to the particular life experience of any one child in the group) . . .

4 By the use of techniques like the 'guessing game' question and answer sessions . . . to elicit key ideas from children rather than informing them of these directly . . .

5 Never defining (for the children) the full agenda of any activity or lesson in advance. Although such curricular agendas were always invoked implicitly by the teachers in the way in which they structured lessons and in their choice of questions to children, they clearly felt dissatisfied if on reflection, they considered that this implicit agenda had limited the lessons' possibilities for children to make their own discoveries . . .

6 Not defining explicitly (for the children) the criteria for successful learn-ing which would eventually be applied to what they had done.
(Edwards and Mercer 1987:33–4)

These strategies appear to stem from ideologies of teaching which Edwards and Mercer identify with the Plowden Report (Central Advisory Council for Education 1967) and Piagetian psychology. Their critique of an unreflective so-called 'child-centred' approach to education, accords with others deriving from different perspectives (e.g. Sharp and Green 1975; Walkerdine 1978; Bennett *et al.* 1984). However, since the fieldwork for these studies and others took place there have been many changes to primary schooling, particularly the introduction of a highly prescriptive National Curriculum. What is inter-esting is that despite the introduction of a prescribed curriculum, all six of Edwards and Mercer's themes still seem to be apparent in the transcription above, and indeed, some may even have been compounded by the lack of con-fidence – the deskilling – which Avis felt with respect to teaching science.

The incident is curious because of the way the guessing game at the start works. It appears that the teacher's aspiration for this part of the session is that the children will produce a number of different attributes of the pieces of paper, including that they are 'the same'. From this she will then seize on the notion of sameness as a prerequisite for a 'fair test'. But if she wants to estab-lish whether the pieces of paper are the same, and in what ways they are the same, surely the most productive question(s) would be, 'Are these two pieces of paper the same?' and/or 'How can we decide whether or not these two pieces of paper are the same?' However, her determination not to give the game away makes it very difficult for the children to understand what is going on. It appears that Robert is not at all concerned. He only wants to get involved in throwing the paper down the stairs as he has seen other children do. Gillie seems unwilling to commit herself and appears to want to wait until she feels safer. Carrie is playing the part of ideal pupil and trying to guess what it is that the teacher wants her to say, but is baffled by the teacher's strategy. The combination of pseudo-open and pseudo-closed questioning is confusing, even to Carrie, partly because it is so inexplicit and partly because the pertinence of any cognitive scaffolding is obscured, at least at first, by being oriented towards all three children. This 'single ability group' actually contains three children whose levels of understanding of the procedures of the classroom seem very diverse.

Edwards and Westgate (1987) note that learning to become pupils is very much a matter of mastering an interactional code, the rules of which are regularly acted on by teachers but rarely explained. Similarly, as Edwards and Furlong point out: 'The deepest level of "common knowledge" is about the proper relationship of teacher and pupil, because without this, the task of establishing procedural competence is difficult and the main business of instruction cannot begin' (Edwards and Furlong 1978:148). Robert and Gillie seem to have made very little progress towards mastering the code. Carrie is playing by the implicit basic rules, but can make very little progress because of Avis's use of obscure variant strategies that seem paradoxically to derive from her low estimation of the children's ability to come up with the answers she is seeking.

As the session develops it becomes obvious that Gillie and Robert are not really involved at all. The children have not worked out the rules behind this engagement. Robert and Gillie keep putting up their hands and are ignored. When they speak, Avis sometimes looks in their direction, but Carrie has realized that bidding with hands up is not part of the rules for a small group of three: she just speaks when she needs to and Avis lets her take her turn in this way. Gillie's and Robert's lack of involvement leads Avis, once she has identified Carrie as a potential achiever, to concentrate almost solely on her, with infrequent references back to the other two.

However, and despite the 'teacher assessment' context, this concentration on Carrie seems less to do with gaining information about her level of understanding and more to do with 'accomplishing the lesson' *qua* lesson; i.e. getting to the end of some imaginary ideal-typical teacher agenda. Ironically, far from directly communicating the content of that agenda – the content of 'the lesson' – this has the consequence of diverting the substance of the encounter away from 'principled' scientific knowledge and understanding to 'ritual' knowledge of classroom processes (cf. Edwards and Mercer 1987). The children have to struggle to understand the teacher's procedural strategy and none of them (though particularly Gillie and Robert) appear to be able to pick up Avis's nuanced use of the conventions of classroom speech. In interview Avis described the trio as 'immature', but it may be that this is not so much because they do not comprehend the work that they are set, as because they do not apprehend the conventions by which the teacher is working. They are like foreigners who, although they may have some knowledge of the words in use, are unable to pick up on the cultural assumptions underpinning them and thus cannot understand what is happening in this society. This impression is completed by Avis's frequent use of mime to cue the children's response. The result of this opaque performance is that any understanding that the children may construct is likely to be on the level of ritual. In trying to understand the puzzling behaviour of the teacher, these children are likely to have little attention left for the content of the session, and their recollection is liable to be determined by the structure of the encounter rather than its substance. This accords with the conclusion of Willes (1983), who found that young children are more attentive to ritual than to substance, and also with our own investigations elsewhere (e.g. Chapter 3, page 41 – 'very good, now do something else').

In this incident there is some principled knowledge at stake. However, even if the children involved had been more proficient as pupils, the guessing game would be likely to remain unproductive because the words and ideas that are being elicited are not at an appropriate level for the children, and the teacher does not provide sufficient scaffolding to enable them to work in their zone of proximal development. Even from the sort of interaction apparent in the opening exchanges it would have been possible to establish fairly quickly that the elicitations were liable to be ineffective; this would then allow the children to be taught directly – introducing straight away the connections between the words 'weight', 'heavy', 'light', 'heavier' and 'lighter'. These could have been demonstrated with the scales, and the children then asked to experiment with the scales to further their understanding and to ensure that there was some degree of handover of the concept. In this way they might not only have learned something, but any observing and questioning at that later stage could have established what they had learned and how they were relating to the new ideas.

In effect the style of the observed discourse not only obscures the scientific principles at stake but also perhaps acts as a camouflage for the teacher's lack of subject expertise. This gives a pointer to another and perhaps most crucial issue. A key assumption of any stepped, 'building block' approach to teaching, learning and assessment (such as that exemplified by the National Curriculum and National Assessment) must be that knowledge exists prior to the teaching encounter, the teacher knows the knowledge, and the teacher can and does transmit the knowledge to the pupils. Similarly, the traditional authority of the teacher derives at least in part from their knowledge of the subject matter, and the transmission of knowledge from teacher to pupil acts as a symbol of this authority. Yet every aspect of Avis's understanding of her role militates against this series of assumptions. Neither as teacher nor as assessor does she see herself directly intervening, and indeed, her perception of her assessor role compounds her non-interventive, non-directive stance. However, this is not to say that the pupils take control of the interaction or the discourse. What we see with Avis is that, rather than give up power, the teacher actually stays even more strongly in control of the discourse. She preserves her control not by offering knowledge, but by withholding it through the question and answer sequence of the guessing game, and by taking what the children say and reinterpreting it with respect to her own agenda.

We shall return to these issues of power, how teachers appropriate and use children's contributions in lessons, and the role of appropriation in structuring learning, in the next chapter – for they can have positive as well as negative implications for learning. For the moment we can note one further intriguing aspect of the guessing game – that of Avis making references to children's experiences at home. That these are met with incomprehension by the children suggests that the home she is alluding to does not really exist.

Edwards and Mercer (1987:33, point 3 referred to above) identify this as a common feature of their observations, while in an earlier study Edwards and Furlong (1978:121), observing older pupils, noted that they had to suspend any knowledge of the topic that they already had, at least provisionally, and generate new meanings within the frame of reference provided by the teacher. Here the children don't 'get it' because they do not understand the 'common knowledge' being invoked – it is simply not as common as teachers suppose.[2] Avis refers to a world of mothers weighing out ingredients and engaging with children in collaborative cooking activities which seems to be unknown to these children. She works hard to give them clues which are nevertheless meaningless for them, and once again the result of these strategies is to place the children in a position of ignorance and non-achievement.

Quite apart from the gender issues underpinning such scenarios, which were not the focus of our study and thus will not be pursued here, they may nevertheless be differentially accessible for different groups of pupils. Even within its own terms, the vision of girls cooking with mothers implicitly excludes boys from this 'common knowledge'. More generally, however, the way in which 'guessing games' work hinges around the tacitness of the assumptions invoked. And, as Bourdieu among others has noted:

> By doing away with giving explicitly to everyone what it implicitly demands of everyone, the educational system demands of everyone alike that they have what it does not give. This consists mainly of linguistic and cultural competence . . . an institution . . . which neglects to transmit the instruments indisposable to the success of its undertaking is bound to become the monopoly of those social classes capable of transmitting by their own means.
>
> (Bourdieu 1973:80–1)

This raises the possibility that assessments such as those in the transcription are not just generally invalid, but by the very opacity of their form are differentially invalid and favour those children who have the cultural capital to recognize the rules of the game.

For the present, however, the key point to reiterate is that classroom assessment is accomplished by a process of teacher–pupil interaction and through the language of teaching. This process is considerably more complex than current policy on teacher assessment, and indeed some of the claims for formative assessment, would allow. This chapter has demonstrated some of that complexity, and we will now move on to explore it in more detail in subsequent chapters, particularly with respect to the impact of assessment on learning, and seek to illuminate some of the positive possibilities of classroom assessment, as well as its problems.

Notes

1 The quotations in this section derive from a tape-recorded interview conducted at the end of the day in which the work took place. 'AT1' = Attainment Target 1 of the

National Curriculum for Science, which is concerned with assessing the children's understanding of the process of science.
2 The same issue applies to test design and development; see Cooper (1992, 1994) for a critique of the use of 'everyday', 'common sense' contexts for maths assessment.

5

The power of assessment: appropriating children's responses for learning, or social control?

Introduction

In this chapter we move on to investigate the ways in which the patterns of teacher–pupil interaction identified in Chapter 4 are established in the earliest stages of schooling and encapsulated in the earliest manifestations of assessment. Initial assessment encounters both exemplify and recursively realize in action the power relations in classrooms and the ways in which teacher–pupil understandings and expectations are constructed and maintained. In turn, however, this social process of continually creating and re-creating norms of behaviour and frameworks of cognitive expectation also acts as the context within which learning can be scaffolded and developed. Thus the dichotomy implied by the title of this chapter is perhaps a little misleading, since our conclusions will be that *both* learning and social control are pursued and accomplished: classrooms could not function if it were otherwise. Nevertheless, we will also suggest that there is considerable room for improvement in how this is done.

An aspect of the dichotomy which requires some initial attention is that of our definition of 'social control', since it is essentially sociological rather than political, though of course the two conceptual fields are interlinked. Common-sense notions of social control in the political sense imply a level of coercion and the unidirectional exercise of power. Clearly there is an element of this (and sometimes much more than an element) in everyday life in classrooms as anywhere else. But power is more usually negotiated over, rather than straightforwardly exercised, and social life in a more general sociological sense could not take place without a significant element of implicit social control; i.e. without most of us, most of the time, taking for granted the norms and assumptions of everyday life. So it is with schools and classrooms. Schools are very significant social institutions which both attempt to impart norms and values in a direct and transmissional sense and, at the same time, establish and realize expectations and assumptions through their pattern of organization and processes of interaction. This chapter will demonstrate that assessment plays a crucial role in these patterns and processes, while also suggesting that it can link forward to learning goals which the teacher may have in mind even if the child does not. A key issue is how the teacher's prospective agenda is 'brought into play' in the present, and with what consequences for teacher judgement and pupil learning. Thus the chapter examines the way in which social expectations and power relationships are used to structure assessment at the early stages of schooling; how these in turn affect the accomplishment of developing pupil identities with respect to understanding and performing the role of pupil; and how teacher appropriation of children's utterances can have potentially positive as well as potentially negative consequences for learning.

This chapter therefore suggests that classroom assessment is a crucial field in which teacher–pupil relationships are realized. The teacher's role as assessor highlights the power relationships that are inherent in classroom interaction, since it is in the process of assessment that what is to count as knowledge is contested and decided. However, as will be clear from the data we present, the child in the featured transcript does not simply aquiesce; she resists the teacher's intellectual and social agenda for much of the interaction while at the same time, through the process of interaction, learning implicit lessons about how she should act in the future. Classroom assessment can thus be construed as a particularly important arena for the social construction of class-room discursive practices. This is especially so when the assessment event in question is part of the child's earliest initiation into the rituals of schooling, as is the case in the extract we present below.

Yet the rhetoric behind much of what is written and said about classroom assessment does not take note of this kind of sociological understanding. In previous chapters we have drawn attention to the fact that classroom linguistic structures make the process of question and answer on which much class-room assessment is based extremely problematic. The issue is further compounded by psychological complexities deriving from the differing motivational orientations of individual children, a topic to which we will turn in subsequent chapters. Here, we develop the idea that contemporary analysis of assessment seems largely to have ignored or forgotten the insights from a long line of sociological research going back to Talcott Parsons, who claimed that evaluation of pupils was 'undifferentiated into the cognitive or technical component and the moral or "social" component' (Parsons 1959:304). The function of schooling with respect to socialization and the importance of assessment within this remains the same, although the processes at work are much more complex and dynamic than Parsons's functionalism would allow. However, this kind of analysis gives a foundation on which to build an argument making explicit the issues of power that are at stake when assessment takes place. Thus in our discussion of the data we draw on insights derived from current sociological work (e.g. Bourdieu 1990; Kreisberg 1992) and relate them to social constructivist analyses of how children learn (Newman *et al.* 1989).

Baseline assessment

The data in the following transcription derive from a 'baseline assessment' interview conducted between a teacher and a pupil new to school – she had joined the reception class the previous day. Formal 'baseline assessments' are becoming widespread in infant schools for both formative and summative purposes. Teachers are keen to establish an initial platform of knowledge about new pupils for the purpose of planning their programme of work, but at the same time the pressure of accountability and the publication of league tables of 'raw' National Assessment results mean that schools and local authorities are also keen to have some basis for establishing what pupils' achievements are when they enter school, so that the 'value-added' by the school can be calculated.

The principle of calculating value-added is contentious, and the practice fraught with difficulties (see, for example, Gray and Wilcox (1995) for a full discussion). It consists of trying to establish what a school can be expected to achieve with a cohort of pupils, by reference to prior attainment, and then comparing this with what it actually achieves – is it better or worse than expected? It can be seen as a technology by which apparently 'poor' schools might be able to demonstrate that they are doing at least as well, if not better, than expected (i.e. with 'poor' raw material); and perhaps that apparently 'good' schools are only achieving what they should be expected to achieve (i.e. with 'better' raw material). It has been most developed with respect to secondary schools, where calculations of the value-added to a pupil's GCSE examination results can be based on measures of prior achievement at age 11. Calculations at younger ages would of course have to be based on measures of even earlier prior achievement. At age 7, the end of infant schooling and the first stage of the UK National Curriculum, calculations would have to be based on what a child can demonstrate when they first enter school: the 'baseline'.

Several approaches to conducting this sort of assessment have been explored by schools and local authorities, including structured but fairly open-ended and formatively intended 'conferences' between new pupil and teacher (sometimes involving parents as well; see, for example, Stierer (1995)). Formal schemes much more obviously oriented to producing measures for calculating value-added have also been introduced by local authorities under the guidance of government (SCAA 1996), though as yet no single practice has been established or legislated for. These more formal approaches revolve around teachers conducting short face-to-face 'interviews' or 'verbal tests' with individual children. Given our discussion so far, the reader will not be surprised that we are extremely sceptical about the validity and reliability of such tests.

The discussion in this chapter is based on the transcription of a less formal baseline assessment interview. It is in effect the teacher's own 'invention' based on what she believes about the value of formative baseline assessment. It has been selected precisely because it is intended to be formative in orientation, but also because it so clearly demonstrates the conflation of the social with the cognitive in children's earliest experience of assessment. The assessment involves the reception class teacher, 'Pat Black' and a 4-year-old pupil new to the school, 'Eloise'. This is the child's second day at school, having joined the reception class in the middle of the spring term. However, it is the first time she has met her class teacher because Pat was absent from school the previous day. The teacher does not explain the purpose of the encounter to the child. This seems to be taken for granted: it is enough that a teacher wants a child to do something, though to help realize the formative intention, some explanation might have been appropriate. As with Avis in the last chapter, therefore, it seems as if the teacher does not want to 'contaminate' the data, though in fact plenty of cues are given during the encounter. Also, at one point, as we note in our commentary, Pat does feel it incumbent on her to explain why she has asked an ancillary helper to fetch her a drink of water – i.e. a non-professional 'social' incident which the teacher thinks is unusual and therefore worthy of explanation. Pat makes unstructured notes as the interview proceeds. She is sitting at a low-level 'small group' hexagonal table. She is sitting next to the wall at one end of the table, with a chair for the pupil on the next hexagonal – i.e. at about 60° to the teacher. Once again, parallel texts are used to present the data.

13:36

T ushers Eloise towards the table and tucks the chair under her so that she sits down.

T   right now then Eloise - could you - do you know who I am?

Eloise shakes her head. While T speaks to her, she takes off Eloise's alice band and puts it back on again. Eloise is perched on the front edge of her chair almost kneeling on the ground, her elbows on the table.

T is controlling the interaction through quite overt physical as well as linguistic means. She has ushered the child into her seat, 'tucked her in' and is now assuming authority over her physical appearance by changing the way Eloise wears her alice band (i.e. hair band).

T   I'm Mrs Black - right and I'm the teacher in here with Mrs Scarlet

Eloise removes her alice band again and replaces it.

Eloise reasserts control over her body.

. . . [brief interruption by another child] . . .

T   now then Eloise could you tell me a little bit about you - how old are you Eloise?

An initially open question is rapidly transformed into a closed question.

Eloise   Four

T   you're four - Eloise - I /am /four/

T writes this down with her right hand as she says it, half facing the child while resting her face on her left hand and her left elbow on the table. Eloise pivots forwards and backwards on the two front legs of the chair.

T writes this as 'I am 4'. T has appropriated Eloise's one-word response and transformed it into an utterance that is acceptable to her and her recording procedures.

Eloise looks at T's hand as she writes, she is curious but seems uncomfortable – fidgety – on the chair.

T   right what's your other name Eloise?

Eloise   Eloise Gray

T   Grade - how do you spell that?

Eloise may be able to write her surname, but it seems unreasonable to ask her to spell it out loud. However, Eloise does seem to understand the question, since she replies directly.

Eloise	I don't know	
T	gee are ay - dee ee- like that Grade ~	T says this quizzically, almost as if she is trying to provide some scaffolding for Eloise's spelling, to see if Eloise can recognize the correct letters. However, Eloise corrects T's enunciation without necessarily recognizing the script.
Eloise	**Gray**	

T looks up across the classroom for a moment. Eloise continues to pivot on her chair, then settles, almost lying with her head resting on her arms on the table.

T	Gray - right - fine - you're four and what do you like doing?	T accepts Eloise's enunciation without making any alteration to the script.
Eloise **13.37**	I like playing with my Barbie	
T	do you?	

T writes. As she does so she turns to Special Educational Needs Ancillary (SENA) and asks for a glass of water: 20 second conversation about this . . . [ ] . . .

T	I like playing - with /my / dolls - your Barbie dolls - what else do you like doing?	Again T has appropriated Eloise's utterance and changed 'barbie' to 'dolls' in the written version. She then reinstates the word Barbie, but this is said quickly and does not appear to be part of the written text.

T writes as she says words. Eloise pulls herself forwards on her elbows out of the chair and rests half crouching on the table.

Eloise	I like playing with my daddy and mummy
T	do you? - right -

T starts to write this down and Eloise watches her subsiding back to previous half lying position.

Eloise	and my brother	Eloise is here engaged in an initiating move, which is uncommon for a child in classroom interaction.
T	and your brother	
Eloise	he's called Oscar	
T	is he?	
Eloise	and he's only two and a half	Eloise is now taking control of the discourse by offering to talk about her brother. This is only loosely a response to T's question. Eloise speaks with marked intonation and some animation, in contrast to her slouching posture. She is clearly interested in talking about Oscar.
T	goodness me =	
Eloise	= he's only small	
T	is he - > and Oscar <	
Eloise **13.38**	> (**) < - is two and a half	
T	who/is/two and a half - he/is/only/- small - right	The words are fairly close to those of Eloise, but the syntax is that of written, not spoken, English.

T writes this down as she says it. Eloise stands up alongside her chair, propping herself up on her elbow on the table, with her chair between her and the teacher; she has moved away from the teacher.

Eloise seems to be resisting T's management of the interaction while being interested in its content. She has obviously deduced that T's writing is related to her own speech and seems to be genuinely curious about the relationship between the spoken and written word. She is initiating again.

Eloise	does that say small?

Eloise points to a word and touches the teacher's paper.

T	it says small -	Rather than merely confirming Eloise's deduction, T

T smiles

T   yes - now then Eloise you sit
           down cos you have to stay sat
           on the chair - and I'd like you
           to do some work -

*T moves back Eloise's chair to allow her to
sit down. Eloise perches right on the front
edge with her knees almost on the floor. T
tears the sheet of paper on which she has
been writing in half and gives half to
Eloise, along with the pencil she has been
using.*

T   now - here's a pencil - here's a
           ruler -

*Eloise picks up the pencil in her left hand
and the ruler in her right.*

T   right - ooo - let me see - we've
           got blue pencils in <u>this</u> basket
           - now Eloise - would you write
           your name for me on the
           piece of paper - off you go

*Eloise puts down the ruler and starts to
write down her name. She writes with her
left hand, and as she does so, she holds her
paper down with her right hand and
stretches across the table, standing up from
her chair. T looks around classroom. As
Eloise finishes writing she sits down, then
slides forward to perch on the front edge of
the chair again.*

T   <u>good</u> girl - right - would you
           like to write in <u>your</u> writing -
           what you like to do -

*Eloise nods and draws her chair in to sit
more squarely at the table.*

T   you write in <u>your</u> writing
           what you like to do =

Eloise   = what do I have to do with
           this?

Eloise points to ruler.

13:39

T   <u>that</u> - you can draw a line
           under your name with that
           rule

T positions ruler at top of Eloise's paper.

T   - would you like to draw a line
           under your name as it's
           important

Eloise draws line with ruler.

could use this as an opportunity for further questioning, e.g. whether she recognizes any other
words, and/or also for positive feedback. However,
what has actually attracted T's attention is Eloise's
behaviour rather than her cognitive performance.
This is now becoming a tacit struggle for classroom
control, and T invokes the need to do 'work' to
legitimate control.

T seems almost ritualistically to be introducing
Eloise to the sacred artefacts of schooling.

T only looks at Eloise as she finishes writing – is T
interested or not? We can speculate that now that
Eloise is 'on task' and therefore controlled, there is
no need for T to monitor her closely. This would
suggest once again that her interest is more in the
socialization of the pupil rather than in gaining
insight into her cognitive and motor skills.

Is this a comment on the quality of the work or the
behaviour? (i.e. the *task* has been done, good or
not). It marks a shift towards more normal evaluative third moves in the discourse structure.

T has asked a typically rhetorical 'teacher question'
– 'would you like to . . .' – which is actually an
instruction. However, Eloise's nodding suggests that
she does not recognize it as an instruction. She takes
it as a genuine inquiry, seems to be engaged with the
task, but is confused by the presence of the ruler and
does not understand the significance of 'your'. T
seems to have an idea of emergent writing which, as
becomes apparent, means nothing to the child.

T invents a function for the sacred instrument. Any
assessment function (can Eloise use a ruler?) is
negated by T positioning it herself.

Another rhetorical question.

T   - good girl - right put that one away now -

Teacher removes ruler and places it in a box on the other side of the table well out of Eloise's reach.

> T recognizes the distracting potential of the ruler.

T   would you like to write what you like doing - you can put I am four - would you like to write I am four - in your writing

> Another open question rapidly narrowed. Eloise is now being asked to write down what has already been recorded by T.

Eloise nods.

T   off you go then

Eloise raises both hands in air and then places right hand on forehead.

Eloise   yes but I don't know how to

> Eloise appears to know about spelling words and she knows that she can't do it.

T   no - you do it in your writing - it doesn't matter if it's wrong <u>you</u> do what you think in your pretend writing

Eloise stands up and leans over the table again to write.

> By using 'pretend' T indicates her desire to see emergent writing, but this word and the word 'wrong' are not really consonant with the rationale behind this approach to teaching writing. Eloise does not have a concept of emergent writing, but quickly catches on to what she is being required to do. What is T now trying to assess? Since Eloise has not practised emergent writing before, T is unlikely to be able to make deductions about her progress to date, e.g. right-left orientation, incorporation of letters or whole words, etc.

T   I - good

Eloise looks up at T, who nods.

T   - good - lovely

SENA returns with water and gives it to T. T turns away from Eloise to receive water and then turns back to Eloise.

> Eloise seems to be trying to write 'I am four' – T reads first word (i.e. I – phonetically eye).

T   I need a drink of water 'cos I've got a headache -

T drinks from mug.

T   right -

T places mug on table away from paper

> T gives a direct explanation to Eloise for what is happening re. the drink, but there has been no explanation re. the purpose of the interaction *per se* – the implication seems to be that tangential 'social' interactions in classrooms have to be explained but the actual purpose(s) of schooling and the task at hand do not.

T   good I am could you do four - d'you want to write four -

> T is 'reading' the first two words 'I am'.

Eloise stands up, T looks at her face directly. Eloise sits down again and writes the number four. As she does this she perches on the edge of her chair.

> This is the numeral, not a 'pretend word'.

T   oh good girl - can you write your numbers you show me what numbers you know

13:40

Eloise   one - two -

T   good

Eloise writes while speaking

> This is evidence that Eloise can understand and write numbers. T now focuses on this and seems to drop the emergent writing agenda. She is responding to what the child can do rather than what she cannot, and has made a very rapid transition from English to mathematics. While this can be seen as a positive response to what Eloise has demonstrated, it may also be confusing to her.

Eloise   three - four - five =

T   = good at counting aren't you?

Eloise   - six -

Eloise looks across the classroom in the

> In what sense is Eloise 'counting' as opposed to reciting and writing? This is the first time that praise is specific; i.e. T giving explicit feedback about what exactly she considers to be 'good'.

direction of noise of a group of children speaking together (reciting something?)

T   good

Eloise looks back to paper, pauses, and nods head slightly six times.

Eloise   eight - **nine** - ten - **eleven**

T   cor you're good at counting

Eloise   two - (*one and) two

T   that's right

13:41

Eloise carries on writing without speaking for 23 seconds, during the last few seconds of which T looks across the classroom. Eloise pulls back her hand from the paper suddenly with a flourish. T looks back to Eloise.

T   well done -

T then looks down at paper

T   oo you've gone right up to <u>fifteen</u> -

Eloise turns paper to show T. T places hands on paper, moving it slightly.

T   goodness me - right - do you know what comes after <u>fifteen</u>?

Eloise shakes head.

Eloise   <u>fourteen</u>

T   fourteen comes before fifteen

T points at paper.

T   fifteen - right <u>well done</u> now then - can you do me some letters?

Eloise   letters

T reaches for new piece of paper.

T   if I tell you some letters you see if you can write them for me - um

T places new piece of paper in front of Eloise.

Eloise   if you write them on a piece of paper then > I (**) <

T   > you can < copy can you

T looks directly at Eloise who nods head.

T   can you see if you can do without - have a try - ay - can you do ay - a - a

Eloise puts pencil in mouth and swivels body

T   - no

Eloise shakes head

Unlike the previous 'good', this 'good' seems to be uttered to attract Eloise's attention back to the numbers – to keep her on task – and is thus about reasserting control rather than providing feedback on work done.

Eloise has recognized and knows the convention, but doesn't appear to know the word twelve. Until this point her recitation of the words could be seen as 'egocentric speech' (Vygotsky 1978), where the recitation of the sequence enables her to construct the written form. However, she is able to write the numbers 13, 14 and 15 without recourse to speech. Her articulation of 'one and two' points to a more sophisticated understanding of the conventions of a decimal system than if she had just been 'counting'.

Eloise is announcing that she has finished the task, or at least wants T's attention; by this flourish she very overtly disengages from the task. In so doing she brings T back 'on task'.

In terms of formative baseline assessment this is potentially a very rich moment. At stake here are whether Eloise understands 'before' or 'after' as prepositions of time, whether she understands that they can be used by analogy to indicate position on a page, and whether she knows the next number in the sequence. T appears only to have considered the third option.

T points at where Eloise has written '14'.

'right, well done' – T makes a 'framing move' (Sinclair 1982) to put an end to the work on numbers and move on to her next concern. She does not pursue whether or not Eloise understands 'before' and 'after', nor indeed whether she knows what comes after fifteen.

Eloise begins to tell T how to structure the task so that she can demonstrate her competence; T interrupts and names the task as copying.

T then defines the task as initially articulated. She stops herself from being seduced into presenting a mechanical task, but it is questionable from the point of view of an initial baseline assessment as to whether she should. It might be more appropriate to test Eloise's recognition of letters in terms of reading, and then copy writing, before expecting her to be able to respond to their dictation.

T   - right

T leans forward to write on paper. Eloise stands up and leans over table resting on her elbows.

T   - that's ay - round and up - that's - what one's that one?

13:42

Eloise   (*p)

T   that's a b

Eloise   b =

T   = - ay - bee ~ > that one <

Eloise   > see <

T   see - good - this one =

Eloise is standing up and moving around the table away from the teacher, with her elbows still resting on the table. As she moves away she speaks.

Eloise   dee =

Eloise is now standing at 90 degrees to the teacher and looking at what T is writing.

Eloise   >ee < eeee

T   >what's that one?<

Eloise starts the ee before the T asks the questions, but lengthens the sound such that she is still making it when T has finished her utterance.

Eloise   eff

T is writing; Eloise raises her right foot off the ground

T   what comes after eff?

Eloise   mmm-

T continues writing – it is not clear whether she is continuing to write the alphabet or is writing assessment notes.

T   what one's that?

Eloise   a - d

T   that's a b =

Eloise   = b =

T   = b b b can you go b b

T   could > you sit down - sit down- b good girl b <

T pats Eloise's empty chair

Eloise   >b b b b b b b b b b< b

As they are both speaking Eloise is moving towards the chair.

T   that's a b -

Eloise finally perches on the front edge of her chair.

T   that one

Eloise   c

Eloise in turn indicates that she cannot/does not want to take dictation, and redefines the task as she wanted to originally.

T has already used both letter sound and letter name conventions, apparently in order to see which Eloise is familiar with. She writes in lower case ('a') but now appears to be concentrating on the letter name (ay = A, phonetically).

Under the influence of Eloise's use of the wrong letter sound, T now switches to using the sound convention.

T returns to name convention and Eloise follows her. However, in doing this T has changed the nature of the task from letter recognition to sequence identification. She cues Eloise with 'ay, bee'. It would seem that this must introduce considerable ambiguity with respect to assessment.

Eloise seems to be quite deliberately distancing herself from T.

Eloise seems to do this so that she keeps hold of the sequence and goes immediately on to the next letter. It appears that the control and nature of the task have now been completely reversed. Eloise is articulating the sequence and T is writing it down. Eloise is standing up, T is sitting down; the effect is that the pupil is standing over the teacher and telling her what to do.

T reasserts control by asking a closed question about the sequence. Eloise loses control by not being able to provide an answer.

T strengthens her control by abandoning the sequence and referring back to previously written letters.

Having reasserted control of the discourse, T now reasserts control over Eloise's body. However, Eloise remains resistant and shows this by her unnecessary repetition, which is said with increasing loudness and aspiration.

T   good

T points to paper

Eloise   <u>b</u> =

T   = d - e

Eloise   e

T   - f =

Eloise   = f

Eloise is now pivoting on the front legs of her chair, knees almost touching the ground.

T   - what comes after the f?

Eloise   ee

T   nearl\ what - that one - do you know what that's called?

Eloise   (**)

T   g it says a

Eloise   g

T   g - ay bee see dee ee eff gee ~

T runs finger along paper as she speaks.

Eloise   **queue**

13:43

T   aitch~

T writes on paper again.

Eloise   eye - kay

T   jay

Eloise   kay =

T   = kay - ell - emm -

Eloise   ewe

T   enn - oh - pee - queue

Eloise is pivoting more noticeably, and stretches her arms across the table.

T   - are -

Eloise stands up and leans across the table.

T   ess - tee - ewe - vee - double-ewe - exe - why

T breaks off, takes hold of Eloise by the waist, pulls the child towards her and puts her onto the chair. She then pushes the chair towards the table so that Eloise's legs are under the table, her stomach is touching the table and she cannot get up.

T   this one's called ~

Eloise   zed

Eloise leans to one side, away from T, resting her head on her right arm.

T   zed - good girl - now would you practise some of those letters for me and we'll see what you can do - which ones would you like to practise?

T seems to have returned to her previous general intention. However, this is now a receptive (reading) task, testing whether Eloise recognizes and can enunciate letter sounds, rather than getting Eloise to write down what T says. Once again she is proceeding in alphabetical order, and also enunciates the sound when Eloise shows any hint of a mistake or slow response to the sequence.

Once again, what does 'after' mean in the context of a sequence of written letters (cf. the numbers sequence above)? Eloise may not understand the preposition, referring to what comes before, rather than after, or may just be unable to recognize the letter.

T returns to the letter name convention. She may wish to demonstrate that the two conventions are in parallel and apply to the same letters, but she does not say so.

Is Eloise responding to the similar shape of the two letters (g/q)? If this is the case, while she misrecognizes 'g' she indicates that she can interpret lower case letters in terms of their names.

T writes letters on the paper in front of Eloise – she is now scripting the alphabet for Eloise.

This alphabetical sequence seems to have taken on a life of its own and T now appears more concerned with reaching the end of the alphabet than with conducting the assessment of Eloise. T writes letters as she speaks them. Eloise seems to have been left behind and her behaviour exemplifies boredom.

Eloise has become physically as well as intellectually disengaged from what is happening. She has become a bored spectator. T does not attempt to re-engage Eloise's interest, but reasserts her control physically.

T's intonation shows she is cueing Eloise's response rather than asking a question.

Eloise is as far away from T as she can be without standing up.

Eloise responds correctly and her role as pupil is re-established ('good girl').

'Practise' seems to mean 'copy', i.e. what Eloise wanted to do in the first place. Can this be construed as a reward for reaching the end of T's agenda?

T has shuffled papers so that another piece
is at the top. Eloise sits up.

Eloise   all of them =

T   = okay then you show me
          how clever you can be - and
          I'll do my bit of writing here

T picks up another sheet of paper.

Eloise   yeah =

T   = off you go then you copy
          some of those letters then

T and Eloise start writing.

13.44

Eloise remains undistracted for almost 30 seconds before looking up briefly towards noise being made by the rest of the class, then returning to the task. After about 50 seconds T looks at Eloise, who is continuing to write. Eloise looks up and meets T's gaze. The interaction then continues for approximately three more minutes as T checks which letters Eloise has copied correctly. It emerges that she can recognize some of the letters probably because of pre-school and/or family experience, e.g. 'i for igloo', 'o for Oscar' and 'r for Rupert' are identified by Eloise in these phrases. Eloise also reveals that she has attended a Montessori nursery school, which she liked and where she was able to choose her own activities.

Appropriating the child's responses

The incident provides ample evidence of the teacher's focus on Eloise's behaviour, with Pat giving overt and repeated attention to controlling Eloise physically, as well as trying to remain in charge of the structure and content of the discourse. Pat seems as concerned, if not more so, with inculcating a norm of 'how pupils should behave' as with ascertaining particular information about what Eloise can do with respect to Reception class curriculum goals. Thus the incident demonstrates the narrowness of much of the debate about baseline assessment and formative assessment – oriented as it is towards a very mechanistic notion of curricular progression. And yet the incident is not so easily categorized; if it is not about objective information gathering, neither is it just about social control in an immediate and coercive sense. It is also about relating classroom control to future learning opportunities. Eloise resists the teacher's control and we can understand the teacher's exasperation with this, though it is interesting to reflect why it is that norms of behaviour, if they are considered important to the creation of an effective learning environment, are not made properly explicit to children new to school, instead of being implicit in the ways in which teachers interact with children in such situations. Perhaps more significantly, however, much information about Eloise's prior experiences and attainment is made apparent by the encounter, along with her orientation to the norms of schooling, and an interesting issue is how Pat interprets this and appropriates it with respect to her prospective pedagogic agenda.

Pat was interviewed immediately after this assessment and again somewhat later, when she was shown a video recording ('stimulated video recall', see

Cowan (1994); quotations given here refer to the initial interview unless they are labelled SVR). Pat's stated objective with regard to the interview with Eloise was assessment:

> I just wanted to look at her concentration and, again, a general assessment, numbers, writing. (SVR).

To be more precise the assessment was to be norm-referenced and diagnostic:

> I was trying to see how far behind or advanced she would be compared to the rest of the class . . .

> *Researcher:* How typical would you say that was of a sort of baseline assessment? – Is that telling you the sort of things that you want to know?
>
> *Teacher:* Broadly yes I, from that I then would go away and plan some activities to try and extend more detail of what I wanted to know. (SVR).

In both interviews Pat seemed happy about the assessment and claimed that it had told her what she needed to know. However, the conclusions she reached didn't always relate to the evidence – her account of the interaction was different from the video tape-recording. For example, immediately after the assessment she characterized its content by reporting the following exchange between herself and Eloise as if it were a verbatim report:

> [Eloise said] 'Yes, I can do numbers.'
> I said, 'Are they different from letters?'
> 'Yes *of course* they are.'
> 'Well why?'
> 'Well they're numbers.'

She also claimed that:

> I think she did know some of her letters and sounds but she hadn't got a clue about alphabetical order.

The whole of the assessment was transcribed, but the reported conversation does not appear to have taken place. This raises some interesting issues with respect to the process by which teachers intuitively summarize and internalize such encounters to inform their future dealings with individual children, and the effect that this has in the present. In this regard we should also note again what has already been recorded in the transcript commentary: what Pat wrote was not what Eloise actually said. Pat, through her recording of Eloise's words, appropriated and changed them to suit her purpose with respect to teaching and classroom control.

Mehan (1979) and Edwards and Mercer (1987), among others, have demonstrated how teachers use appropriation in order to control and manage the pacing and sequencing of lessons. The practice results from the 'tension between the demands of, on the one hand, inducting children into an established, ready-made culture and on the other hand developing creative and autonomous participants in a culture which is not ready-made but continually in the making' (Edwards and Mercer 1987:163–4). It involves teachers eliciting the words of pupils and then re-presenting them in acceptable forms to accomplish a satisfactory lesson. We have noted examples of this earlier in the book, and in particular that Edwards and Mercer (1987) show how teachers use pupils' responses as a 'resource' when sequencing and structuring the teaching process. Pupil utterances are incorporated into the teacher's evolving sense of 'where the lesson is going' and the teacher feeds back a reshaped version of 'what-has-just-been-said' or 'what-has-just-happened' into the teaching and learning encounter in order to 'move the lesson on'.

Now it might be argued that this is only a contextualized manifestation of what happens in most communicative acts. Grice (1989) has proposed a 'cooperative principle' whereby communication occurs through people assuming that what is being said makes sense and constructing a reading of it that fills in any gaps.[1] This principle is what makes social interaction and communication possible, since to voice interpretations aloud would seem tedious and pedantic in ordinary conversation. However, in situations where the listener is very concerned to 'get it right', especially where a text produced by the listener becomes some kind of acknowledged record (e.g. assessment), there may well be an important purpose in articulating the interpretation. In principle this might allow the participants to verify the interpretation and negotiate the record. In classrooms, and from the point of view of the teacher, appropriation in this sense might also be seen as part of the process of scaffolding learning that can take place during teaching or indeed in dynamic assessment (Newman *et al.* 1989; Brown *et al.* 1992).

Vygotsky's (1978) theory of learning depends on teacher and pupil creating a zone of proximal development where what the child can do alone is extended and transformed by the intercession of the teacher. This external, i.e. socially contextualized and constructed learning, 'awakens a variety of internal developmental processes that are able to operate only when the child is interacting with people in his environment and in co-operation with his peers. Once these processes are internalized they become part of the child's independent developmental achievement' (Vygotsky 1978:90).

The process whereby internalization takes place has been termed 'appropriation' by Leont'ev (1981). Newman *et al.* (1989), in their detailed study of Vygotskian approaches to teaching and learning, point out that appropriation is a two-way process. Both teacher and learner need to be receptive to what the other is doing or saying and to appropriate it. They claim that teachers should build on children's participation in activities that they do not fully understand by elaborating on what they do achieve. From this theoretical perspective, rather than the differences in understanding or interpretation causing trouble,

> the participants can act *as if* their understandings are the same. At first, this systematic vagueness about what an object 'really is' may appear to make cognitive analysis impossible. However ... this looseness is just what is needed to allow change to happen when people with differing analyses interact. It is the key element for the process we call 'appropriation'.
>
> (Newman *et al.* 1989:62, original emphasis)

Thus in this version of appropriation an element of ambiguity and uncertainty is both inevitable and essential, since it creates the 'mental space' in which both parties work in order to 'make sense' of 'what is happening', thereby creating the process by which knowledge is internalized through the act of interpretation. Clearly, however, a struggle for understanding is not necessarily the same thing as a struggle for comprehension over the social rules which govern the engagement within the struggle for understanding, and it is here that more clarity and transparency are likely to be of benefit. In this respect the emphasis of a cognitive science version of appropriation is on mutuality and a power relationship that is more self-consciously open than that apparent in the transcript here. In turn, the interpretations that the participants formed and the way they become the internally recorded and remembered 'text' which will provide the 'script' for the next encounter, depend on the agendas which the parties are pursuing.

Nevertheless, this contrast and tension between appropriation for purposes of social control (accomplishing the management of the lesson) and appropriation for purposes of scaffolding learning is intriguingly represented in the data reported here. Interestingly, Newman *et al.* point out that teachers' work is prospective – that is, they know in curriculum terms what the children will need to know later. This may well be the case with Pat in our example, but her focus seems to be less on Eloise's development of the culturally devised tools of schooling and more on the way that her behaviour might be made to converge with that of an ideal pupil. The effect of Pat's appropriation is to use the discourse to assert her authority. Moreover, accompanied as it is by repeated physical interventions exemplified by moving Eloise's hair band and forcibly placing her in a chair, it is reasonable to conclude that socialization into the routines of schooling was Pat's primary concern in this instance.

Thus the evidence suggests that although the overt purpose of this assessment was to find out what Eloise knew, understood and could do, at a more tacit level the assertion of the teacher's authority, her right to decide on what counted as significant or appropriate, indeed to decide what had actually been said by Eloise as well as how she was sitting and even how she was dressed, was the main purpose of the interaction. Immediately after Eloise walked away Pat turned to the researcher and, unprompted, gave her verdict:

> We've been allowed to wander and do what we want when we want – she doesn't sit down . . . So – we're – we're going to need training into that – sometimes we choose and sometimes we have to do what everybody else does.

In the subsequent interview Pat did talk about the cognitive agenda, but the socialization issues continued to be salient. Even in the later stimulated video response interview Pat stressed her concern with 'trying to get her to conform to the expected types of behaviour' rather than with her understanding, and confirmed that this was a very important factor for her in the assessment:

> Researcher: To what extent do you feel that you were actually trying to get her to conform?
>
> Teacher: Quite a lot I think I haven't ver/I don't very often grab a child twice and sit on the chair and go grrr like that, you know. (SVR)

So what might appear to be an assessment of cognitive capacity and current attainment is also in Parsons's (1959) terms an exercise in assessing the 'moral' character of the child and seeking to mould it into a more acceptable form.

The transcription yields other insights with respect to the interface between good work and good behaviour. The justification for the regimentation of children in classrooms is that it enables them to concentrate on their work. Therefore children are told to sit down so that they can get on with their work. However, in this instance work is invoked to facilitate classroom control rather than the other way round. This is apparent initially since Eloise is actually performing the 'work' that the teacher has set her; her only deficit is in her conformity to the accepted norms of classroom behaviour. Elsewhere in the transcript, as long as Eloise is responding to questioning according to Pat's plan she is allowed to stand up, but as soon as Pat loses control of the discourse, Eloise's posture becomes important. In this case school work legitimates social control rather than social control enabling school work to take place. However, it is also important to recognize that the teacher does not simply assert control and retain it. There is a tacit struggle going on which becomes overt on several occasions.

Thus we might also speculate as to the meaning of the incident for the child. Given that she is new to the school, one might expect the teacher to offer some sort of explanation of what is taking place, but there is none, except when she is given the writing implements and told that she has to sit down because she is going to do some work. In Edwards and Mercer's (1987) terms, the 'ground rules' are never made clear. Indeed, the whole affair must be very puzzling for Eloise. For example, she has already given to the teacher an account of what she likes to do, and this has been written down, and yet she is then required to repeat it in 'her' 'pretend' writing, a strange request from someone who obviously can write very well to someone who cannot. Eloise may be similarly confused by the changeover from language to number, and the interchangeability of the two conventions for referring to letters.

Returning to Parsons's (1959) recognition of the lack of differentiation between the evaluation of the cognitive and social elements of early schooling, we can nevertheless move beyond his functionalism by examining the data in the light of more dynamic theories of social reproduction, in particular those of Bourdieu (e.g. Bourdieu 1990). Bourdieu's key concepts are of *habitus*, *field*, *cultural capital* and *practice*, and all his work could be seen as an investigation of the way in which they interrelate: '. . . concepts of *capital*, accumulable social-symbolic resources, *field*, the arenas of social life and struggle, *habitus*, embodied social structures that serve as principles organizing practice' (Collins 1993:117).

An important part of Bourdieu's theoretical project is to get away from the simplistic dichotomies of determinist or individualistic theories of social practices by proposing a reflexive sociology. So systems which are themselves structured by social processes have the effect of structuring further processes. This allows for a more sophisticated understanding of the relationship between, for example, cause and effect, and the way that the present practice of an individual or group relates to their past and future. Thus practice is seen not only to result from structures that are inherent in the field, being brought into play by the people who act there, but also to modify and produce further actions (cf. also Giddens 1979).

According to Bourdieu, school is one mechanism whereby society ensures that inequalities are reproduced and maintained. Moreover, by hiding the social function behind its cultural function, it legitimizes the social hierarchy and status quo (Charlot *et al.* 1992:19). These notions of the recursive realization of social life, combined with the social reproductive functions of schooling, lend added significance to the incident discussed here. Pat brings to the interaction practices which are informed partly by her theorization of teaching which values pupils' autonomy and spontaneity, but more especially by her implicit understandings of what is the proper behaviour of a school pupil. Their occurrence at the very beginning of Eloise's school career brings into sharp focus their potentiality for acting on Eloise's understandings of what it is to be a pupil and so socializing her into the expected role.[2]

Pat's explicit ideology was often expounded in interviews. Talking about the induction of the rest of the children into the class, Pat was at pains to stress that she wanted the children to be 'organizers and planners' as much as she was:

> ... some teachers ... feel that they have only got control when the children are conforming to what they want them to do. I'm quite happy that the children tell me what to do sometimes.

She went on to explain how she was attempting to encourage the children to learn:

> Basically what I feel is if I've done my bit by organizing the room and it's accessible to them, their height and they know where everything is, then they should be given the freedom to actually go to that area or that area if they want to.

These statements seem at odds with the observational data reported here. Pat very clearly did want Eloise to conform to what she wanted her to do. However, the issue is not so much one of 'bad faith'; rather, it results from the competing prospective agendas with which Pat has to juggle. Thus we can speculate that Pat focuses on Eloise's behaviour and does not remember the details of the assessment accurately, because she is not really concerned with them. At this stage of Eloise's school career, Pat's prospective knowledge of 'what is to come' is oriented towards future classroom management rather than future cognitive development, because one is taken to be the precondition for the other. It is more important at this stage that Eloise becomes a good pupil than that Pat actually learns particular things about her, since Pat's view of learning is that it occurs not so much as a result of direct instruction (even if tailored to individual needs) but rather is produced when children are placed in a suitable environment. However, to utilize such an environment, children have to learn to be pupils. Thus when Pat commented on Eloise's progress in the SVR interview some months after the events transcribed, she did not talk of her academic progress but of her ability to conform. In turn, the practices that Pat had engaged in with Eloise and that we have seen in the transcript would act as organizing principles for continuing and future transactions.

Summary

The discussion has highlighted some of the complexity of what is at stake in baseline assessment. The analysis has enabled us to study the exercise of classroom power 'from the perspective of how it inserts itself in . . . knowledge, how it is inscribed in the body within particular social practices, in organisational forms and how it produces specific material and lived effects' (Giroux 1988:196). Clearly, policy discussions of baseline assessment and 'value-added' approaches to infant and junior school evaluation are far too simplistic. More important for the discussion here, however, are:

1 our identification of different prospective agendas for how teachers construe their appropriation of children's classroom utterances; and
2 the way in which assessment provides a key interactive context for the struggle for power in the classroom.

Kreisberg's distinction between *power over* and *power with* may be useful here. Kreisberg (1992) distinguishes between what he terms coercive *power over*, based on domination, and *power with*, which is 'characterised by collaboration, sharing and mutuality' (p. 61). In a situation such as described in this chapter, the exercise of power is not unidirectional or uncontested, but neither is access to power equal. By strategies such as denying the child a voice the teacher is not only exerting *power over* in the present but setting in motion the expectations and actions that will perpetuate the practice. A consciousness of issues of power and a view of learning which sets the establishment of *power with* as an aim would seem to be a prerequisite for developing the possibilities of this kind of informal assessment. In the following chapter we develop this idea further as we examine the different motivational orientations which children might have towards schooling and learning, the different factors to which they attribute success and failure, and the differential access to power which different children have, with respect to defining the outcomes of assessment events positively or negatively.

Notes

1 cf. also Garfinkel's (1967) notion of the 'etceteras' which it is the task of the ethnomethodologist to investigate.
2 The 'ideal pupil' is also a gendered notion. The reaction of Pat to Eloise, the only girl in the class who challenges her, is very different from the rather more indulgent attitude she takes towards several boys who are lively in the classroom. (For a fuller treatment of this issue see Walkerdine 1978 and Clarricoates 1987.)

6

Formative assessment and learning: where psychological theory meets educational practice

Introduction

One of the key arguments in favour of developing and extending the practice of formative assessment is that it will aid learning. This has become a virtually unchallenged axiom, even mantra, of proponents of formative assessment. It is also intuitively very appealing: provide pupils with feedback on their strengths and weaknesses and they should be able to improve their performances and achieve more. Yet, as we have noted with Sadler in Chapter 2: 'even when teachers provide students with valid and reliable judgements about the quality of their work, improvement does not necessarily follow. Students often show little or no . . . development despite regular, accurate feedback' (Sadler 1989:119). Taking into account what we have already reported in previous chapters, there must be some doubt about just how 'valid and reliable' teacher feedback is, and this may go some way to explaining the nature of the problem which Sadler has identified. More importantly for our purposes here, however, is our contention that formative assessment should not simply be construed as a set of sequential procedures with, perhaps, some 'unreliable' information being fed back to pupils; but rather should be conceptualized as a continuous process which has potentially negative, unintended consequences, as well as potentially positive, intended consequences.

Given the focus on learning, it is also rather surprising that more attention has not been given to the extensive psychological literature on achievement motivation and attribution; that is, on studies of what makes a difference to student motivation, and to what factors students attribute their academic success and failure. It is to this literature that we now turn, before then subjecting the various psychological theories embedded within it to the test of classroom practice provided by our data. This chapter will thus review some highly relevant literature on attribution, motivation, and their relationship to learning; examine further classroom assessment incidents in the light of this literature, and explore the ways in which teacher feedback might have negative as well as positive consequences for learning, despite the teacher's best intentions; and then look at the limitations of a purely psychological perspective, particularly with respect to how theories of learning need to be situated and developed in the context of the social dynamics of the classroom. The chapter will thus bring to bear and integrate both psychological and sociological perspectives on the practice of formative classroom assessment, while at the same time interrogating those perspectives with evidence from the classroom. Our intention is to generate a better understanding of the problems and possibilities of formative assessment by examining the interactive educational context in which learning takes place.

Achievement and motivation

A key issue with respect to the impact of feedback on motivation and learning is the way in which 'reinforcement' is understood and applied. In particular, as we suggested in Chapter 2, too narrowly behaviourist a view is unlikely to have the desired effect. Researchers such as Ames (1984), Dweck (1989), Nicholls (1989) and Weiner (1984) have established that many of the practices that are routinely adopted by teachers as 'positive reinforcement' to enhance motivation, may actually result in children avoiding intellectual tasks, approaching them with limited confidence, and not persisting in the face of difficulties.

Attributions

Thus, for example, Weiner (1984) has argued that the most significant factor in determining learners' motivation is to what they attribute their success or failure. The theory is complex, but in essence relies on the idea that there are three main dimensions to any of the attributions that people make. *Locus* refers to whether they see responsibility lying with themselves or with external factors; *constancy* to whether they see it as confined to one event or domain as opposed to being of wider significance; and *responsibility* to whether or not the factors can be controlled – be they perceived as internal (i.e. personal traits) or external. In all of these a distinction is made between stable and unstable factors. The consequences of an attribution also depend on whether it is being made for a success or a failure:

> Success at academic tests and tasks attributed to stable factors such as high ability result in higher future expectancies than does success ascribed to unstable factors such as luck. In a similar manner, failure attributed to stable factors such as low aptitude results in lower future expectancies than does failure ascribed to unstable factors such as low effort.
>
> (Weiner 1984:25)

However, as Vispoel and Austin (1995:399) point out, it is 'a fundamental principle of attribution theory . . . that success and failure are not mirror images'. In other words, the fact that success is attributed to one factor does not mean that failure will receive the same attribution.

Goals

Carol Dweck has built on the work of Weiner to formulate a different theory. Attributions for her are not so important in themselves, as in the kind of attitude they engender in the learner. In particular she sees motivation as being bound up with the types of goal that students have. Her main concern is with achievement goals which are connected with the task at hand (they may be underpinned or countered by more general non-achievement goals such as being popular or having fun). She makes a distinction between two kinds of achievement goal:

(a) *learning goals* in which individuals strive to increase their competence, to understand or master something new; and

(b) *performance goals*, in which individuals strive either to document, or gain favorable judgments of, their competence or to avoid negative judgments of their competence.

(Dweck 1989:88–9)

There have been a considerable number of studies conducted both by Dweck and her associates and by others over the last two decades, mostly in experimental settings (see also Nicholls 1989; Urdan and Maehr 1995). Drawing on the evidence of these studies, Dweck has built up a detailed picture of the contrasting approach to schooling which children with each of these goal orientations have. In summary she has found that children with *learning goals*:

- choose challenging tasks regardless of whether they think they have high or low ability relative to other children;
- optimize their chances of success;
- tend to have an 'incremental theory of intelligence';
- go more directly to generating possible strategies for mastering the task;
- attribute difficulty to unstable factors e.g. insufficient effort, even if they perceive themselves as having low ability;
- persist;
- and remain relatively unaffected by failure in terms of self esteem.

She has further suggested that learning goals are prevalent in pre-school children, are fostered by collaborative work, and encourage personal (ipsative) standards of success, i.e. comparison with previous performance or with task criteria. Those who show a preference for learning goals are said to be 'mastery oriented' (Dweck 1989:111).

On the other hand, pupils with *performance goals*:

- avoid challenge when they have doubts about their ability compared with others;
- tend to self-handicapping so that they have an excuse for failure;
- tend to see ability as a stable entity;
- concentrate much of their task analysis on gauging the difficulty of the task and calculating their chances of gaining favourable ability judgements;
- attribute difficulty to low ability;
- give up in the face of difficulty;
- and become upset when faced with difficulty or failure.

Dweck has also found that performance goals are developed in the early school years and become prevalent by the middle years of schooling; that they are fostered by competition and encourage normative standards of success, i.e. comparison with peers.

Thus a tendency to adopt performance goals is not in the long-term interest of the learner. Unsuccessful children quickly become demotivated and even successful ones, especially girls, are liable to suffer from low confidence which, if persistent, results in what has been termed 'learned helplessness' (Licht and Dweck 1985). Dweck claims that rather than using performance goals to create confidence through success, it is better to inform pupils specifically of what it is that is causing their lack of success and to create an emphasis on learning goals and personally challenging tasks. Her analysis incorporates a clear critique of behaviourism which resonates with our earlier criticisms outlined in Chapter 2, and to which we will return in the next chapter. She argues that high aspirations and achievement are fostered by a tendency to:

(a) **think strategy** i.e. to engage in task analysis that focuses on strategy formulation, particularly on challenging tasks, under evaluative pressure and when obstacles arise;
(b) **think progress** i.e. to adopt challenging standards that are based on personal progress vs. inflated norms; and
(c) **focus on past and future success**, and on effort and strategy as causes of and cures for failure.

(Dweck 1989:110)

Dweck's analysis accords well with that of Nicholls (1989), whose designations 'ego involvement' and 'task involvement' are broadly coterminous with performance and learning goals.

Rewards

A different focus, on reward systems, is taken by Mark Lepper and his associates (e.g. Lepper and Hodell 1989). They found that extrinsic reward systems have detrimental effects on intrinsic motivation, especially when initial interest is high; i.e. extrinsic rewards can be seen as a 'bribe' which skew motivation, particularly when they are offered merely for task engagement:

> Very few of the experiments in which subjects are initially intrinsically motivated have yet found any reliable method for using extrinsic rewards to increase intrinsic motivations further, whereas a number of investigations have found that such rewards may be important in enhancing interest among subjects that do not find the activity of initial intrinsic interest.

(Lepper and Hodell 1989:78)

Their analysis, based on several experimental studies, indicates that superfluous reward systems adversely affect performance, particularly of those aspects that are not central to the reward and when a creative rather than routine response is demanded. Moreover, children who become used to extrinsic rewards tend in future not to choose activities where these incentives are not attainable, and also favour less demanding activities. Lepper's work would suggest that the cultivation of intrinsic rewards, besides being important for enhancing student motivation, also promotes more effective, deeper and longer-lasting learning, an argument which is developed at length by Gardner (1993).

The data: two transcript extracts, four classroom incidents

Such analyses, deriving from experimental settings, beg many questions about the way in which teachers construe and construct assessment and feedback opportunities in the classroom, and it is to these questions that we now turn. They will be explored in the context of transcript evidence deriving from feedback given by a teacher to two children following a spelling test, and two others engaged in handwriting practice. Thus the first transcript features feedback following the spelling test and focuses on the way in which the teacher appears to seek to 'protect' the children involved from what he seems to believe could be the negative impact of his assessment. However, this emphasis on 'protecting the child' does not necessarily lead to the intended outcome. The second extract, featuring feedback on handwriting practice, focuses even more closely on the social construction of the outcome of assessment, and demonstrates the way in which some children may have more impact on that process of social construction than others. In both extracts the right-hand commentary column focuses on the potential impact of the teacher's feedback in the light of the theoretical issues of attribution and motivation just discussed; but the following analysis goes beyond this to explore the ways in which the social context and practices of the classroom mediate this impact.

The teacher, Chris Brown, teaches one of two parallel Year 2 classes (6- to 7-year-olds) in the school. The first two incidents portrayed take place on a Tuesday morning in February. In the second two terms of Year 2 (i.e. spring and summer terms) the school policy is to give weekly tests in spelling and mental mathematics. On the day in question there was a postgraduate teacher-training student in the classroom who had taken responsibility for working with two of the four small groups into which the class is divided. The other two groups were engaged on independent work. While Chris did not necessarily review the results of every test in the detail we report here, in interview he called the featured assessment interviews 'unremarkable' and confirmed that he saw them as typical of his practice. He intended to see every child over the course of the morning and indeed did succeed in doing so. The test was marked out of ten.

10:00

T is sitting on an upright chair in the corner of the classroom. He has just called up Eliane and now sits with his record-book of spelling test scores on his lap, and Eliane's book in his hands. Eliane stands by his side. Her hands are behind her back; her left hand holding her right wrist and her right hand clenched in a fist; her head is on one side looking at the book. The teacher is pointing at the book with a pencil held in his left hand.

T	now look at this you've got nine right that's really good - isn't it - now family do you know what's missing from there?

Eliane's dress and demeanour make her look rather formal. She seems fairly relaxed but somewhat reserved.

Positive feedback for high score, though the 'isn't it' suggests concern that the child may not appreciate this.

Specific closed question

Correctly answered

Eliane   i

T looks up at Eliane

T   an aye yes- (*like that isn't it)

T writes in her book

T   - so how come - how come that escaped yesterday then

T transfers book to left hand and points at it with his right.

T   how come you missed it out then - just one of those things - that happens

A potentially stimulating metacognitive question, asking the child to reflect on the process of misspelling the word, but no space left for an answer; indeed T goes on to answer his own question – 'just one of those things'. The question therefore seems to derive from his conversational style and personality rather than a theoretically informed view of the value of such a question in promoting learning.

Eliane takes a step backwards and leans backwards, nodding her head

Moving away from the interrogation?

T   - don't you know it should have an aye in it?

Why ask this again? Eliane has already correctly identified her mistake. Is T engaging in some sort of intuitive reinforcement?

Eliane nods

T   yeah so - so what did you score last week do you remember?

T doesn't ask about other possible difficulties or focus on any successes – nine out of ten is taken to be indication enough of full understanding – T creating performance goal orientation?

T removes the book from his list and points to the list with his right hand. Eliane moves forward and looks at where he is pointing.

Eliane   ten (**)

T   you got - oh - you were - yes - last week - you were absent - you only got six - because - you didn't learn them did you - so - nine is better than six - so - what do you have ~

T offers an acceptable account of why Eliane got a relatively low score on the previous test. He answers his own implicit question – 'why the low score?' – by reference to an unstable factor: absence and hence lack of opportunity to learn. Ipsative assessment – 'nine is better than six'.

Eliane   a merit mark =

T   = off you go then have a merit mark then - well done

Improvement earns a merit mark, overt behaviourist 'reinforcement', though Lepper's work would suggest this is unnecessary, even counterproductive.

T points at Eliane who begins to walk away whilst he is still speaking.

There is a break in the transcript while T copes with a child's medical problem

This whole interaction has lasted under a minute.

10:02

Now Timmy is standing by T. He has adopted a similar posture to Eliane except that his fist is not clenched and one foot is

slightly on top of the other. T has his mark
sheet on his lap with a small pile of exercise
books stacked on top of the sheet. He holds
Timmy's book in his right hand, pointing to
it with his pencil in his left hand.

T   here we are - Timmy Patner

Tim   I knew I'd got nine or eight - or
         something like that =

T   = six

T looks directly at Timmy, who does not
meet his gaze.

T   - did did you f\ - find it a bit of
         trouble then?

Tim   yeah

T   which bits did you find did
         you find the four extra words a
         bit difficult did you?

Timmy nods.

T   OK shall we look at those then
         - difficult - you nearly got right
         - there should be an ell there

T writes in book.

Tim   cut

T   yes you've got diffi<u>cut</u> with an
         ell it goes cult you see -

T looks up at Timmy again, who still does
not look at him.

T   OK - and s\ night was fine -
         f\family you had one go and
         crossed it out - tried again and
         gave up - yes

Tim   no it's just I didn't get enough
         time to do it =

As he speaks Timmy makes a circular
motion with his right hand which he then
withdraws again behind his back.

T   = oh dear never mind yes - we
         were a bit rushed yesterday
         weren't we - fam/ i/l y

T writes as he is saying this.

Tim   yeah I was going to do that but
         I couldn't - >(**) <

Timmy points to where the T is writing as
he says this. He then withdraws his hand
again.

10:03

T   > oh < were you - oh well
         never mind because -

T looks up at Timmy who this time meets
his gaze.

Initiation by pupil; Timmy seems anxiously assertive – 'getting his retaliation in first'.

T is quite blunt in his response; his subsequent utterances and behaviour suggest he may feel he has been too blunt.

T again asks diagnostic question but then answers it himself.

T's tone of voice now suggests a concern with this pupil's confidence – there is a sufficiently large number of errors to warrant concern about affecting the pupil's confidence, but not so many that they cannot be addressed individually.

Social and cognitive initiation by Timmy could be taken as an indication of Timmy's high level of potential and visual discrimination skills. He can read 'cut' as a separate part of the word he has written. In terms of formative assessment this is probably the most useful cue T has had. Could he have made more of this both in terms of assessment data and pedagogy/motivation? This is potentially both an assessment moment and a feedback moment.

Timmy refuses to accept this fairly negative characterization – he is not a person who gives up – he just didn't have enough time.

T accepts Timmy's interpretation. An agreed account of the causation of error has been negotiated, again beyond the pupil's control, i.e. lack of time. Is T still concerned about confidence/motivation? He is keeping Timmy 'on board'.

This gesture could be interpreted as a vindication of the teacher's willingness to acquiesce to

T   it was possibly my fault - for
        not giving you as much time
        as we had last week - but - and
        surprise -

T writes in book again.

T   we need to just - that was one
        of the hardest wasn't it sur-
        prise - OK and friends - a little
        aye - do you think - do you
        have a good practice of these
        words - did you?

Tim   yes

T   good - all right so you tried
        your hardest - that's all I want
        you to do - try your hard\

*T puts his left hand lightly on Timmy's
right shoulder as Timmy takes one step
away from T.*

T   now -

*T removes hand and closes Timmy's book,
placing it with the class set in a plastic con-
tainer at his right foot.*

T   don't go away - yet - smile -
        (*that's better) -

*T looks closely at Timmy's face. Timmy
smiles.*

T   you always look so worried all
        the time -

*T looks at name on cover of next book on
his lap.*

T   could you go and ask Mark to
        come and see me please

*T touches Timmy again on the right shoul-
der and Timmy walks off, still with his
hands behind his back.*

Timmy's account of why he failed to get the word right. For the first time Timmy feels secure enough to look the teacher in the eye. T develops the scenario offered by Timmy and they agree an acceptable excuse for the errors; moreover, one that according to attribution theories would best preserve Timmy's motivation.

This question about 'practice' is focusing on strategy. Timmy seems to have done what T has suggested and it has enabled him to get the majority of the words right. However, T chooses not to emphasize the link between strategy and partial success; instead he uses it as a lead in to a different attribution (effort) which now has the effect of sandwiching the potentially negatively received error analysis between positive comments. This means that the maximum effort attribution is associated with the failure rather than the success.

Overt behaviourist intervention – instructing Timmy to modify his behaviour, and (hence?) his perception of the interaction.

Reiteration of concern about Timmy's confidence. T seems to be seeking reassurance for himself that he has not frightened Tim.

Assessment and learning take place in a social context

These two brief incidents portray examples of the routine, ('unremarkable') formative classroom assessment of 6- to 7-year-old children. The teacher has marked the work, distinguishing correct from incorrect spellings, and is now feeding back his assessment to the pupils as well as showing them the acceptable versions, thus trying to enable them to succeed on a future occasion. However, from the way the participants behave it is apparent that this cognitive agenda has to be accomplished within a social context involving particular individuals whose understandings and feelings create many complications. The interaction is accomplished in a micropolitical situation where actions and attitudes are determined not just by personal feelings but by issues of relative power, as highlighted in the previous chapter. Furthermore, the incidents are realized within a well recognized discourse structure which we have also explored in some detail earlier in the book.

With respect to the issue of feedback *per se*, the teacher, Chris, seems constantly to be feeling his way forward, making judgements about the effect of his management of feedback on the pupils: on their understandings of how they have performed, and on the emotions that are thereby induced. Our analysis contained in the commentary in the right-hand column above is validated by Chris's own reaction to watching the incidents on video. With respect to Eliane he said:

> The reason I said 'how did it escape?' is that I know she's quite sensitive. If you ever say, 'Look, you made a mistake on this,' she may just have that bottom lip tremble. I think if you say that it's escaped, well, obviously, she's let it get it away, she just hasn't perhaps applied herself so well . . . I think that language with her – is cos of that reason – the way she reacts to how I ask the question.
>
> (SVR interview)

So Chris is conscious of dealing not just with a child who has nine out of ten, but with an individual who will react differently from other individuals. This makes the accomplishment of classroom assessment a much more complex matter, relying as much on teachers' knowledge of the child over time as on their understanding of the subject matter they are teaching and assessing. Within his school Chris is seen as a teacher who has a very good understanding of children and excellent relations with his pupils; we can see in the extracts examples of his skilful use of intuition and his ability to build on the store of his social relationships with the children. Yet for all his intuitive skills, Chris's negotiation of the process of these assessment incidents might have been more productive. Good openings are made but, because they do not seem to be informed by theoretical understanding, they are more social than professional or reflective; Chris seems concerned to 'manage' the interaction rather than intervene in the learning process. In short, teaching in general and formative assessment in particular are located within a social context and structure of discourse which renders self-conscious, theoretically informed intervention extremely difficult to carry out and sustain. Thus feedback can appear to be entirely intuitive and a product of the teacher's personal relations and style. In saying this the intention is not to criticize Chris, but to identify the demands of the classroom context in which formative assessment is being accomplished. The 'theoretical resource' which informs Chris's actions, insofar as there is one, seems to be a rather generalized commitment to child-centred 'gentleness', coupled with behaviourism (reinforcement through extrinsic rewards), rather than an understanding of the relationship of assessment to learning. Nevertheless there are potentially positive as well as negative outcomes from these interactions, and clearly, such intervention will have an impact on learning, intended or not. Thus in the following section we will look at the incident involving Timmy in more detail and examine it in the light of the theoretical positions that have already been elaborated.

Timmy and attributions

The assessment of Timmy is exceedingly rich in attributions (see Table 6.1). Chris initiates six statements that might lead directly to attributions and Timmy initiates one (the third).

In all of the statements except the last there is a process of negotiation going on which refines the agreed attributions. Teacher and pupil collaborate to suggest that task difficulty caused by the teacher's choosing hard extra words and not providing sufficient time was responsible. These are both unstable attributions. Other attributions are tried out and rejected, but even these are unstable; both Chris and Timmy seem to be at pains to establish that unstable factors are paramount.

At first sight this carefully constructed edifice seems then to be undermined by Chris's final remark when he talks of maximum effort in the context of Timmy's failure.

> *Researcher:* Right you were saying that was a hard one to write, why were you saying that?
> *Teacher:* It's [laughs] I mean I have to stop to think about it – I mean it always sounds like you've got to put ess ee are surprise instead of ewe surprise that's the (*) I suppose . . . it is a tricky one (**) just the nature of the word – I mean . . the thing is I know I know he spells very well yeah.
> *Researcher:* He spells well.
> *Teacher:* Yeah he is he's a you know weller speller –
> *More of the videotape is shown*
> *Teacher:* I think that confirms it you see, yes, you tried your hardest 'cos that sums it up what I've just said hopefully – yeah in kid-speak.
>
> (SVR interview)

Chris seems to be assuming that saying 'you tried your hardest' is understood by the child to be an attribution of failure to the difficulty of the material rather than to the child's lack of the necessary ability. Yet according to Dweck

Table 6.1 Statements leading to attributions

No.	Statement	Suggested attribution	Initiator
1	did you find the four extra words a bit difficult	Task difficulty (teacher influence)	T
2	tried again and gave up – yes	Effort	T
3	no it's just I didn't get enough time to do it	Teacher influence	C
4	it was possibly my fault – for not giving you as much time as we had last week	Teacher influence	T
5	that was one of the hardest wasn't it	Task difficulty	T
6	do you have a good practice of these words – did you	Strategy/effort	T
7	all right so you tried your hardest – that's *all* I want you to do – try your hard\	Effort/ability	T

(1989), this focus on maximum effort and being *seen* to be making an effort may not be helpful. The phrase 'you tried your hardest' when applied in the context of failure is more likely to lead to an attribution of insufficient ability. This brings us back to a central concern of the book – whether teachers and children share a common understanding of assessment incidents. Chris, by using the term 'kidspeak', seems to be suggesting that he aims to empathize with the children in his class, yet children of this age are likely to differ in their capacity to differentiate between ability and task difficulty (Nicholls 1989), and a key point for teachers of infant children to remember would be that attribution is unlikely to be unambiguous. Whether unambiguous attributions *could* be accomplished is another matter, but clearly they cannot be assumed.

More positive impact might have been achieved by a concentration on the positive aspects of achievement in Timmy's test: i.e. by dwelling on his effort in terms of the six words he got right rather than the four words he got wrong. In this case, however, Chris did not believe that Timmy had worked particularly hard on the words he got right, as opposed to those he got wrong; rather, 'he was doing what he'd normally do'. Thus Chris thought the six correct spellings were words he had previously learned, and therefore to have praised his effort there would have seemed rather too insincere to Chris. However, there is another way in which Chris could have concentrated on the positive in Timmy's work, and that would have been to pick up on the recognition of the word 'cut' in his mistake. Again the opportunity provided by the stimulated video recall interview enabled him to spot this himself.

> *Teacher:*   That was good actually – yes I mean 'cos he actually said cut for himself before I said the word cut I suppose cut so it's quite good that he actually realized his mistake as I (**) it was good – yes – I'm happy with that.
> *Researcher:* You're happy with what exactly?
> *Teacher:*   About the way he's um dealt with that word the way he's explained it to me. As soon as I told him there was a mistake the point where he actually got to it before I got to it, yes that's right or as I told him he got it yes so he you know that's good . . .
>
> (SVR interview)

The recognition of the word 'cut' allows an insight into how it might be possible for Chris to work with Timmy in his zone of proximal development, since although Timmy has spotted that this letter cluster spells something else, he has not been able to apply this sufficiently well to get the whole word right. The sort of scaffolding that would therefore help Timmy at this point would be to discuss other words that contain the sequence 'ut' and to contrast them with words that contained 'ult'. The problem is whether any teacher would be able consistently to apprehend and grasp such opportunities as they occurred. Again Chris offered some insight into the way this reorientation of teachers' thinking might take place.

> *Teacher:*   I felt that if he'd have learnt them he wouldn't have actually made those few little errors, those little miscues –
>
> (SVR interview)

When invited to elaborate on the idea of the miscue Chris said:

> I quite like the term miscue because it sounds, you know, I can't actually tell you why – 'error' just sounds so harsh and final and a brick wall doesn't it – it sounds, it's unsurmountable – but a miscue sounds like you just strayed off a little bit. I think as, as, as, you know, as a word it's, it's a nicer word.
>
> (SVR interview)

In several months of close contact with the research project, this was the first time Chris had used the word 'miscue'. He had obviously come across the concept, but it was only in the context of long reflection induced by the researcher that he used it. Significantly, too, it was only after he had spotted that he had missed the opportunity to make use of Timmy's 'difficut'. Furthermore, Chris's orientation towards the word was on the level of it being less harsh than 'error' or 'mistake'. It fitted in well with his objective of caring for the child: 'it's sort of me making a big effort to be nice and considerate'. Once again the basic 'backcloth' to these sorts of interaction seems to be the assumption that assessment is a rather nasty business and the child must be protected against its worst effects, rather than assessment being perceived as potentially positive if well-structured and conducted.

However, the power of the notion of the miscue is that it enables teachers to make principled interventions in children's learning. The concept was first articulated by Goodman, who initially also propounded its attractiveness as a replacement for the word 'error': 'in order to avoid the negative connotation of errors (all miscues are not bad) and to avoid the implication that good reading does not include miscues' (Goodman, 1969:124). However, miscue analysis presents a powerful technique for diagnosing strengths and weaknesses in reading.

> Shifting the focus in this analysis from errors as undesirable phenomena to be eliminated, to miscues as the by-product of the reading process, has made possible a revolution in viewpoint in which both the reader and the reading process may be regarded positively. The reader, particularly of the native language, may be regarded as a competent user of language whose language competence is reflected in miscues produced as a proficient reader and at all stages of acquisition of reading proficiency.
>
> (Goodman 1976:103)

The idea of working with miscues could obviously be helpful to a constructivist view of knowledge, as they provide gateways into the zone of proximal development and enable teachers to help children build on their current understandings. However, this would depend on teachers' interventions being driven by understanding of how children might learn rather than by a desire to protect children's motivation. Yet it is not enough to provide a theoretical framework that might assist teachers in analysing children's work such that it enables them to construct new meaning based on current knowledge and understanding; it must be done in a way that takes account of the multiple factors that concern both teachers and pupils in the process of formative assessment, including both motivation and the need to 'accomplish the lesson'. Moreover, in formulating this framework we must make sure that it is contained in terms that are accessible to those infant teachers who see their role as much in terms of 'caring' as in terms of 'educating'. We shall return to these ideas later in the book.

Performance goals and extrinsic motivators

A recurring theme in these extracts, and indeed in much of the data we have collected, is the pervasive influence of behaviourist ideas. This is nowhere more apparent than in the prominence given to devices such as stickers, smiley faces and merit marks. These, along with the widespread adoption of systems of 'assertive discipline', would suggest that in both academic work and behaviour, primary schools are continuing to rely on performance-goal frameworks and extrinsic tokens of success, even when a more critical-descriptive feedback would be merited by the work in question.

Chris thinks that merit marks are appropriate for certain children only, those who 'need to have some sort of physical reward, if you like, or need some sort of thing they can do, to say I've done this'. Because of this, he makes the classroom competition visible: when children receive a merit mark they colour in a square on the class chart:

> They go away smiling but this way they actually do something mechani-
> cal – physical I mean they colour in the team points – with this display I
> think it's quite important – suddenly you get quite a lot of team points
> after spelling tests and suddenly the thing changes and the graph changes
> so it's a visual thing you know – and everyone is – I might say equal but
> everyone is seen as being equal in spelling tests . . . children would see it
> and you know 'Oh and so and so's got a team point,' you can hear them
> all whispering. I think it's good for some people to hear their name men-
> tioned.
>
> (SVR interview)

However, Chris has to work with a school policy which insists that merit marks are given and collected weekly to count towards a school-wide compe-tition between teams. So despite his reservations about the utility of merit marks for all children, the existence of this policy means that they are necess-arily applied to all children. As we have seen, the work of both Dweck (1989) and Lepper and Hodell (1989) would suggest that such extrinsic reward sys-tems might harm the motivation of children and contribute to their adopting performance rather than learning goals. Moreover, the behaviourist context seems to set up a climate whereby even in a promising situation for formative assessment such as the incidents cited, where time has been made to look at mistakes (or miscues) with individual children, the opportunities are not always grasped. Many teachers still seem to hold a tacit view of assessment in behaviourist terms and 'fall into' that mode of operation as first recourse, focusing on the social situation and classroom management – the surface manifestation of problems. So, for example, when Timmy resists the impli-cation of error due to lack of effort and offers evidence of understanding (cut), the teacher attends to the excuse, rather than to the evidence of achievement and understanding.

Two further examples: feedback on handwriting

Having explored the relevance of certain psychological theories for our study of formative classroom assessment, we now want to move on to interrogate the theory more critically. We wish to move beyond a simple 'application' of theory to practice, in order to test and develop the theory in the light of practice, particularly with respect to the complexities of the social context in which, and the social interaction through which, psychological processes are realized.

The transcript again features Chris providing one-to-one feedback to individual children – Bella and Mario. The incidents portrayed take place on a Friday morning in March. In line with school policy, the children engage in a weekly handwriting practice, consisting of copying a selection of words several times from a sheet of paper into their handwriting books. The words are chosen to demonstrate a particular letter cluster or are otherwise connected to current work in hand. When the children have completed the task, they bring their book up to the teacher for assessment before continuing with finishing incomplete work from the previous four days.

T is sitting on a chair. A queue of three children is waiting to see him. Bella is the first in line. She has given him her handwriting book. Throughout the beginning of the interview Bella has her left hand up to her head and is fiddling with her hair, twisting it round her finger. Her body is arched with her chest thrust forward and her buttocks back. She is rocking back on her heels with her toes just off the ground.

There is a great deal of tension in Bella's body. This suggests that she is also feeling very tense about the judgement she is about to receive.

11:16

T   the line's moving again chaps
Teacher edges children back into a line.
Bella   I had to do them (*lot) =
Bella points to book.

Although Bella initiates, she does so rather tentatively.

T   = would that be fair to say this
             is probably not your best page
             in this book

T is positioning this piece of work as a failure rather than a success.

T looks up from book to Bella, nodding as he speaks. Faye who is behind Bella in the queue looks over Bella's shoulder at the book.
Bella   mmm
Bella nodding.

Although the children are bringing their work up and ostensibly having a private conversation with T, the context is nonetheless public in that other children in the line are party to it. Was Faye's interest aroused by T's opening remark, which might be conceived as a prelude to a negative assessment?

T   did you find it a bit tricky
             today?
Bella   mmm
Bella nodding.

The attribution for failure is being established.

T	why - cos they're quite long words?	T is suggesting that the main reason for failure is task difficulty, an unstable attribution, which attribution theory claims would have a positive effect on Bella's motivation.

T   why - cos they're quite long words?

Bella   mmm

Bella nodding.

T   OK -

Pause for six seconds while T writes in Bella's book.

T is suggesting that the main reason for failure is task difficulty, an unstable attribution, which attribution theory claims would have a positive effect on Bella's motivation.

T   I can see you've tried Bella well done good

Bella stops fiddling with her hair.

However, he is now suggesting that she has tried hard; attribution theory would suggest that in the context of failure this would not help Bella's confidence.

T   - so long as you try - all right I'm gonna give you a team point for that cos I can see you've tried and you've had to <u>cross</u> out and do it again so it must've been quite hard - yes ~ - well done - now -

T mimes the crossing out with his finger and then begins to flick back through the pages of the exercise book.

The extrinsic reward is given for Bella's effort rather than her achievement – behaviourist reinforcement?

T justifies his deduction that she has tried hard – interestingly it is the crossing out, usually seen as a negative feature in written work, that is used as evidence. To what extent does this emphasize that this is effort in the context of failure?

11:17

T   when your mum came to see me the other day =

Bella   = mm

T looks up at Bella, who meets his gaze. Mario, who is behind Faye in the queue and until now has been watching events in the rest of the classroom, moves round and looks at Bella's book.

T   = she she was not happy that your <u>last</u> topic book about toys was not finished -

Bella nods.

T   a lot of things were - and you came and said you were going to try harder - and I've looked at your topic book this time -

T points to Bella's topic book which is on the book rack next to him.

T   and most of the things are nearly finished aren't they -

Bella nods.

The focus has now changed from this individual piece of work to a more general appraisal of Bella's work on this topic. T is using the chance of seeing Bella 'alone' to give her feedback on his marking. Mention of Bella's mum raises the stakes of the assessment. T has revealed in interviews that he is of the opinion that Bella's mum is over-anxious and that this makes Bella lack confidence. He sees her as underachieving because she is so worried about failure: his task is therefore to reassure her parents and to boost her confidence.

Reference to the previous book makes this ipsative assessment, but the emphasis is on finishing rather than on quality of work.

T   in fact most of them <u>are</u> so you actually have made a big difference haven't you -

T takes piece of paper from Bella.

'Nearly' and 'most' operate to make this again not quite a success. This is an interesting grey area: despite all her effort is Bella still not succeeding; or is she almost succeeding as a result of almost enough effort?

T   so your <u>mum</u> should be pleased - so what've you got to do next?

Bella   (**) (*some writing) =

The assessment is over and Bella is being directed to more work. Apart from her initiation at the start of the incident Bella has communicated entirely through nods or 'mmms'.

... [ ] ...

T	look through your topic book and <u>see</u> what needs doing yes

Bella walks off.

T sees Faye to solve a problem over the order in which she does her work (14 seconds, not transcribed). Then Mario reaches front of the queue. He hands his book to T.

T	Mario where's the bit of paper you were copying from please?

The whole incident has lasted just over a minute.

Mario walks off and returns with paper to T's right-hand side. T opens out book and taps it.

T	- come on Mario - you should have that already - come and stand here

T points to left-hand side. Mario moves round. T touches Mario on arm.

T says this with some annoyance. Mario has been standing in the queue for some time and yet does not have all the necessary documentation.

T has been able to look at the book while Mario was away. He seems to have decided that it is not very good.

11:18

T	right did you find this a bit tricky by the looks of it?

Jason, who is behind Mario in the line, repositions himself slightly so that he can see Mario's book.

As with Bella, T's first comment assigns this to the difficulty of the material, again using the word 'tricky'.

Throughout Mario's assessment Jason looks at his book and at T, moving slightly when his vision is obscured by Mario's back.

Mario	mmm
T	mmm - seventeen - nineteen - twenty - two oh OK - what did you find the hardest thing about it -
Mario	hardest thing - was that one

Mario points to the book.

These are the words that Mario has had to write. T is asking about the <u>process</u> of writing, potentially a fruitful way of exploring what it was about the handwriting that Mario found difficult. However, instead of focusing on process, Mario concentrates on the most difficult item.

T	was it - is it - is it cos the words are quite long -
Mario	mmm
T	and you find (*that they) keep going - and you want to s\ =
Mario	= yeah and you get yer finger aching
T	yeah - OK

T does not receive the answer he requires and therefore uses a 'reformulator' (French and MacLure 1983), which has the effect of moving from an open question 'what did you find . . .' to a closed one 'is it cos . . . ?' In this way he has taken control of the discourse.

T is prompting again about the process but in a rather closed and directive fashion ('you find', 'you want'). Mario responds, but it is difficult to say whether the sore finger affected the quality of the handwriting or was merely a consequence of the difficulty. T does not probe further.

Mario holds up his hand and waves his finger. T writes in book. At this point another T enters and engages T in a conversation about the whereabouts of a member of the school support staff. T continues to write whilst she talks to him. (Not transcribed 29 seconds.) As the other T is still talking but has retreated towards the door, Mario says loudly.

T seems at first to be annoyed by the intrusion, but prolongs it by asking 'How's it going?' and prompting a further narrative from T2.

Mario	(*) that's the best I've done in my book

Mario appears annoyed that his time has been interrupted and speaks across T2.

11:19

T	- just a (*moment then) Mario	The tone of this utterance suggests that it is not to be construed as an admonishment, T is just asking Mario to be patient.

Meanwhile other T continues to speak (not transcribed 10 seconds) before leaving.

T   sorry Mario - what did you say?

Mario   that's the best piece of writing

T   well I was going to say that - yes - I mean I mean - sometimes it's looked a bit neater, but - I think as you've tried so hard I think I'm going to give you a team point =

... [ ]. ...

T shuts Mario's book and taps it with his finger.

T   right Mario well done - team point - put that away - look in your basket for what you've got to do next

Mario turns and begins to go.

Mario   (*) I'll do that

The tone of this utterance suggests that it is not to be construed as an admonishment, T is just asking Mario to be patient.

This is said much more animatedly, in sharp contrast to the previous statement. T appears to have returned to annoyance with the intrusion and to be affirming that Mario's irritation was justified. Significantly, Mario's interruption marks a shift in the way the piece of work is viewed.

Mario's suggestion appears to have had an effect. T appears to have been persuaded that the work is more meritorious than he did to begin with. Mario has been determinedly ipsative in his view. Indeed, he appears to have applied very sophisticated success criteria to the work, persuading T to weigh the difficulty against the neatness. Though this juxtaposition is not articulated overtly, it seems to be the socially constructed outcome of the interaction, with T agreeing that he was 'going to say that' although in the past Mario's work has 'looked a bit neater'. T seals the change with a team point. Is this necessary? Lepper's work (Lepper and Hodell 1989) would suggest that this is precisely the wrong moment to introduce an extrinsic reward, as the pupil's intrinsic pleasure with the results might be deduced from his judgement of the work as 'the best'.

Social context and the construction of psychological processes

Once again we are faced with two incidents that at first sight may seem rather insignificant, yet they constitute exactly the sort of myriad routine inter-actions which lay down the 'sediment' of student identity and self-esteem with respect to the processes of schooling. And below the surface, complex issues are being played out. We have already drawn attention to general issues of attribution and motivation. Our particular focus here will be to look at the differential effects that these two short incidents might have on the pupils' developing motivational orientation, and the differential consequences that the same broad teaching approach may have for different children. In particular, are these children's experiences contributing to the acquisition of learning goals and hence to 'mastery orientation', or to performance goals leading to learned helplessness or to being 'failure-prone' (Covington 1984: 84)? Having explored these questions we will move on to reflect on the further development of theory with respect to the realities of classroom life.

Comparing the two incidents suggests that in broad terms Chris is concerned about issues of confidence and motivation, but because he interprets Bella's and Mario's responses in different ways, he adopts a different specific strategy towards the two pupils concerned – an impression which is confirmed by other data. His different evaluation of the motivational orientation of each pupil is revealed in what he reported to their parents:

> [Mario's] confidence has always been strong, academically he has improved well. He now takes more care and pride in his work and really beams happily when he discovers a new skill.
>
> (Extract from report to parents)

> [Bella] is more self-motivated than before, as she sees successes more often . . . she has an over-cautious approach to her work and tends to worry.
>
> (Extract from report to parents)

These comments were included in Chris's annual report to parents as part of a summary of the pupils' achievement at the end of the school year (i.e. after the events shown in the transcript). In terms of the motivation literature cited earlier, they suggest that Chris sees Mario as having learning goals: he 'beams', not when he is praised, but when he acquires a new skill. The term 'self-motivated' applied to Bella would also suggest learning goals, but the rest of the statement rather counteracts this. It has overtones of behaviourism ('as she sees successes more often'), and her caution and tendency to worry are unlikely to be caused by learning goals which are claimed to provoke the opposite reaction. In conversation Chris confirmed that he thought Bella was always most concerned about living up to her parents' expectations. This evidence suggests that Bella is seen to be operating with performance goals. However, what is of most interest here is not that she already has a potentially problematic motivational orientation but that *it appears to be amplified by the interaction*.

The literature on attribution and goal theory would suggest that two main issues are at stake: is this piece of work to be viewed as a success or a failure; and to what is performance attributed? Table 6.2 summarizes the statements that potentially have most bearing on Bella's motivation.

The first three comments refer to the handwriting work and establish fairly conclusively that it is a failure. The third comment needs to be seen in light of the following extract from an interview with Bella. Crossing out is definitely not neat, and Bella sees neatness as the prime test of good work.[1] The interview extract below demonstrates this and other issues which we will return to later:

> *Researcher*: OK, so what do you think makes work good – how can you tell if work's good?
> *Bella*: 'Cos Mr Brown says and Miss Peach says about it.
> *Researcher*: Right, but you wouldn't know otherwise?
> *Bella*: No.
> *Researcher*: So you don't know, when you're taking up some work to show – you don't know whether it's going to be good or bad?
> *Bella*: Because if if they, they (*) give me a team point or not then it might, might give me a tick.
> *Researcher*: A tick's not very good then?

Table 6.2   Bella

Statements suggesting success/failure	Analysis
T = would that be fair to say this is probably not your best page in this book	failure
T did you find it a bit tricky today	failure
T and you've had to <u>cross</u> out and do it again so it must've been quite hard	failure
T and most of the things are nearly finished aren't they –	failure/success
T in fact most of them <u>are</u> so you actually have made a big difference haven't you	success/failure
Attribution	
T did you find it a bit tricky today	ability/ task difficulty
T why – cos they're quite long words	task difficulty
T I can see you've tried Bella, well done, good	effort
T so long as you try	effort
Rewards	
T all right I'm gonna give you a team point for that 'cos I can see you've tried	extrinsic
T in fact most of them <u>are</u> so you actually have made a big difference haven't you	intrinsic?
T so your <u>mum</u> should be pleased	extrinsic

Bella: No.
Researcher: No, OK – what does – what do you think they're looking for then when they're deciding whether to give you a team point or not?
Bella: To see if it's neat.

(Tape-recorded interview)

With respect to the second issue, that is, the statements which lead to attributions, although not completely clear cut, these tend to resolve themselves into an attribution of high effort, which in the context of failure acts as a 'double-edged sword' since failure has occurred despite the effort (Covington 1984:90). All this is compounded by further features which raise the stakes for Bella – the fact that she is being assessed in the hearing of the children in the queue, notably Faye, and also that her mother, whose attitude Chris recognizes as at least in part a cause of Bella's anxiety, is mentioned.

Now while we know that Chris's actions are constrained by school policy, if he wishes to foster learning goals he would be advised to promote intrinsic rather than extrinsic rewards. In fact the analysis in Table 6.2 suggests that he does the opposite. Moreover, Lepper and Hodell (1989) suggest that with respect to the evaluative function, the provision of extrinsic rewards for task involvement (i.e. trying hard) rather than for achievement, actually harms intrinsic motivation. Similarly, with the social control function they claim that:

. . . the central issue is whether the introduction of extrinsic rewards leads children to view their engagement in the activity as extrinsically

constrained and instrumentally controlled rather than intrinsically motivated. If so their subsequent intrinsic interest in the activity, in terms of
this third process, will be reduced.

(Lepper and Hodell 1989:86)

Bella's behaviour and the interview data would suggest that this was indeed
the case.

The situation with Mario is rather different. As we have seen, he appears to
have a strong inclination towards learning goals, which this incident serves to
reinforce not so much through the action of the teacher as through Mario's
own assertiveness in seizing the opportunity presented by the interruption
and taking charge of the assessment situation. The interaction begins in a
remarkably similar way to that with Bella, but Mario's own intervention shifts
the agreed understanding of the work from failure to success. The task difficulty attribution is accepted, but is now seen less as an excuse for failure than
as a reinforcement of success. Similarly, Chris's comment about trying 'so
hard' in the context of success now activates the other side of Covington's
(1984) double-edged sword and serves to contribute to Mario's positive self-
image. On the level of the reward system too, Chris's use of an extrinsic reward
has a different effect. Mario's evident intrinsic pleasure at progress makes it to
a certain extent redundant, but the fact that it is now a 'bonus not a bribe'
(Lepper and Hodell 1989:70) means that according to those authors it should
not harm intrinsic motivation (see Table 6.3).

The differences between the possible effects of the interactions on Bella and
Mario are particularly intriguing. They could be ascribed to the individual personality features of the children, but this does not take us very far; rather, the
social context and structure of the interactions present more interesting explanations. To begin with it is worth noting that certain aspects of this extract
conform to much stereotypical behaviour noted by gender research. Chris's
rougher handling of Mario (he begins by berating him for his lack of a piece
of paper) contrasts with his gentle treatment of Bella. The tendency of teachers
to see girls as lacking in flair and to reward them for effort even in the context
of failure is well documented both by experimental research in the field of educational psychology (e.g. Licht and Dweck 1985) and in more ethnographic
studies (see Walkerdine et al. 1989).

The gender of the two children also bears on a further issue with which we
will engage in more detail, namely the issue of power relationships in the
classroom. Although they are both pupils in the same class, the orientations
to power of these two children are very different. This is manifest in many
ways, not least in the fact that Bella barely speaks, whereas Mario not only initiates but even interrupts a teacher. As noted at the end of Chapter 5, the
importance of the pupil's voice being heard in the classroom is a key issue with
respect to the relationship of assessment to teaching and learning, and is the
focus of Kreisberg's (1992) study of power. Kreisberg makes a distinction
between coercive *power over* and *power with*, which he claims is 'manifest in
relationships of co-agency' (p. 85) and is the 'power that empowers' (p. 175).

Concepts of power and resistance are similarly employed by Bloome and
Willett (1991). They quote a transcript in which they say interaction itself

Table 6.3   Mario

Success/failure		Analysis
T	right did you find this a bit tricky by the looks of it	failure
Mario	(*) that's the best I've done in my book	success
Mario	that's the best piece of writing	success
T	well I was going to say that – yes – I mean I mean – sometimes it's looked a bit neater	success/ failure
Attribution		
T	right did you find this a bit tricky by the looks of it	ability/ task difficulty
T	was it – is it – is it cos the words are quite long –	task difficulty
T	I think as you've tried so hard I think I'm going to give you a team point =	effort
Rewards		
Mario	(*) that's the best I've done in my book	intrinsic
Mario	that's the best piece of writing	intrinsic
T	I think as you've tried so hard I think I'm going to give you a team point =	extrinsic
T	right Mario, well done – team point	extrinsic

contains tacit definitions of aspects of classroom life: 'These definitions are not static, nor are they merely given by the teacher or the school. They are continuously *negotiated, contested and evolving.* The various definitions can be viewed as multiple and sometimes conflicting versions of reality presented' (p. 228, emphasis added). We have already reviewed in Chapter 5 the way in which classroom power is contested but nevertheless is inscribed in knowledge and recursively realized through classroom interaction. Here it is the negotiation and contestation evident in Mario's intervention that causes the relationship with Chris to evolve from the 'power over' position evident with Bella and at the start of Mario's assessment, into the 'power with' category. Mario has identified an area where he can have an impact on the socially constructed outcome of the interaction, and he moves to realize it. Bloome and Willett recognize that despite the teacher's seemingly greater share of power in the classroom, he/she may not have control over all the discourse: 'Rather than assuming that the teacher is powerful and dominant, a finer analysis is needed to make clear in what discourses the teacher is powerful and in what discourses he/she is not' (Bloome and Willett 1991:230).

This teacher is powerful and dominant because of his position in organizing and managing the class and in assessing children's work, but he also has an ideological commitment to a child-centred approach which involves his 'making a big effort to be nice and considerate' (tape-recorded interview). Mario is assertive enough to make his case, but Bella is silent and is not able to access this power. In other words, despite any general commitment to pupil-centredness that a teacher such as Chris might have, the motivational orientation of different children means that access to a share in that power is not equitably distributed; in turn, the motivational impact of teacher feedback is likely not only to be differentiated, but also to compound the process of differentiation. Thus, Mario's tendency to focus on learning goals means that he is not so vulnerable to the verdict of his teacher, and it is this that allows him the confidence to disagree and to negotiate. Paradoxically, Chris's gentleness and desire to bolster Bella's confidence by reinforcing her performance goals have the effect of denying her power. In such cases the role of teacher as assessor emphasizes unequal power relationships. Chris's gentleness and potential openness to pupils' disagreements will not help a child such as Bella, who is caught in a powerless situation by her dependency on other people's judgements.

This is clearly a very important issue with respect to formative assessment. It would seem that if teachers wish to encourage autonomy and boost confidence through formative feedback, a critical analysis of motivational issues contextualized in the micropolitics of the classroom is necessary. Returning to the issues identified in Chapter 5, it can be argued that the power relationships required for effective formative assessment mirror the ideal of Kreisberg's 'power with'. The teacher remains in a privileged position and takes the prime responsibility for providing feedback on performance, but the aim is to foster self-monitoring in the pupil. The learned helplessness which arises from performance goals makes pursuit of such autonomy and empowerment extremely difficult, for, as Elliott and Dweck (1988:5) point out: 'helpless children react as though they have received an indictment of their ability, but mastery oriented children react as though they have been given useful feedback about learning.' Our data concerning the dynamics of classroom interaction suggest how this might be realized in action, but also highlight the limitations of simply applying this sort of analysis to the classroom. Categories such as 'helpless' and 'mastery oriented' are not given and immutable, but can be seen to be created and reinforced by patterns of interaction. Thus Mario elicited descriptive/ipsative feedback and demonstrated his preference for this when interviewed:

Researcher: What isn't helpful?
Mario: When he doesn't speak to me a lot about the work . . . when he just says – very good, Mario.
Researcher: Right – what sort of things are helpful then?
Mario: Helpful like when he tells me about my work.
Researcher: What sort of thing did he say?
Mario: Like, erm, I think you've done much better this last week or something. (*)

(Tape-recorded interview)

In the videotape transcription Mario shows he has a good understanding of the situation because he is able to balance task difficulty with the appearance of the handwriting. Although it might not look so neat as previous work, because the task is more difficult, the work is better. Mario has his own success criteria in contrast to Bella who, as the interview transcription reveals, seems to rely purely on her teacher to tell her when something is good or not. Even worse, it is the presence of extrinsic rewards that acts as the indicator of whether or not things are good. Bella's reaction was not an isolated case. As we have reported in other chapters, many of the teachers and children who were questioned during the study offered similar perceptions of extrinsic rewards. This is particularly significant with respect to the debate about the development of motivational styles. The children in this study are still young (the oldest are 7). Their experience of what constitutes good work is limited, and their capacity to differentiate between difficulty, ability and effort is, at the least, underdeveloped. The availability of an easy way of telling whether or not work is good through the giving or withholding of extrinsic reward means that they are not encouraged to think about criteria in any principled way.

Summary

In previous chapters we have identified some key sociolinguistic issues with respect to the social construction of classroom assessment. This chapter has attempted to develop our understanding of the problems and possibilities of facilitating learning through formative assessment in the classroom. It has done so by reviewing relevant literature in the field of achievement motivation and then subjecting it to scrutiny by analysing detailed evidence of how teachers and pupils interact in the context of routine assessment 'incidents'. The chapter also represents a critique of approaches to formative assessment where the complexity of the situation is minimized and interaction is seen in purely cognitive terms. It suggests that an attempt to understand formative assessment must involve a critical combination and coordination of insights derived from a number of psychological and sociological standpoints, none of which by themselves provide a sufficient basis for analysis, and that such considerations need to be contextualized in the actual social setting of the classroom. In the next chapter we move on to examine some of the circumstances in which teachers ask more open questions of their pupils, genuinely seeking to elicit new information rather than 'right answers', and the implications that this more divergent form of interaction can have for formative classroom assessment.

Note

1 More accurately, Bella's main criterion of good work is whether it is judged to be good by a teacher, but she believes that this is the criterion they apply.

7

Ask a genuine question, get a genuine answer

Introduction

In this chapter we return to look at the patterning of classroom speech in more detail and in particular to look at instances where circumstances lead the teacher to ask what might be termed 'genuine questions'. A feature of most of the transcripts we have presented so far is that very few words are actually spoken by pupils. The overwhelming quantity of talk comes from the teacher, despite the fact that the ostensible purpose of their utterances is to elicit responses from children. This pattern appears to be an almost inevitable part of the IRF structure of classroom interaction.

However, in parts of the transcripts, for example elements of the baseline assessment with Eloise and the feedback to Timmy and Mario, the discourse has a different quality, and rather more conversational than scholastic discourse structures prevail. The fundamental difference in these cases is the lack of a third move or, where a third move is used, it takes the form of an acknowledgement of the response rather than an 'evaluate'.[1] Significantly, it is precisely at these moments that the child begins to initiate, elaborate, expand and explain and thus provide the text for a potentially more rounded assessment. In the case of Eloise, a reason why the IRF structure is not wholly followed might be that in her first week of schooling she has not yet learned to conform to the rules. However, it is not possible for children to remain in ignorance of the rules for long, nor, as we suggested in Chapter 4, would it be desirable or helpful to them (cf. Robert and Gillie's problems). For teachers too, IRF structure is useful in many situations – coping with large groups of children, limited time, and a fixed curriculum. IRF provides teachers with the control necessary to guide the course of the lesson and push it towards a conclusion. In such circumstances a conversational structure would be liable to degenerate into disorder, and the space available for deeper cognitive processes might be taken up with talk irrelevant to the principles at stake (Edwards 1992).

However, when teachers and pupils are involved in formative assessment a more detailed elicitation is desirable, and a situation where pupils are only guessing at what the teacher wants to hear is unhelpful. Yet IRF discourse, grounded in the exigencies of teaching rather than the promotion of learning, seems to frustrate attempts that teachers might make to exercise a different form of control and elicit more 'genuine' or 'authentic' responses. Since our interest in this book is classroom assessment, we have been focusing on teachers eliciting information from children to reveal what they know, yet in the course of the research study we observed very few sustained examples of this occurring other than through IRF discourse. The predisposition of pupils, and especially of teachers, towards IRF seemed to be so strong that it was difficult for them to break out of it. IRF seems to be what Bourdieu (1977) describes as a 'structuring structure' recursively brought into being by, and at one and the same time structuring, the field of the classroom.

There have been a number of suggestions made as to how teachers might avoid the IRF structure. Many involve teachers consciously adopting particular strategies or unlearning what they already do – see, for example, the contributions of Douglas Barnes, David Wood, Neil Mercer, and Tony Edwards to the National Oracy Project (Norman 1992). However, some of our data enables us to show instances where different, more elaborated pupil speech occurs without conscious effort on the part of the teacher. In other words, it provides examples of 'naturally occurring' contexts where IRF is transcended and enables us to evaluate the potential of such situations for formative assessment. This usually occurred in situations where the teachers concerned were asking more 'genuine' questions than might usually be the case in routine classroom discourse; e.g. where they were trying to ascertain what had gone on in a situation which they had not observed (perhaps children working with a trainee teacher, or with a parallel teacher brought in to assist with special needs), or where they were preparing for a situation which they could not easily predict and control (e.g. a visitor coming in to speak). We shall now examine some of these situations in detail.

Questions about a science experiment

In the following transcript the class teacher is working with a group of seven Year 2 children (6- to 7-year-olds), attempting to find out how much the children have understood of a science activity that they did with a trainee teacher. They were asked by the trainee teacher to carry out and write up an experiment collaboratively. Although the class teacher planned the activity jointly with the trainee and has seen her lesson report, he was not with the children when they conducted the activity, so he did not observe it directly and, as far they are concerned, he knows very little about it. This means that one of the usual features of IRF discourse, that the teacher is only asking questions to which s/he already knows the answers, is not quite the case here. Interestingly enough, however, in the light of what other teachers reported in interview (see Chapter 3), the teacher is very much working with the group, and trying to appraise the group's overall level of understanding and readiness to proceed, rather than working with individuals.

The children and T are sitting on chairs grouped around a large table. Each child has an exercise book in front of them.
. . . [ ] . . .

T   and you put warm water in three bottles all at the same time did you?

T makes three movements with the flat of his hand.

Cs   yeah

T   now was the warm water the <u>same</u> for each bottle?

Angela   yes

T   was it exactly the <u>same</u> warm water?

Elspeth   no =

C   = yes =

Elspeth   no =

Elspeth and Greta shake heads, Charles and Ella nod.

T   no - why not?

T looks at Elspeth.

Elspeth   because it was poured in at different times

T   it was poured in > at different times <

Jon   > yes but only < about - a few seconds =

Jon gestures with his right hand.

Ella   = the first one was > (**cold water in) < -

T   >would that make any difference - <

Ella   and the and the second (*)

T   = but how did, how did Miss Tawney make warm water cos she - she had the kettle on and it boiled that's boiling hot - how did she make it warm? =

Jon   = > she left it - <

Jon gestures with both hands.

Elspeth   > she put a bit of cold water in <

C   > (**) <

Jon   she left it =

T   = so she poured some water out to make some room and . . . [ ] . . . she put some cold water in to make it warm - so - am I right in thinking . . . [ ]

The phrase 'all at the same time' is significant. T is initiating a debate about whether the variable of initial temperature was controlled – was it a fair test? However, his position as outsider is interesting, as the question can be construed as one that is seeking information rather than 'testing' pupils' knowledge. The response of the children may well be determined by their interpretation – whether T does or does not know the answer.

There is disagreement amongst the group on the issue. Could it be that Elspeth and Greta have seen the phrase 'all at the same time' as a cue and are not therefore seeing the question as 'real'?

Elspeth's response may have been prompted by T's previous statement 'all at the same time'. She evidently has a fairly sophisticated idea of how the initial temperature would need to be controlled. This is the sort of critique of working methods that is required in science at a higher level. T's repetition seems designed to encourage debate.
Jon acknowledges Elspeth's point but considers the inaccuracy negligible.

Ella is continuing her turn, which means that T's question does not appear to be answered.

T is asking a different question. (Miss Tawney is the trainee teacher.)

The children are arguing about the exact content and sequencing of events. They seem to be responding to T's questions as a genuine

... she had - did she have a
kettle then full of warm water?

Charles   yes

T   and how did she know it was
warm, how did she test it - or
didn't you see that?

Elspeth   we didn't > see it <

Charles   > didn't see it <

Elspeth and Charles shake their heads.

T   OK so she came back with a
kettle full of warm water and
she poured it into one two
three - more or less at the same
time ~ =

*T mimes pouring into three vessels with his
left hand.*

Jon   yeah it was only a few seconds

T   right so are you happy then
before you covered the bottles
- all the water in the three bottles was of the same warmth

*T makes a threefold gesture with the palm
of his left hand held vertically.*

Cs   yeah

T looks around group.

. . . [ ] . . .

T   OK - so - you had three - you
happy with that - did you -
was there a lid put on the
bottle

Cs   yeah

T   so what happened next? - I've
got three bottles now with
warm water in - all the same
height ~

*T repeats his threefold gesture and then
holds his index finger and thumb apart as
if holding a small bottle.*

Cs   yeah

T   all the same bottle shapes ~

Cs   yeah

T   so they're all - so it's _fair_ is it?

~-

*T moves his left index finger abruptly from
right to left parallel to the ground. The children nod.*

T   OK - who can tell me what
happened next -

*Fiona raises her hand. T looks at Angela,
then back to the centre of the group.*

enquiry. T is appropriating the children's
responses and tentatively synthesizing them
into an acceptable composite which also attends
to his prospective teaching agenda.

This has a slight rising intonation and could be
interpreted as a question. T is establishing the
degree to which the variables were controlled.

Jon responds as if to a question, reiterating his
original observation.

This elicitation has invited the group to cement
the consensus over the issue of whether the
difference in time between the pouring of the
water into the three vessels made any difference
to its temperature ('warmth').

They agree that there was no difference.

Another question to which T does not know the
answer, but by asking it he assigns significance
to the issue.

T is restructuring pupils' responses in order to
attach significance to the control of variables.

This leading question establishes a boundary
between the idea of a 'fair test' and other aspects
of the investigation.

A typical 'framing move' followed by a very
open elicitation – but one which is an invitation
to bid, perhaps to keep the quiet pupils 'on their
toes'.

T   Angela - what happened next? - three bottles lids on what happens next?

T holds his left palm perpendicular to the ground. T looks back at Angela.

> T has decided who will speak and thus is still retaining control over the discourse, but the question remains a very open one.

Angela   and then we put the material (**)

T   OK - so - what material did you put on?

Angela   we put - cotton **and** =

Jon   = and nothing =

Angela   = (*) and - and nothing

Cs   nothing

T looks at centre of group.

> 'Material' – a key scientific term and integral part of the process is introduced by a pupil. The 'OK' in response seems to be an acknowledgement rather than an 'evaluate', though T seizes the opportunity to extend the description – 'what material?'

T   nothing - why did you put nothing on one then - why did you leave that one =

Jon   = um - to see if with nothing on

T looks at Jon and nods.

> 'Why?' – an invitation to explain. During 'normal' classroom discourse this would almost certainly be interpreted by pupils as a question to which T knew the answer and which they would have to 'get right'. Here it is treated as a genuine inquiry.

T   = so what =

Jon   = (*to see if it's) still warm =

Jon leans forward

T   so what - so you wanted to see what would happen - with nothing on it - now did you <u>predict</u> what would happen? - did you just sort of - oh right - did you just <u>predict</u> - did you sort of say I think this is one is gonna stay the warmest the longest=

9:52

Ella   = yeah I (*) - and / the / fur / will / be / hotter / than / all of them

Ella points to her book with a pencil.

> T is acknowledging and extending by recapping and appropriating. He has reshaped what has been said, but interestingly, rather than giving a more specific rendition of what the Cs stated, he has been less specific – 'you wanted to see what would happen'.
>
> However, this openness then allows him to introduce and illustrate the word 'predict' which is being marked as specially important.
>
> Ella appears to be reading from her book.

T   the fur will stay the hottest the longest will it - OK

T nods as he speaks; Ella nods at the same time.

T   - anyone else have a prediction - what did <u>you</u> predict?

T looks across at Greta

Greta   the fur (*is the warmest) (*)

Greta also speaks slowly and deliberately. T nods.

> In Ella's account the variable of time remains implicit.
> T reformulates the prediction so that time is included but it remains entangled with the other variable of temperature. 'OK', acknowledges Ella's contribution and acts as a marker that she has said enough on this.

T   now was your prediction correct?

Cs   yes

> Again there is no evaluative move: the focus is on eliciting the scientific process, rather than endorsing a correct observation.

T   right so who can tell me what happened in the what happened section -

Ella and Charles raise their hands. T points to Charles's book.

. . . [ ] . . .

T   what do those three numbers tell you?

Angela   how warm it was

Charles   how warm it is

T points to Charles's book with his left hand.

T   so which one is the warmest?

Jon   the third

C   uh

T   what the largest number?

Jon   yeah cos it's thirty four

Charles   thirty four degrees centigrade
=

Charles turns to face T.

T   = did you test the temperature of the warm water before you did the experiment and then test it afterwards - do you know what it started off as?

Charles   no

C   yes

Jon   we all felt it before

T turns towards Jon.

T   did did you not - you didn't do it with a thermometer though?

T points to Jon's book.

Jon   no

T   no - OK so when did you check on the temperatures then - how long did you wait -

Ella raises her hand. T looks across at her. She puts her hand down.

T   yes

Ella   about one hour

T   about one hour - and then you went back and tested it -

Ella, Elspeth and Greta nod their heads.

T   OK and were you surprised at the results - that the fur kept > it <

C   > no <

T   you were surprised =

Elspeth   = no =

However, this follow-up marker ('right') effectively affirms the observation as correct.
'The what happened section' – T alludes to his routine formulation of the 'results' section of pupils' reports.

T probes for understanding of the symbols of the Celsius system.

These two reformulations, under the normal rules of teacher–pupil talk, would suggest that although 'how warm it is' and 'the third' are not wrong answers, they are also not the answer that the teacher wants.

Charles interprets the symbols correctly.

However, T seems satisfied with the pupils' responses and does not evaluate them. The sequence does not follow IRF, and the effect of this is that all three children's contributions seem to be seen as valid. Instead of the evaluating move T now returns to a question whose answer he does not know. However, it appears to carry with it the implication that he thinks a pre-test should have taken place.
Jon's interjection shows that for him the test took place even though it was not done with a thermometer. He thus reveals an understanding of the purpose of the check.

Ella bids and is invited to contribute by T. This sequence accords very closely to IRF, but under normal IRF rules T's repetition 'about one hour' would imply a wrong answer, i.e. 'try again'. Here it formally marks the next stage in the scientific process.
This is an interesting metacognitive question, which is also a genuine one. Whether the children were surprised or not might help T to see how knowledge derived from the experiment was integrated into what the children already knew. Either answer might serve as a cue to getting the children to theorize.

T   = no =
Elspeth   = no
. . . [ ] . . .
T   so what does this tell you   We have now come from the particular, this
           about fur then - what does this   individual investigation, to the general know-
           tell you about <u>fur</u> -   ledge about fur and the insulating properties of
                                               materials. The pupils are asked to draw infer-
9:54   ences.

Elspeth and Ella raise their hands. T looks
across at Elspeth. Charles puts his pencil in
his mouth.
T   yes
Elspeth   that it's the warmest   'OK' may be an acknowledgement or it may be
T   it's the warmest OK   an evaluate. It is difficult to tell from the into-
Jon   but the fur isn't really the   nation.
           warmest
                                                Jon takes it as an acknowledgement on which he
T looks towards Jon.   can improve.
Jon   - if you don't put it the fur side
Jon holds out both his hands.
T   oh if you turn it inside out   T interprets and articulates Jon's mime.
           would it =
Jon   = if you put it the other way
           around - then the fur showing
           =
T   = so =
Jon   = it won't do it cos the (**)   Jon seems to have an understanding that the
           (*air) =   insulation properties of the fur are connected
T   = oh =   with the way air is held next to the hot body.
Jon   and it all comes out
During these utterances Jon has been ges-
turing with both hands, miming a turning
inside out.
T   right - so did you you have the
           fur on the inside then =
Angela   = yeah   Angela is involved, albeit fairly passively, in the
T is making spherical gestures with both   reasoning.
hands.
T   = and then you had sort of,
           like, the skin bits or whatever
           it was on the outside - so if you
           take it the other way around   T is now appropriating and interpreting Jon's
           so the fur's on the outside ->   statement by rephrasing it and providing a logi-
           you think it wouldn't be < the   cal extension.
           same
Jon   > so it wouldn't be fair < - so it   Jon is rephrasing again using, significantly, the
           wouldn't be fair   vocabulary T used earlier, an example of a pupil
T   so that's something to try out   appropriating from the teacher.
           isn't it perhaps maybe - per-
           haps next time you should
           perhaps get two bottles two   This speculation about where to go next can be
                                                seen as an attempt to intervene and extend the

	bits of fur - > fur inside fur outside < -	children's learning at the level of general ideas rather than specifically situated scaffolding.
Jon	> I'll do it at home <	
T mimes bottles with his right hand then taps Charles's book with his pencil		Jon is obviously very engaged in the problem.
T	see what happens OK - OK now - right =	T puts in another boundary marker – he is going on to something different and therefore does
Jon	= Miss Tawney said we have to =	not accept whatever Jon was going to say.
T	= Charles read out we think this happened because - read what you've put please	
T points to Charles's book		T is ensuring that the session moves on.
Charles	the one with the fur was the hottest and the one with nothing was cold and the one with fur and cotton trapped air	This is the same theory that Jon has already expressed.

The interaction continues in similar fashion for another 3 minutes

Assessment as interview

Although this transcript relates to a relatively complex activity, the teacher's intentions were clearly directed towards assessment. In an interview shortly afterwards he stated:

> I was assessing there that they actually understood what they were doing – and what the results meant so they'd come back with a conclusion . . . I suppose in the short term – is – if they know something about insulation for a start and they realize that some materials keep the warmth in better than others. So that's the main conclusion I expected, anything beyond that is a bonus obviously.

The evidence of the transcript would suggest that the bonus was obtained: all of the children seem to have succeeded at the task, and some at least – Elspeth, Charles and Jon – have some understanding as to why the materials have the properties observed. Moreover, Jon is able not only to demonstrate some sophisticated reasoning, but to take his understanding further during the course of the assessment event. Indeed it is possible, even probable, that the same is true for the rest of the group. The means by which the teacher enables this to happen might therefore be seen as a successful combination of assessment with teaching.

A crucial aspect of this transcript is that the work that is being assessed was not set by the assessor, so his relationship to knowledge about that work is different from usual. As mentor to the student teacher, the class teacher (Keith) would have been aware of what the activity was about, but he was not present when the investigation took place, being engaged with another group of children. However, what is most significant is not what he actually knows about the activity, but the children's beliefs about his knowledge. As far as they are concerned, he does not know the answer to many of the questions he is posing and they are therefore genuine questions. Whether this is the case for all the pupils at the start of the transcript is unclear, but by the end it seems to have been generally accepted. As we have suggested in the commentary, this impression is maintained and reinforced for most of the time by Keith's avoidance of an evaluative third move.

However, although this might not be IRF, neither is it exactly ordinary conversation. The structure would seem to approximate more to that of the interview where the interviewer takes responsibility for structuring the interaction, but there is usually no third move. When a third move is observed here, its purpose is acknowledgement and facilitation of the discourse rather than an evaluation of the answer. Just as it would be inappropriate for an interviewer to comment on the veracity or validity of an interviewee's statements, so here the teacher is concerned mainly with eliciting a response. When he repeats or rephrases a child's statement this seems to have the function of seeking clarification of what has been said and assisting them to refine their thought or to reach consensus. Further elicitation, after a suitable framing move ('OK', 'Now', 'Right') then moves the discussion on to another focus. Thus, contrary to the normal IRF rule, repeated questions do not seem to be interpreted as an indication that the previous answers are wrong: when Keith attempts to probe individual children about the factors that help insulation, they reiterate what has already been said and do not attempt to guess at other answers. Thus the structure of the talk seems to allow some of the control for the content of the speech to lie with the children, whilst enabling the teacher to adopt a facilitating and structuring role which keeps the exchanges relevant to the task in hand.

The teacher's questions are genuine but they are not naive. They are motivated by a deeper understanding of the scientific issues at stake, coupled with a prospective curricular agenda, rather than knowledge *per se* of the events about which he is enquiring. Here, then, is a different form of classroom interaction that does not follow the standard IRF pattern, but in which both teacher and pupils appear to be competent. Willis (1992:122) makes a distinction between questions and pseudo-questions dependent on whether the questioner knows (K1) or does not know (K2) the answer:

> A given utterance may be treated as a K1 or a K2 elicit. How it operates in the discourse depends not simply on the structure of the initiation but also on how the participants choose to regard it. An *evaluate* tags the opening elicit as K1 and, if this is a common feature of the discourse, tells us a good deal about the relationship between the participants. An *acknowledge*, on the other hand, tags the opening elicit as K2, which is likely to be the norm outside settings like the classroom and the quiz show.

However, much of the time in this transcript a lack of feedback means the questions are tagged as neither K1 nor K2. There is some use of an 'acknowledge', but generally the teacher avoids both, either reiterating the response as an 'acknowledge' or proceeding straight to a reformulator. In some cases he probably knows the answer and in some he does not, as he was not there when the practical work was done. The situation might therefore be characterized as a third form (K3!) where the lack of a third move tags the question as Socratic.[2] Here, whether the questioner knows the answer or not becomes less important, as the purpose of the question or elicitation is the same in either case: to clarify what is being said, encourage a consensus and provide a supportive structure to the interaction. The asking of the question, that particular question and not another, assigns meaning to the answer. Knowledge of the specific answer may be unimportant, but knowing the direction in which the group must travel is vital. It might be possible in this context for the teacher to restrict himself to only asking questions that have a right answer; but by directing attention towards the process that the pupils have experienced and where they are the experts, he is getting them to reflect on their own thought. The teacher has in mind an overarching theory related to the school science curriculum, in this case a notion of thermal conductivity, but the pupils provide the context, situating the knowledge, so that the teacher's questioning can prompt them to generalize and theorize.

This seems to be remarkably close to what Bruner (Wood *et al.* 1976; Bruner 1985) describes as scaffolding; the teacher collaborates with pupils to provide an external model of the internal processes of thought. Moreover, it is the teacher's repeated refusal to use third move evaluators, but rather to use reformulators, that puts him into this role. Thus it might be argued that it is the participants' expectations that the pattern of interaction will conform to IRF, that makes successful scaffolding in the primary school rare (cf. Askew *et al.* 1996).[3] Pupils do not necessarily react to questions as scaffolds, because they expect them to be followed by an evaluate. Just before the transcribed section of the assessment above, it is for a short time unclear whether the children are demonstrating their principled knowledge or are engaged in the ritual of trying to guess what the teacher wants. What establishes for them that the ground rules might include this type of elicit (K3) is the teacher's display of ignorance about what actually did happen concerning the trainee teacher's use of warm water. In turn, the teacher is able to reap the benefits in terms of gaining greater access to the children's ideas.

In this transcript the teacher displays considerable skills in handling the discussion, but interviews with him afterwards confirmed that the avoidance of the evaluate or its careful transformation into an acknowledgement demonstrated a tacit knowledge of what might be productive, rather than a premeditated and deliberate strategy. Moreover, this approach was unusual rather than typical, and seemed to emerge from this particular situation. The quality of the interaction, then, depended on the serendipitous occurrence of a suitable context, rather than by design.

Before moving on from this transcript it is important to clarify the effect of the lack of an evaluate on the event as assessment. Although it meant that each utterance was not judged immediately after it was produced, it did not mean that the children remained in the dark as to how well their efforts matched up to the teacher's standards of quality. Instead, this evaluation was delayed until the end of the session and then took a more global or holistic form: 'Right I think this is lovely . . . I'm actually – very pleased with the way you've explained to me – and I think I understand what you're doing now . . . you've actually told me . . .' Since Keith was happy with what they had done, there was no specific feedback for individuals on, for example, what was especially good or what could have been better. But had the teacher uncovered misconceptions it would have been extremely difficult to give more specific feedback to individuals at that juncture. In this case the delayed evaluation reflected the group's overall reasoning and understanding rather than being attached to each individual utterance. However, such feedback may still be of more meaning and use to the individuals in the group than that contained within a usual IRF structure. As we have seen, IRF can be overly ritualistic and lacking in real import, but some 'group oriented feedback' may nevertheless lead individuals to focus on principle rather than procedure because the substance of the discourse is more engaging. Such a possibility will depend on the creation of a context where a different discourse structure is produced and where sufficient time is spent with the group to make delayed evaluation possible.

Questions about Jamaica

We observed another example of how a particular context can give rise to unusual classroom discourse in a Year 1 (age 5–6) classroom in an inner city school of great ethnic and cultural diversity. A small group of seven children who regularly work together with a 'Section 11' support teacher[4] were doing a mini-project on Jamaica, as part of the geography curriculum. The class teacher had arranged for the group to interview the support teacher, who was born in Jamaica and who had just been to Jamaica to visit her relations. The teacher set the group the task of preparing suitable questions to ask and, because of the way in which this opportunity had presented itself, also identified English work that could be assessed – specifically, English National Curriculum attainment targets 1.4c and 2.3f on 'speaking and listening' and 'reading'.

The group had already looked at some books on Jamaica by themselves, and now the teacher is working with them. This context creates several interesting features. In particular, the task is authentic in that the questions are being formulated for a real purpose: if the questions are not sufficiently good, the children will not discover what they need to know about Jamaica. Also, the teacher is eliciting questions, not answers. Once again the teacher retains overall control of the discourse and is the one who determines when a question is sufficiently well formulated to be written down – she does the writing. However, as in the previous example, there is an important issue of knowledge at stake, and what she does is contested. The teacher and the seven children are clustered around a flipchart which already contains some questions that they have formulated, and the teacher is writing up the questions.

Rebecca (*do they) have schools in Jamaica?	Rebecca is suggesting this as a question to ask. The fact that the children are being asked to

T	well - what do you think?
Cs	> yes <
C	> schools in <
T	do you remember - did you see any schools in the books that <u>you</u> looked through?
Cs	yes
T	right - is there any question <u>now</u> that - you know that they have schools in Jamaica but can you ask a question about the schools in Jamaica?
Fatia	I know
C	do they - do they
C	what does it look like in schools in Jamaica?
11:40	
T	OK - can you be more a little bit more specific - can you ask >something <=
C	> miss < =
Etienne	= > what does < that mean =
T	= think of something - about - I mean - think of something that we do at school - and then think - well - do they do that in Jamaica?
Etienne	did do they like do write\ writing when when you've finished at the holidays when the holidays are finished - like you like like you - you tell us to do writing
T	right so I tell you to write about what you did at the week-end - yeah - but maybe what you =
Fatia	= miss, I've got a
T	OK
T points to Fatia	
Fatia	have they got - have they got -
Etienne	(***)
... [ ] ...	
Fatia	have they got trolleys?
T	have they got trolleys
Fatia	bug\ - buggies
T	buggies- what would you do with a buggy?
Cs	(laughter)
Thandi	push the babies

formulate questions rather than answers immediately changes the nature of the discourse. T's response is a negative one; she does not consider the question to be a very good one, but rather than being a standard evaluative feedback move, it is conversational or argumentative.

The classic reaction to an unacceptable move from the child would be to reformulate the question. However, here T is scaffolding the children's own reformulation by directing their attention to what they already know. The fact that the children are being asked to pose the question has turned the discourse on its head.

Once again the issue is whether the questioner already knows the answer to the question. This time, though, the roles are reversed. T wants the children to formulate a genuine question!

T's suggestion that the children focus on the pictures they have seen prompts a visual question.

T asks for reformulation but uses a word, 'specific', which is not understood. Throughout this transcript she seems to be making no concessions to the age of these children.

Etienne is assertive in asking for a definition of 'specific'.

T tries to make the word 'specific' more concrete by giving an example of how they might in this case be more specific. However she does not really explain the word such that it might become part of the children's vocabulary – interestingly enough, given previous observations about teachers' prospective agendas, her objective is that they comprehend her here and now, rather than that they learn new vocabulary.

This is an acknowledge rather than an evaluate. The question does not appear to be sufficiently well formulated to be accepted by T.

T may be expecting Fatia to reformulate Etienne's question about schools.

In the event, the question is not about school; T reiterates it as an acknowledge, though Fatia interprets this response as 'try again'.

T appears here to be asking another question because she does not understand what Fatia means to say. This is thus a genuine question. Throughout this transcript and others in this

T	oh for <u>babies</u>
Fatia	yeah
T	oh we'll ask that

T goes to write on flipchart.

Etienne	miss -

11:41

T	why do you ask that question Fatia?
Thandi	she wants to know how =
T	yeah I know she wants to know but why did you ask it - what made you think of that - what made you think about - what made you think that - they might have buggies - to move the babies around in - why did you think that - no - no idea - OK

Fatia shakes head. T makes to write on flipchart.

T	ummm - any more questions -
Thandi	miss
T	Fatia um Thandi
Fatia	> (*why do you keep doing that *) <
Thandi	do they - do they have - what kind of - what kind of curtain (*)
T	what kind of ~
Cs	curtains
Thandi	do they have a shutter - or a curtain
T	oh - right - do they have shutters or curtains - umm - we'll have to ah add that one to the question about houses won't we =

11:42

Thandi	= yeah

T writes question on flipchart.

Cs	do/they/have/shutters/or/curtains/for/their
T	right - in their houses I'm going to put
Cs	in/their/houses
T	right -
Etienne	can I have a (*drink)
T	can you hang on - hang on - it's nearly lunchtime -

class it is apparent that T often asks questions which are aimed at improving her own understanding of what the children are saying. Sometimes she cannot hear them, sometimes she has difficulty understanding their accent, and sometimes the cultural references escape her. Here it seems to be merely a case of her not expecting the change of subject but she finds the question a good one.

Earlier T had asked the children to be 'more specific'. They have now moved from the very general to the very specific. T is asking an extremely demanding metacognitive question, but nevertheless it does appear to be a genuine one. However, Fatia is stumped by it and seems to interpret it as a negative response to her original question – she does not read the question as soliciting further information, but as indicating that the first question was inappropriate. She seems to be expecting IRF, whereas Thandi's response suggests that she has recognized this as a different situation.

'OK' marks the boundary as T gives up on eliciting an answer from Fatia.

Thandi starts to ask a closed question but corrects herself and reformulates the question in mid utterance. She has benefited from the earlier interventions of T re. asking questions which would call forth description rather than yes/no answers, and has thus reached a stage where she is able to monitor her performance in the moment of production (cf. Sadler 1989).

The question is accepted without modification and without any ostensible praise. The fact of acceptance is possibly seen as making a linguistic evaluation redundant. Although T holds the power to decide what counts as acceptable, she preserves the conversational and collaborative form of the exchange by not making a recognizable verbal evaluation.

Children read as T writes.

T has added her own contribution to the question.

Despite the collaborative nature of this event T still preserves her authority of the organization of the classroom and the movements of the chil-

T	right - let's go back to the one about schools - try - well we know that they have schools in Jamaica - but they might not > be the same <	dren, a role which complicates both the social and the linguistic context. T has not forgotten the original topic of schools. This is a recapitulation of the point they had reached.
Thandi	> what sort of < I know =	
T	= Thandi, sit down here please I can't talk to you when you're over there =	Once again the organizational role intrudes and T's interjection prevents Thandi's question from being asked. This allows Etienne to get in. He has remembered the previous cue and asks a more specific question but a closed one.
Etienne	do they have playgrounds in the schools?	
T	have a think -	
C	no =	This may be a response to the closed nature of the question or it may be a reference back to her previous statement.
Thandi	= they might have	
C	they might	
T	right -	

T reaches over to Thandi, who places something into her hand.

T	think about what sort of quest\- we know that they have schools in Jamaica but what sort of > questions - you could ask <	The parallel agendas of facilitating question making and controlling behaviour continue.

. . . [ ] . . .

11:43

T points to Thandi.

Thandi	what do they have in their school	
T	well - what do you mean - what kind of - what are you thinking about cos they could just - Mrs Magenta could just give you a long long list of the things they have in their school and you would just fall asleep it would be so long - I mean she could be talking about - nails or -> pins or pencils - crayons <	Thandi suggests a very open and unfocused question. It may be that Thandi is taking as read that it refers to the school playground. Whether she does or not, T does not accept it as sufficiently clear and demonstrates why it is not. Nina Magenta is the Section 11 support teacher.
Thandi	> I know one < - what - what kind of - what kind of playgrounds	
Fatia	(***)	Thandi has taken Etienne's original question and has put it in a more acceptable form, i.e. open but specific.
Thandi	what kind of playgrounds do they have?	
T	what kind of ~	
Thandi	what kind of playgrounds do they have - do they have no poles or > do they have <	T accepts the question in this form. This refers to the equipment in this school's playground.
Etienne	I know something	

| Thandi | do they have no slides or do > they (**) < |
| T | right - you just tell me the first part of your question - what kind what kind of |

This is a clear indication that T has not heard/understood the word 'playground' and is using a strategy to elicit the question in parts from Thandi. One cannot keep asking for clarification in multilingual classrooms when dealing with people whose variety of English is not necessarily familiar. This may also be a context where teachers avoid an evaluate move.

Thandi	playground do they have
T	what kind of <u>playgrounds</u> do they have in Jamaican schools?
Etienne	in Jamaica

It seems that at last T has decoded the word 'playgrounds'.

T writes

| Cs | what/kind/of/playgounds/do/ they/ < |

11:44

| Fatia | >what's that (*) - every time you write that (*) - |

Fatia appears to be asking about the question mark.

| T | Fatia - just wait |

Fatia points at writing.

| Cs | have/in/have/in/in/Jamaica |
| T | Jamaican schools - right in any |

Etienne stands up and moves closer to flipchart.

Etienne	playground
T	right - Rebecca
Rebecca	umm
Fatia	miss you've just made a mis-take - look =

Fatia's attention is not confined to the question mark. She physically touches the flipchart as she speaks. This act of intervention shows that even though T is determining what counts as an acceptable question, her actions are not uncontested. The context is open enough to enable children to initiate speech.

Fatia points to flipchart.

| T | = it doesn't matter - it's |

T alters writing on flipchart.

| T | right Etienne sit down |

Etienne sits down.

T does not appear to welcome the correction in this case. Nonetheless she does make the alteration.

Another initiation.

| Etienne | what did - you write there? |
| T | oh we've just written what kind of playgrounds do they have in Jamaican schools |

T engages in appropriation for learning purposes, by use of the plural 'we'. Nevertheless there are strong grounds for claiming that the activity has been one of genuine collaboration between teacher and pupils.

The session continued for another nine minutes, during which further questions were suggested and refined.

Assessment as debate: questions about questions

The class teacher, Gaynor, was able to come to several conclusions about the children's attainment in this session: 'Their use of language is actually quite sophisticated. I mean I think to do this at six is quite good, really, and especially some of the stuff Thandi was coming out with ... I know that they've got that skill.' Once again we note that although there was some differentiation between the children in the allusion to Thandi, the conclusions were mostly about the group as a whole. Gaynor went on to say that she saw the session as useful, as by intervening, she had enabled the children to learn more about how to ask productive questions. However what is most significant for our argument is the context: here the pupils' task is to devise questions, rather than to respond to them; in turn, this has influence on issues of knowledge and knowing, as well as on the structure of the discourse. Gaynor's actions have the effect of positioning her as having no more substantive knowledge about Jamaica than the children; what she might be expected to know is counterbalanced by the group's previous activity of looking through books. As with Keith in the science transcript, her knowledge or lack of it is not directly relevant to the task in hand, since it is her colleague, not herself, who will be the authority. However, this is not to say that she is not therefore in a position to shape and control what is going on. She assumes the role of arbiter of what is to become the accepted question because, although she does not have specific knowledge of the answer, she does have more global knowledge of what makes a productive question; and it is this mixture of knowing and not knowing which seems to condition the discourse.

Gaynor, like Keith, avoids the usual form of the IRF interaction, but unlike him, she is leaving the children in no doubt as to her judgement of their efforts as they occur. However, this is conveyed through a response that encourages either reflection on what has already happened ('what do you think . . . do you remember – did you see any schools in the books that *you* looked through') or anticipation of what might happen ('Mrs Magenta could just give you a long long list of the things they have in their school and you would just fall asleep it would be so long'). Like Keith's delayed evaluation, such an approach avoids focusing the children's attention on guessing what the teacher has in mind. Rather than being an evaluate, moves such as these form counterarguments which prompt children to further thought and reasoning. Unlike incidents reported in previous chapters when the teacher seemed concerned to be gentle with the children by avoiding negative evaluations, here Gaynor is paying them the compliment of putting their ideas to the test by arguing against them. The extent to which such a strategy will succeed must be dependent on the relationship that the teacher has developed with the children; in particular, and with reference to some of our discussions in previous chapters, it would seem to require the teacher to exercise *power with* the children in order for them not to be engulfed by the weight of her argument. Gaynor appears to have been able to establish this with some, if not all, the children in this group.

Assessment and the third move

In both these transcripts the teachers' utterances were more successful as elicitations than they usually were, since although they spoke more than the children, the proportion is more even than on most other occasions when they were observed. Interestingly, the only occasions when there appeared to be even more child speech were 'show and share' sessions, when children were telling their news to the class and where once again the teachers' questions were genuine and aimed at producing and acknowledging the children's speech rather than directly evaluating it. The association of a larger pupil text with the frequent absence of an evaluate move recalls a distinction made by Douglas Barnes (1976). He claimed that what actually stops children from revealing what they know is the threat of critical feedback: 'If we perceive other people as threatening critics, ready to judge us and show up our inadequacies, we are likely to put on a display, to concentrate on external acceptability of what we say and do' (Barnes 1976:110). This observation is similar to that of Bruner (1985:32–3): 'What is obvious . . . is that there must needs be at any given stage of voyaging into the zone of proximal development a support system that helps learners get there. If tutors are not seen as partners in advancement, but . . . as sources of punishment, then it may have disastrous consequences for the candidate learner'. However, Barnes's suggested solution was to overcharacterize the distinction between *replying* to pupil utterances and *assessing* them:

> When a teacher *replies* to his pupils he is by implication taking their view of the subject seriously, even though he may wish to extend and modify it . . . teacher and learner are in a collaborative relationship. When a teacher *assesses* what his pupils say he distances himself from their views, and allies himself with external standards which may implicitly devalue what the learner himself has constructed. Both reply and assess are essential parts of teaching; assessment is turned towards the public standards against which pupils must eventually measure themselves, whereas *reply* is turned towards the pupil as he is, and towards his own attempts, however primitive, to make sense of the world . . . If a teacher stresses the assessment function at the expense of the reply function, this will urge his pupils towards externally acceptable performances rather than towards trying to relate new knowledge to old.
>
> (Barnes 1976:111, original emphasis)

The problem is that Barnes's notion of assessment is at variance with ours. He focuses on the summative purpose, what might be termed the outcome of the assessment, the giving of the judgement, and the degree to which this converges with external fixed criteria. However, we are also interested in the formative purpose, involving not just the giving of a judgement, but the whole process of reaching, negotiating, sharing and communicating a series of interpretations and judgements of the work. We would claim that the 'collaborative relationship' between pupil and assessor and 'trying to relate new knowledge to old' are legitimate constituents of formative assessment. Thus our point is that it is probably not possible to hold to an absolute distinction between *replying* and *assessing*, it is a matter of degree and interpretation; but neither is it desirable. The issue is for pupils to learn from and through assessment. What Barnes describes as *reply* is the kind of dialogue that we have observed above, namely where pupils are encouraged to indulge in what he terms exploratory talk because the third move is on the whole not used by the teacher to give evaluative feedback. With Keith the reply is the facilitation and probing of the interviewer; with Gaynor it is the counterargument of the debater. The paradox is that both teachers had the intention to assess and, we would claim, that was what they were doing.

Key elements of classroom control are still present in both these transcripts, as is the evaluative function of the interaction, but it is not overemphasized by the ritualized use of superficial evaluative feedback. These two transcripts also suggest that both the context and the linguistic structure of the interaction play an important role in opening up teaching, learning and assessment. Contexts where teachers are able to ask genuine questions produce a discourse structure where teachers are able to maintain a guiding hand on the interaction but where pupils are also able to become more fully involved. Potentially, these are situations where teacher and pupils can properly collaborate to produce what approximates to a best performance. This cannot only act as a more valid basis on which to make judgements, but can also indicate the path to improvement which must be the fundamental principle of making assessment more formative. However, these two transcripts also indicate that this process is problematic. Although the contexts in which they took place were deliberately set up by the teachers concerned, they had no systematic plan to create similar situations, and their exploitation of them was tacit and to a certain extent haphazard. Moreover, the degree to which the children involved were able to profit from the situation depended on their ability to recognize that the teacher's questions were genuine and that the usual rules of classroom interaction were not in place.[5] Contrast, for example, Thandi with Fatia, who is thrown by Gaynor's question about the thinking behind her question. This once again raises issues about how children recognize differences in discourse structure and whether or not they feel empowered by this. We shall return to these issues in the next chapter.

Caterina's book

This notion of a 'best performance' provides the theme for the next transcript. This incident took place once again in Gaynor Sable's Year 1 classroom. Most of the children in the class are speakers of other languages, notably Portuguese, Chinese and a number of African languages. There is some provision in the school for additional help with English for speakers of other languages, partly through in-class support and partly through the withdrawal of small groups. Much of this work is done by Nina Magenta, the Section 11 support teacher. A small amount of her time is also available for short term individual tuition using 'reading recovery' methods, most recently with Caterina, the pupil featured in the next transcript.

As usual, the children in the class had spent part of Monday morning writing about what happened at the weekend (their 'news'). There is a wide range of achievement in writing: two or three children produce a hundred words or so of well structured narrative with fairly standard spellings; at the other extreme some children are only just beginning to distinguish written text and pictures in their independent writing. The strategy for reviewing work consists of the child reading their text back to the teacher, who may write a version of it at the bottom of the paper. The rationale behind this approach is that of developmental or emergent writing, where even the 'scribblings' that toddlers produce are seen as writing (cf. what Pat in Chapter 5 described as 'your writing'). One advantage claimed for this approach is that it enables teachers to set the same task for children of very divergent attainment and thus to differentiate by outcome; moreover, 'working from what children do achieve in writing helps one to assess positively and to see the tremendous amount of learning children display at each stage of development' (Browne 1993:35).

The assessment of Caterina's work proceeded much as described. Although this is ostensibly an assessment, to begin with Gaynor did not really evaluate the work; indeed, apart from writing down a fair copy she made no response to it. Her lack of speech was mirrored by the pupil, who merely recited her text. Part of the problem was that the teacher was frequently interrupted by children and events in other parts of the classroom: the demands of running the class rather than the assessment of Caterina were what were taking the teacher's attention. Thus we must infer from the first part of the interaction (not transcribed) that the teacher judged Caterina's news to be adequate and unexceptional.

Suddenly, however, the teacher remembered that the support teacher had told her earlier that day that Caterina had been making very good progress. At this point Gaynor sent Caterina to fetch her reading recovery workbook, i.e. to review work which the teacher had not had a direct role in producing. The teacher is struck by the discrepancy in quality between the work produced in class (i.e. Caterina's 'news', which is very poorly written and spelled) and the work produced under the guidance of the support teacher. Once again, with this transcript, the teacher is in a position of relative ignorance and is asking genuine questions about what the pupil has done, and how she has done it.

13.42		This is the first of several inquiries about the process of the writing. It is a genuine question in that the work was neither set nor supervised by T.
T	yeah let's have a look at this - did you write this all on your own?	
T looks up at Caterina's face. Caterina nods.		Until now T had been looking at Caterina's work rather than at her face. She is now seeking Caterina's gaze. A great deal of Caterina's communication is through nodding and shaking her head. It is possible, however, that she is also speaking, though we are not able to discern this on the recording.
... [] ...		
T	(*what does it say then)	
Caterina	I/like/to/play/a/lotwith/my/ (*bike)	
Caterina points to the book.		As with the news, the child is being asked to read back her writing, though with a different rationale: rather than needing the child to say what the words are in order to decode them, T is checking that Caterina can read the text and possibly trying to ascertain the extent of the support she received from Nina.
T	did you find any of those words difficult - to spell?	
13.43		
T looks at Caterina. Caterina shakes her head. T looks back at the book.		A question which might lead from the correctly spelt words to some more diagnostically useful information, but only if answered positively.
T	(*) did you find that easy to write - that sentence?	
As she says this T looks up at Caterina, who meets her gaze and nods.		Another question about the process, in effect a positive reformulation of the previous question.

Caterina   I/like/to/play/with/my/dolly/
             and my sister
. . . [interruption] . . .
T   were there any words you
             found difficult to spell
13.44
Caterina   no - if I - if I - if I don't know
             the letters to spell (*then **)
*As she says this Caterina points to the
book.*
T   Oh - I see - so if you don't
             know what the letter is ~
T looks up.
Caterina   yeah - I just didn't know that
T   Mrs Magenta writes it for you
Caterina nods.
T   but you haven't written a (*)
             Mrs Magenta hasn't written
             any letters down here has she
             - and you did this all by your-
             self that's > really < . . . [ ] . . .
             that's really really good - it's
             very good
T looks into Caterina's face.
T   which do you think is your
             best writing - which are you
             most pleased with?
. . . [ ] . . .
*T touches the news sheet and the book in
turn. Caterina looks puzzled.*
Caterina   (*) this is not <u>mine</u> - oh yeah
             it is
*Caterina puts her hand to her mouth. T
smiles and Caterina smiles and points to
the workbook with her pencil.*
Caterina   this one
T   this one
Both T and Caterina nod.
T   why's that?
Caterina   because - it's - because - it's
             written - erm - no - no wrong
             wrong things
13.45
T looks at paper and nods.
T   right - do you think that you
             could - do this writing more
             like this?
*T points to the paper then to the workbook
and looks up at Caterina who nods.*
Caterina   (**)

The reformulation means that it would only be productive of more dialogue if answered negatively. Despite the nod, Caterina seems unsure how to respond to such questions, possibly because she is not used to them, so she begins to read again.

The same question is repeated. It refers to different words but also suggests that T is after some more substantial answer than a nod or shake of the head. This time it evokes the longest non-read response from Caterina, as she finally gets the message that T would welcome more elaboration. It seems that T is able to hear more than is audible through the radio microphone; however, her response would suggest that she too is having to interpret Caterina's intentions. 'That' appears to refer to one word on the page.

T seems to be able to deduce from the markings on the page the amount of help given by the support teacher, concluding in this case that the intervention was minimal.

This is the first descriptive or evaluative statement made by T about either this book or Caterina's news.

T is seeking to draw Caterina into the process and to make her assess her own work.

To begin with, Caterina denies that she wrote her news. It could be that if she claims the poor writing of the news she might lose the status she has won as a result of T's praise. Alternatively, having focused back on the work in the book, Caterina seems no longer able to identify with her news, suggesting that it was done with little engagement. Caterina's puzzled expression, followed by embarrassed laughter, would point to this second explanation. 'Why's that' is another open question which is important to establish what Caterina's criteria are. As seems apparent, there may be many reasons for preferring the book work, so her reply will be important in order to assess what is important and salient for her. Her reply seems to be an indication that accuracy of spelling is the most important thing for Caterina.

Obviously there was a great deal of difference in the context in which the two pieces of writing were done. For the news there was no one there to scaffold Caterina's writing. How could she make the second piece more like the first under such different circumstances?

The question seemed to require an affirmative answer, but Caterina is probably unsure as to

T	what was har\ d'you - what what was was there anything difficult about this?	how she might achieve such a thing. A nod would therefore seem to be a safe response. T poses the same question as was asked earlier but in a slightly different form. A much more definite answer is given.
Caterina	yes	
T	what	
Caterina	writing words and spelling them	
T	spelling them right - but you know a lot of spellings here don't you - you have a lot of words you can spell properly	T is pursuing the theme of inconsistent spellings. At this point she seems to be claiming that having spelt a word correctly once you should always be able to do so.

Caterina nods.

T	you see look - there's the word with ... [ ] ... <u>with</u> - there which you've spelt brilliantly - you've spelt right - but here you've spelt it you've spelt it differently	'With' is to be the concrete example as it occurs in both pieces of writing.

T is glancing from book to Caterina.

Caterina	because I didn't - because I didn't remember them words	Caterina explains – T's reasoning has made her enunciate her difficulty clearly – that she cannot remember the spellings at the time she needs them.
T	you did ~	

T moves ear closer to Caterina's mouth.

Caterina	<u>not</u> remember	Caterina is now very clear.
T	you didn't remember - oh **right** -	

13.46

T	if you saw that word on its own <u>with</u> would you know how t\ would you know what it said?	This question is leading to T giving Caterina a strategy for spelling.

T points upwards, to pieces of whole class collaborative writing stuck up on the wall. Caterina looks up.

T	so if you were to look up there - right - if you think if you thought well I know how to spell (*I used to know) how to spell with - an \ and can't remember how to write it so if you were to go and look for it round the classroom would you recognize it if you saw it?	The strategy involves making use of the resources in the classroom.

T is modelling the thought process that Caterina would have to have at the time in order to operationalize the strategy. The model involves a kind of egocentric speech. |

Caterina nods. T nods and points down at Caterina's book and then looks up again.

T	you would - so maybe what you could do instead of writing that - which is just nothing is it - el ee em - you know that doesn't spell with - if you	The work that Caterina has just completed is evaluated and found wanting, but this is done in

know that you w\ if you
know that you can read the
word with then you could go
and look for it couldn't you
(**) rather than just writing
anything - yeah

the context of the strategy which is being reiterated in detail.

The model is being re-presented in the form of a set of instructions.

T turns the pages of Caterina's book . . . [ ]

. . .

T   look at all your other words
           (*) all your other words you
           could do the same couldn't
           you - if you know if you know
           that you can read that word
           then you could go and try to
           find it in a book or written
           anywhere around the class-
           room and then write it down
           properly yeah -

The strategy is repeated once more and made to apply generally to other words. The first line of this speech also suggests that T is introducing the idea of drafting, though she is not actually getting Caterina to do it with the current piece of writing (her news).

13.47
Caterina nods.
T   do you think so?
Caterina nods.
 T   OK
T holds up the workbook.
T   this is very nice writing
T closes the book.
T   (*that's it) OK - shall we hand
           this back to Mrs Magenta
           now?

Even though Caterina is obviously very pleased with the outcome of the interaction and enjoys the praise she receives, she still appears somewhat tentative and still avoids actually speaking. The reiteration of the praise rounds off the interview.

Different context, different assessment

Earlier in this chapter we suggested a link between a discourse pattern that deviates from IRF and potentially more rich and productive assessment dialogue. However, the issue is not so much the elimination of the evaluate move, i.e. the pattern of IRF *per se*, but *any* ritualized form of interaction. Caterina does not expect a great deal of feedback in the normal course of events, and seems to think that low level emergent writing is what is being asked of her. She has not understood that it is supposed to lead to the more standard form of writing that she produced with the support teacher, Nina. Caterina's ability to transfer her knowledge from one context to another is hampered by her inability to recognize that this is required. The problem can then be ascribed in part to the nature of the methods of assessment that were routinely employed in each different context.

After Caterina fetches her workbook, produced in another context, the class teacher, Gaynor, is genuinely interested and therefore asks genuine questions. The discrepancy between Nina's judgement of Caterina and her own leads her to make a more conscious effort at assessment. She has come across something outside the normal classroom routines and this prompts her to deliberate (Eraut 1994).[6] By comparing the two performances, not only does Gaynor gain a more valid insight into what Caterina can do, but she is also able to feed back to the pupil in a very positive way. The process of deliberation seems to stimulate not only a different discourse structure but also a different form of practice.

Nina's scaffolding has enabled Caterina to achieve what she would not have managed to achieve unaided. The issue is to what extent Caterina has appropriated and internalized the ideas that Nina offered in scaffolding her learning. The evidence of the poorly completed news sheet would suggest that she had not. Gaynor's intervention is therefore designed to provide further scaffolding to support her in this. Her metacognitive questions seem aimed not only at uncovering for herself the processes at work when Caterina is producing her best work, but also at alerting Caterina to these processes. Moreover, she provides a model of the actions that would enable the pupil to improve by providing a sort of 'think aloud' text for Caterina to follow, which accords with Vygotsky's notion of egocentric speech where 'speech and action are part of *one and the same complex psychological function*, directed toward the solution of the problem in hand' (Vygotsky 1978:25). Thus she is providing a further intermediate stage between the social accomplishment of the task (achieved with the help of Nina) and its internalized accomplishment. Gaynor's intervention seems calculated to offer up for appropriation ideas which might enable Caterina to improve her work in the process of its production (cf. Sadler 1989, quoted in the previous commentary and in previous chapters).

This interaction is also relevant to some of our previous analysis. Whereas the ritualized practice of hearing children read back their work whilst writing out a 'correct' version, without any evaluative comment, might be seen as protecting the child from negative reinforcement, Gaynor's later interventions are reminiscent of the practices suggested by Dweck cited in Chapter 6. Caterina is encouraged to:

(a) *think strategy* (i.e., to engage in task analysis that focuses on strategy formulation, particularly on challenging tasks, under evaluative pressure and when obstacles arise); (b) *think progress* (i.e., to adopt challenging standards that are based on personal progress vs. inflated norms); and (c) *focus on past and future success*.

(Dweck 1989:110)

Gaynor's capacity to make an appropriate intervention hinges on her ability to arrive at a valid judgement of the level of the child's competence. This is not easily arrived at, because the performances that Caterina routinely accomplishes are not indicative of this competence. The poor classroom conditions created by frequent interruptions obviously make it much more difficult for Gaynor to work with individuals in the way that Nina does. Nina confirmed in interview afterwards that she gave the minimum amount of help needed to enable the successful completion of the task, i.e. sufficient scaffolding, but not too much. Such interventions would have been difficult for Gaynor to make when, as on other occasions we observed (e.g. questions about Jamaica), she was monitoring work in hand. Newman *et al.* (1989) make an important distinction between these two situations. Nina is able to use what they call 'dynamic assessment' (Feuerstein 1979; Brown *et al.* 1992), whereas Gaynor is engaged in 'assessment while teaching'. They suggest that 'in dynamic assessment the goal of teaching is subordinated to the goal of determining the child's independent level of achievement', whereas in assessment-while-teaching, 'The teacher subordinates assessment to instruction' (Newman *et al.* 1989:80). This would explain why Nina's determination of Caterina's level of competence, and Caterina's demonstration of it, might be more accurate. However, Newman *et al.* go on to claim that:

> *Giving too much help is usually not a critical problem for teaching.* If the children get help with a problem when they do not need it, the worst that can happen is that they become a little bored and perhaps want to get onto something new or into something inappropriate. A teacher can afford to err in the direction of giving too much help, but the consequences may be far more disturbing if too little help is given.
>
> (Newman *et al.* 1989:87, original emphasis)

This is an important point, but Newman *et al.* fail to recognize an aspect of the problematic nature of teaching while assessing. In the example that we have reported, Caterina is failing to progress in class and has continued to produce performances well below her competence because the teacher consistently provides too much help in the form of taking responsibility for producing the 'correct text'. The teacher has not recognized that Caterina can do more, and Caterina has not recognized the class 'news writing' task as a situation in which she should do more. Interestingly enough, the situation which Newman *et al.* suggest as being most likely to produce fine grained assessment-while-teaching is question and answer sessions, where 'if the children fail to answer adequately, the teacher can reframe the question, thus providing more help' (Newman *et al.* 1989:88). However, as we argue throughout the book, this is easier said than done.

Summary

Elements of each of the three transcripts investigated in this chapter suggest ways in which more effective formative assessment practice might emerge, though in each case the psychological and social complexities of real classroom contexts mean that any conclusions remain problematic. The notion of asking genuine questions links all three examples, and seems to be a crucial factor when teachers are eliciting a response from pupils that not only provides insight into their current state of understanding, but is also potentially useful in stimulating further learning. Such situations seem to provide a context where pupils interpret the questioning as genuine and begin to attend to the principles at stake rather than the ritual of question and answer. Certain contexts, such as those where the teacher is assessing other people's work, can help to indicate that questions are genuine, but these are not always available. In such cases the only option would seem to be for the teacher explicitly to make their pedagogy clear to the pupils. Teachers therefore need to be clear about the processes of assessment and to attempt to communicate them to their pupils. Adopting a variety of linguistic patterns, a 'contingent response' (Cordon 1992; Wells 1992), especially asking questions about pupils' processes of thought and action, and making explicit to children what they are doing and why, would seem to be a fruitful way forward. Understanding derived from these practices might then be further enhanced by giving pupils chances to model these assessment strategies themselves, by putting them in the role of assessor to their peers through groupwork and reciprocal teaching (Brown *et al.* 1992). Furthermore, the discussion of the processes of assessment which would result might also allow opportunities for making explicit issues of power and motivation that we discussed earlier. Our analysis has highlighted the collaborative nature of formative assessment; if it is to be effective, pupils as much as teachers will need to understand what they are doing. The next chapter takes up this theme and develops it further.

Notes

1 We use the nouns 'evaluate' and 'evaluator' to apply to an explicitly evaluative third move in the IRF sequence (see Willis (1992) cited below).
2 Socrates is no naïf, setting out on a first unguided and an untutored philosophical journey, every time we meet him. He has been on the journey before, and knows at least some of the paths and pitfalls. His questioning of his companions is guided (informed and structured) by a prior understanding of the territory to be traversed and possible routes through it. This prior knowledge may be deliberately understated, or held in tentative fashion, but it clearly exists. Without it Socrates would be useless as a guide' (Pateman 1998:5).
3 A study by Askew *et al.* suggested four reasons for the absence of scaffolds: '1. Scaffolding precluded by use of directive teacher strategies; 2. Scaffolding excluded by initiative being given to pupils; 3. Teacher/pupil discourse but no real interaction; 4. Conditions for scaffolding present but not noticed by the teacher' (Askew *et al.* 1996:3). Each of these would seem to fit well with our analysis.
4 Section 11 refers to the legislation under which extra resources can be provided to schools with large numbers of children whose first language is not English.
5 This problem invokes Bernstein's (1996) notion of a 'recognition rule' and raises issues about whether the ability to identify such a situation may be unevenly distributed across social categories. However, although intriguing, this issue is not within the scope of our immediate argument (but cf. Cooper, forthcoming, for a discussion of the issue with respect to National Curriculum test items).
6 This is similar to the tension that Brown and Macintyre (1993) observe between the preservation of a 'normal desirable state' in the classroom and the idea of progress.

8

Constructing and integrating assessment and learning

Introduction

Our intention in this chapter is to start drawing together the various elements in our analysis of formative classroom assessment, and in particular to try to demonstrate some of its more positive aspects. Then, in the final chapter, we will conclude the book by summarizing and articulating different models of formative assessment. We have argued that classroom assessment is socially constructed: that is, assessment 'events' or 'incidents' are accomplished through, and situated within, the everyday routines of teacher–pupil inter-action in the classroom. Furthermore, such incidents are to a large extent cir-cumscribed by the taken-for-granted discourse structure of teacher questions and pupil responses. In such circumstances we might define formative assess-ment in terms of its positive intent, but we cannot be sure that such intentions will always be realized. Thus our position is that assessment will always inter-act with, and have an impact on, learning and motivation, but that impact might be negative as well as positive. Having established the problematic nature of much classroom assessment in Chapter 4, we went on to explore the 'double-edged sword' of assessment in some detail in Chapters 5, 6 and 7, demonstrating its positive possibilities along with the many difficulties inher-ent in trying to operationalize such positive intentions.

In this chapter we present data which illustrate how a focus group assess-ment can generate a great deal of information about children's knowledge and understanding, while at one and the same time contributing to the process of creating that understanding. The data demonstrate how much talking chil-dren can and will do, when given the time and space by a teacher prepared to listen and observe. Such talk not only provides evidence of the children's progress to date, but also simultaneously scaffolds the learning of the group as they interrogate each other about the nature of the task and collaborate to accomplish it. In the following transcript extract, therefore, what we see is a teacher very much conducting an 'assessment' rather than 'teaching', in terms of the role she plays and the discourse structure recorded. She asks a few key, open questions, and mainly watches and listens to how the four children in the group try to accomplish the tasks set, making notes as they work. However, this is not a mechanistic 'information-gathering-to-inform-future-planning' exercise, which has no impact on the children while they are doing it. Rather, the very act of engagement with the task prompts the children to discuss what they are doing and hence produces evidence of learning which might not otherwise have occurred.

We should emphasize that the following extract is by no means 'perfect' in terms of the critique of classroom assessment that has been developed in previous chapters. It still contains much 'teacherly' activity, particularly with respect to the artificial and potentially confusing nature of the task itself. The teacher sets up a maths task by asking for 'help' in sorting out some leaves. She wishes to ascertain whether or not the children understand the concept of categorizing and sorting and, if so, how they will go about doing it. Now for a start, the leaves are not real; they are made of paper and have been cut out and coloured on one side only. Furthermore, why should a competent adult require the help of 5-year-olds to 'sort them out'? So there is much in this example that is reminiscent of the 'common knowledge', and the 'suspension of disbelief', that teachers routinely invoke when managing classrooms. Much of the discourse also demonstrates that many other forms of shared knowledge are relied upon by teacher and pupils alike to accomplish the interaction, including turn-taking and sometimes competition over and rejection of turn-taking. Furthermore, the teacher sometimes seems to miss certain contributions, or at least not act on them, perhaps because they do not fit with the sequential development of the task which she has in mind (i.e. her prospective agenda of moving from one sort-category to another, in turn). She also has a tendency to privilege the contributions of one (male) member of the group (Justin), who comes across as the most capable, although a different interactive dynamic could well produce the same impression for the girl in the group (Megan). So this is very far from a 'perfect' example of formative classroom assessment; but perhaps it is as close to it as we can reasonably expect a busy teacher in a real classroom to get. It is a 'naturally occurring' example which offers us the opportunity to observe the different form of discourse structure, and its impact on the children's learning, which emerges when a teacher is prepared to watch and listen, rather than 'teach'.

The transcript is of a focus group assessment incident which takes place in a reception class (4- to 5-year-olds) on a Thursday morning in October. The other pupils in the class have been assigned to various activities by the teacher and she is now concentrating on the focus group of four children – three boys and a girl. The teacher is sitting at a low (pupils') octagonal table with the four children. Justin is sitting on her right at an angle of about 120° to her. Megan is next on his right at 120° to him. Frank is next, standing behind his chair at 120° to Megan, and Ricky is last as we move around the table, sitting next to Frank, and opposite the teacher. On the table there is a pile of (paper) leaves in a variety of shapes, sizes and colours. The teacher has a notepad in front of her. The children are looking at the table, except for Frank, who is watching some classmates working with construction toys behind him.

10:02

T   now then - gosh - what a lot of
           leaves

*Frank sits down, still looking behind him.
T is laying out leaves on the table.*

T   I've got a problem with these
           leaves - Frank

*T looks at Frank and he turns to face her,
then she looks at the children individually,
and gestures with her hands towards the
paper leaves on the table.*

T   my problem is that I've got so
           many of them that I don't
           know how to sort them out =

Megan   = I > know<

*T looks at Megan and then back at the
leaves. Justin turns to look at Megan and
smiles, while Frank and Ricky are now
looking straight at T. T now pushes the
leaves forward towards the children.*

T   > and I < hoped you could <
           try and help me decide <

Megan   > I I know <

T   how to sort them out > so
           what I want you to do <

*T points to leaves, still looking at the
leaves. Megan moves some of the leaves
around on the table. Ricky is sitting
hunched over the table, his chin resting in
his left hand, and then his head drops
onto the table.*

Justin   > different colours <

*Justin leans right forward on both his
elbows and begins to touch the leaves.*

T   is have a look at them and see
           if you could decide

*Frank now stands up and leans over the
table to look at the leaves. Frank and
Justin look at the leaves and begin to touch
them. Megan looks on.*

T   how > you would sort them
           out <

Justin   > the same colours <

*T looks straight at Frank. Ricky now also
leans forward to his left to pick up some
leaves. All four children are now moving
the leaves around the table.*

T   and get yourself a little pile -

Megan   > (*can't) <

T   > of them < =

Frank appears to be more interested in what the
children behind him are doing than in what is
happening on his own table. T's naming of him
focuses his attention for the moment.

The leaves are not real, and unless the children
have been very unobservant they would have
noticed the teaching assistant making them – if
they need sorting out, she or T could have done
it. The problem is one that has been created by
T. Nevertheless, although the children are relatively new to school, they understand what is
required of them, without further explanation
or justification. They are already socialized
enough to 'read between the lines' of the
teacher's explicit utterances.

Megan is not only focused but is almost ahead of
the game; she cannot wait for T to finish her
introduction before starting the task. However,
T is not deflected into a 'traditional' IRF structure. She carries on describing the task without
providing any cues as to how to do it. NB she
doesn't just ask the children to help 'sort them
out', but 'how to sort them': she is asking for criteria. Ricky is not looking at the centre of action
and appears not to be listening. Justin indicates
he too is not prepared to wait for T to finish her
sentence, but moreover he is not content just to
make a bid for attention (Megan: 'I know'), he
offers an answer. His utterance and action suggest he understands the concept of sorting, that
one can do it by a variety of criteria – in his case
colour – and, perhaps, by wanting to make the
criteria for sorting public, that he expects the
group to be working cooperatively. He seems to
appreciate that this is not a situation which
simply calls for a correct answer to be uttered,
but for something to be done by the group.
Frank too is now engaged by the activity.

'You'; this is now a task for the children though
it is not clear whether she means 'you' as a group
or 'you' as four individuals. However, once
again, she is not deflected by Justin into providing an evaluate or indeed any cue, though Justin
is keen to contribute his idea.

Ricky is having to reach over a long way in order
to get any leaves. 'Get yourself' seems to be suggesting that each child is expected to work individually.

Justin	= you can have that one =

Justin passes a leaf to Frank, who is still standing up.

T	= and see if you can decide how you would ha/sort them cause there are so many of them aren't there <

This remark suggests that Justin interprets the little pile idea as being part of the sorting task. He is assuming each child will have a pile of a different colour, and by his utterance and action is sorting not only his, but Frank's.

T writes on the notepad in front of her whilst the children are still sorting through the leaves.

10:03

Frank	you can - you can - kind of g g get the ones that - that are green and put them together (**) =

Frank contributes tentatively. Justin, Megan and Frank are now working on the principle of each being the collector of a specific colour, though T has not confirmed this as the task. Justin has done the 'teaching'. Ricky appears at this point just to be taking any leaves he can manage to get hold of.

T writes in her notepad.

Megan	= oh I want the pink

Megan is standing up and holding up a pink leaf. Justin turns towards her.

Pink for a girl?

Justin	yeah you have the pink
Megan	that's not my right shape

T writes in notepad.

Justin	you don't not not the right shape - > just the same colour <

Although following Justin's suggestion that they sort on the basis of colour, Megan is applying shape criteria to her selection as well. However, because she is talking through her thought process Justin is able to reassert the notion of sorting by colour alone. One might speculate as to whether Megan's remark is 'egocentric speech', scaffolding her own learning (Vygotsky 1978), or whether she is responding to Justin and her intention is modification of the evolving classification system.

Frank	> (**) <

T looks at Justin. The children continue to collect leaves from the table top.

... [ ] ...

Frank	> (**) <
Megan	I've got the pink

T looks at Megan, still standing.

Megan seems to accept the colour criterion.

T	well, you just sit down when you've got your little pile <

T signals for Megan to sit down.

Justin	> there's a pink one Megan (*) <

Justin reinforces his choice of selection criteria through helping Megan.

Justin passes a leaf to Megan.

... [ ] ...

Frank sits down and then stands up again. Ricky reaches out to pick up a leaf from across the table. T looks up at Frank while he is talking.

Frank	now you can - now you can get some yellows and then you've got some yellows > you can put them<

Frank is also talking through his selection process, possibly seeking evaluative cues from T.

Justin	> there's some more (*) Megan pink pink <

Justin gives Megan another leaf.

Frank   > (***)<
Megan   >(*I don't want **)<

Megan throws the leaf that Justin has given her on the table and throws her arms in the air. T speaks without making any eye contact.

T   well you decide and then I'll talk to you about it when you've got your pile of leaves that the ones that you wanted

Once again, Megan appears to be rejecting this leaf because although pink, it does not conform to her shape criterion. Is this a decision that is based on mathematical or aesthetic principles? Or is she just fed up with being patronized by Justin?

T still bides her time – no evaluate is forthcoming.

Ricky is still choosing leaves and stretching over the table to reach them. Frank is still standing up. Megan is sitting still. Justin also reaches over the table to pick up another leaf. T reaches out and turns a couple of leaves over.

T   - cos there are lots of them aren't there - so it takes quite a long time to sort them all out

The others have stopped sorting and appear to be happy with their piles.

10:04

Frank   (*) some big ones

T glances down at Megan and Justin's piles. Ricky leans forward across the table in Justin's direction.

Ricky   (**) got to get
Megan   oh Justin - that's orange
Justin   no - I'm doing it how I want

Ricky reaches right across the table and picks up a leaf that is just in front of Justin.

T   right - are you finished then?
Justin   yeah

Megan moves a leaf over towards Frank, who passes it on to Ricky. Justin moves a leaf over towards Frank.

Megan   I've got the pink
Justin   I've got the brown

Justin turns towards Megan. The children are now all sitting down with their piles of leaves in front of them, except for Frank, who is standing up looking directly at T. T is now looking at Justin.

T   > tell me what you've got then Justin <

Frank   > I've got different colours< =
Ricky   = I've got different colours =
Justin   = brown

T puts her left hand across to Justin's pile.

T   you've got the brown ones -

T starts to lay each leaf out separately as

This much more recognizable 'teacher comment' is actually an instruction, or at least an encouragement, to the group to continue until there are no more leaves left in the middle.

This is the first time that size is mentioned (or at least implied) as a criterion. NB three criteria have now been introduced – colour, shape and size – and all three have come from the children (one each from Justin, Megan and Frank). But without an evaluate from T, and like Megan's earlier application of shape, this suggestion of size does not deflect the search from the initial criterion of colour.

Justin's reaction seems to be a response to Megan's dismissive comment. She implies he has made a mistake (mis-sorting a colour as orange not pink); he retorts he is employing a different category system that she doesn't know about.

Justin asserts control once more, though in fact some sorting is still taking place – 'are you finished' is treated by the children as a teacherly cue to a final flurry of activity.

Why ask Justin first? Because he said 'yeah' to begin with and therefore was first with a bid? Because he is sitting next to T and is in a sense 'first in line'?

Frank and Ricky seem to recognize that they have different colours, so they understand the concept of sorting-by-colour, but they haven't actually done it.

An apparently neutral feedback – though confirming Justin's successful completion of the task.

she speaks to him. The other children appear to be looking at Justin's leaves.

T   let's have a look - how many brown ones did you find then?

Justin   four

T   four -

T moves Justin's leaves across back in front of him. Frank points in turn to each of Justin's leaves with his left hand. T turns to Megan.

T   what about you then Megan - which ones did you sort out?

Megan lays out her leaves.

Megan   pink

T   you had all the pinky ones the pinky-red ones

10:05

T inclines her face to look up at Frank, who is pointing to each of Megan's leaves in turn.

T   > what about you, Frank - what did you <

Megan   > I had five <

T   five

Frank   I had different colours

Frank lays his leaves out in front of him, apparently now sorting them out on the basis of colour.

T   ohh - and are they all sorted then - how did you decide on - having all different colours then?

Frank   cos I (*saw) a gre/green and some yellow and some oranges and some reds and some - and some yellows

As she hears Frank's response to her question, T writes in her notebook, which is in front of her. While Frank is speaking, Justin and Megan are looking at his pile of leaves. Ricky is resting his head in the palm of his right hand. He then starts to rub his face with both hands.

T   right so you had all the different colours what about you ummm - Ricky =

Justin   = and some browns

T   what colours have you got then no/ er Ricky?

Further confirmation coupled with additional probing.

Frank appears to be counting Justin's leaves.

T appropriates and changes Megan's word. Why 'pinky-red ones'? Is this just reception class baby talk thought appropriate for a girl, or is T trying subtly to correct Megan's definition of what counts as 'pink'? In fact some pink leaves have ended up on Ricky's pile, but it is not clear whether Megan has rejected them on the grounds of shape or colour (not pink enough, by her definition). T assumes it is the latter. This is the first recognizable evaluate which T has uttered, which also acts as a teaching intervention, though it may be based on a misinterpretation of what Megan has done. T asked Justin how many he had. Megan isn't going to let her turn pass without the same amount of interaction with T, or to let T think that not only does she not know what 'pink' is, but that she also can't count.

Even though he had a mixed pile, it seems from his words and actions that Frank can recognize and name different colours and perhaps is able to understand the notion of sorting by colour. Why he didn't do this presumably revolves around the social dynamics of the pecking order involving Justin and Megan. T appropriates Frank's explanation by recognizing 'all the different colours' as a category in itself. This positively evaluates his knowledge of colour and dignifies his attempt at the task; there doesn't seem to be much hint of the usual 'neutral' teacherly feedback which actually implies 'all very well but not what I wanted'.

Justin's remark seems to be directed at Frank's listing of colours in his pile. T is not deflected and continues to focus on Ricky; however, instead of asking 'how' he sorted out his pile, she asks a more specific question, to ascertain

Ricky   well I've got all > the different
          < colours too

*As Ricky speaks to T he is touching his
leaves in turn. Frank is still standing up
from his chair whilst leaning on the table.*

Ricky   I've got browns, yellows -
          orange -

*All the children now look at Ricky's pile of
leaves. Ricky is going through his leaves
placing each one on top of the other, effectively making a new pile and moving them
from one pile to another.*
. . . [ ] . . .

T   right OK - lets put them back
          again -

10:06

*T moves Justin's pile to the centre of the
table. The other children push their piles of
leaves into the centre too. Frank is still
standing up. T turns over some of the
leaves as she speaks.*

T   now a lot of you decided to
          sort them by colour that time
          didn't you you decided that
          that was a good way put those
          two back as well Frank can you
          -

*T points to some leaves in front of Frank.
He picks them up and places them on the
central pile.*

T   I wonder if there's another
          way you can think of to sort
          them =

*Ricky leans over the table and Megan puts
her hand up.*

Justin   = the same <u>shape</u>
T   the same <u>shape</u> that would be
          a good idea wouldn't it?

T looks at Frank as she says this.

Frank   the same colour

*Frank looks at T and puts the palms of his
hands together. Ricky is sitting with his
chin cupped in both hands, moving his
body from side to side.*

T   now let's see if we can do what
          Justin   decides   on   same
          shapes -

*Justin, Megan and Frank reach for the
leaves.*

whether or not he knows the colours in front of
him. In doing so she has reduced the intellectual
demand of the question, presumably because
she thinks Ricky has not understood the intellectual demands of the task.

Ricky also seems to be able to recognize different
colours, but it is not clear whether or not he
understands the notion of sorting.

Ricky's response has been cursory enough for T
to conclude she will get no further. She marks
the end of an implicit 'stage 1' of the task, and
in doing so, confirms that sorting the leaves out
is not a 'real' task - she didn't really need 'help'
in a once-and-for-all-sense of sorting them, then
putting them away. Justin, Megan and Frank
seem to understand this. It not clear whether
Ricky does, though he follows T's lead in joining
in putting the leaves back in the middle of the
table.

'A lot of you'? Two of you, with Frank half joining in. This speech is marking sorting by colour
as 'done'. T is now after sorting by some other
attribute. She 'moves the lesson on' by appropriating the children's words and actions, integrating them, and employing them with respect
to the management of the task (cf. the discussion in Chapters 4 and 5).

Nevertheless, in moving the task on, T still asks
an open question. There is no cue about what
the next category might be.

Once again Justin is impatient to get started and,
unlike Megan who puts her hand up, realizes
that he doesn't have to bid, just speak, simultaneously   appropriating   Megan's   previous
contribution regarding shape, for himself. T
affirms his idea with a 'classic' evaluative
response: bracketing the teacher role completely
is difficult - she has managed it for about three
and a half minutes. Frank, meanwhile, is still
focusing on colour - has he understood the
question?

Justin is confirmed as the agenda setter. While in
one sense this can be seen as an interesting
example of the pupils themselves taking control
of the agenda and genuinely engaging with the
nature of the task, Megan might feel justifiably
aggrieved.

T   so see if you can sort them according to the same shape

Ricky also starts to lean over the table, out of his chair, and sort the leaves.

Frank   that's the same shape isn't it

Frank looks straight at T and holds a leaf in each hand.

T   mmm it is

T nods.

Justin   doesn't matter if they're the same size (*)

T begins to write in her pad. Megan reaches over to the far side of the pile.

Megan   oh (**)

Justin is leaning over and looking at Megan's pile.

Justin   oh no where's another one this shape - where's another one this shape -

Justin looks up and sighs.

10:07

Megan   err - (*that's the one)

Megan reaches over and retrieves a leaf from Ricky's end of the table.

Frank   I've got some - I've got some, Mrs Rose

T, who has been writing, looks up at Frank. Frank makes a pile of leaves in front of T. Ricky pulls in his chair and sits down.

T   well keep them in front of you

T looks up briefly at Frank but carries on writing.

Frank   I can't find any more

Ricky   Mrs Rose

T   > yes Ricky < -

T glances up but keeps on writing. Frank turns to Ricky and starts to sort Ricky's pile of leaves.

T   right well sit down on your chair then we can have a look - at the ones that you've chosen

T gestures with right arm that Justin and Megan should stop leaning over the table and sit down. Meanwhile, Frank is moving Ricky's leaves.

T   no um - er - just let Ricky do his own please - you don't have to do it for him he can do

Ricky seems slower and more peripheral; socially he knows that something has to be done but educationally doesn't seem to understand the task. Frank, despite his 'false start' earlier is now apparently demonstrating understanding of the concept of shape, and perception of particular shapes, the very act of engagement – doing and talking – possibly helping him in a way which seems not to be benefitting Ricky.

Confirmation without evaluative affirmation? T is trying to move back into her 'assessment' role. Megan introduced the idea of shape, and Frank size; Justin, having appropriated shape, reintroduces size, thus taking on board the others' ideas and feeding them back for the benefit of the group. He is almost substituting for T who is trying simply to observe. A casual (though not strictly correct or fair) 'assessment' of the interaction might nominate him as leading the group and getting 'all the right answers'; nevertheless he could be said to be scaffolding the group's learning.

The repetition suggests this was not egocentric speech but a question to Megan. Justin is assuming that the task is collective so it is appropriate both to ask for, and give, help. His assumption of group leadership again provides scaffolding for the group's learning: whether the speech is egocentric or not, it provides a thought model for the rest of the group.

Frank is more oriented towards his own accomplishments and also seeks to refer to T: he seeks her positive evaluation. There is a contrast here with Justin's utterances which tend to be addressed either to Megan or to the group in general and facilitative of the task in hand.

Having attracted T's attention Ricky says nothing else, although T allows him sufficient time to say whatever he wishes. Perhaps because she is writing, and previous experience suggests this is an important thing that teachers do, he feels unable to continue with what he may perceive as an 'interruption'. In turn T is concentrating on writing her notes and perhaps doesn't give him the attention she should. In the meantime Frank appears to have identified a leaf that is to be Ricky's shape and is moving away all the other leaves.

Frank and Ricky are good friends. T has indicated in interview that she feels Frank tends to dominate Ricky and not allow him to do things by himself. However it is a moot point, even several minutes into the interaction, whether the children perceive this to be a collaborative task, or an individual task with which they can nevertheless help each other.

it on his own I think - can you sit on your chair?

Frank sits down. T looks up in Ricky's direction.

T   right have you finished Ricky?
Ricky yeah
T   right what shape are the ones you chose can you show me?

. . . [*brief interruption by other child*] . . .

T   what sort of shape are those Ricky then
Ricky they're sort of a star shape
T   they <u>are</u> a bit star shaped aren't they? - Frank can I have a look at yours?
Frank well a lot of them are star shape as well

Frank holds up a leaf to show T.

T   they are are they like the ones Ricky's got then?
Frank (*)

Frank turns to look at Ricky's pile of leaves . . . [brief interruption by another child] . . .

10:08

T   are they like Ricky's star shaped leaves or are they\ is there anything different about them?
Frank they're a bit (*) -
Megan <u>bigger</u> =
Frank up and down and (*) =

Frank runs his fingers along the outline of the leaf, still holding it up.

T   = and what about Ricky's - why aren't they the same as Ricky's?

Frank scratches his head and he reaches over to touch Ricky's leaves

Frank cos him - are bumpy (*)

Frank reaches over to Ricky's leaf again and then back to his own fingering them at the edge.

T   his are bumpy ~
Frank (*) there
T   right I see - OK Megan what about you
Megan mine are this shape

Megan holds up a leaf, turning it around in her hands.

T   what shape's <u>that</u> then?

Although she did not encourage the original initiation by Ricky, it is to him that T turns first – perhaps thinking that she should have given him more attention a few seconds before.

This is a direct question about the shape of the leaves that Frank has sorted out for Ricky. Just as with T's previous direct question to Ricky about colours, this may establish whether he understands and can describe different shapes, but will not reveal if Ricky understands sorting.

They are copies of field maple leaves.

T's stress on 'are a bit' indicates Ricky has given a satisfactory answer, though not a 'correct' one. This is close to an evaluate, and T moves on to the next person rather than extending the sequence.

Frank's leaves are copies of sycamores.

T indicates 'yes, but I want more than that'; in other words, she has been led to expect more from Frank, but not Ricky. She provides scaffolding to the task by directing Frank to compare and contrast, the salient difference between field maples and sycamores being more one of size than shape.

Megan has focused on the salient difference, and uses Frank's utterance as a cue.

Frank sticks to shape as the independent variable. He wants to get his point across, and ignores Megan's interruption, correct or not.

But shape doesn't distinguish sufficiently. T tries to draw this out by reiterating the need to compare and contrast. In doing so she indicates once more that Frank hasn't yet got 'the point'.

Frank, however, is sticking with shape, though this could be as much a function of the social situation as his lack of understanding of the task – Frank was, after all, the first pupil to mention size some minutes previously, though T did not seem to pick this up. Now it may be that his commitment to shape derives in some way from his refusal to accept the validity of Megan's intervention. Also, of course, 'stage 2' of the task was to sort by shape, not size; T made this very explicit in her response to Justin's suggestion.

Once again, T feels she has got as far as she is going to with Frank, as previously with Ricky, so she marks the end of the interaction and moves on.

Megan's leaves are copies of sweet chestnut leaflets.

'This shape' isn't sufficient – T is pushing for Megan to articulate shape vocabulary.

Megan   that sort of an <u>oval</u> shape

Megan is turning the leaf around in her hands as she speaks.

T   (*a bit) like a long oval isn't it-
yes that's right yeah except its
got - what's that at the top?

T points to the top of Megan's leaf.

Megan   a point =

T   = yes and ovals don't have
points do they?

Megan   no

T smiles.

10:09>

Justin   they have - **curves**

Justin describes a curve with his finger on the table. T nods and writes in her notebook. Ricky has begun to play with one of his leaves.

T   yes that's right Justin - they
have curves that's right - right
Justin and how did you decide

T has been writing still whilst saying this. Ricky now lays his head on his arm on the table and continues to play with a leaf. Megan is holding all her leaves in a 'fan'.

Justin   they're curvy like Ricky's

Ricky sits up again

T   they are a bit so what's - why
aren't they the same as Ricky's
then?

T points to Ricky's leaves.

Justin   because they're **longer**

Justin runs his hand along the leaf. T nods her head.

T   they are longer aren't they -
did you think you have more
curves or less curves than
Ricky's?

Justin   there's **more** curves

T   and maybe - can I have a look
at yours Ricky - just a minute -
one of yours

T reaches forward to pick up one of Ricky's leaves. Ricky pushes one towards her. She brings the leaf very close in front of Justin and looks over it herself. Justin brings his head close to it.

T   has he got curves or has he got
points?

Justin   he's got points

'Oval' is a fairly accurate description, but T thinks Megan can provide more detail still; her probing is not of the 'guessing game' variety, however; rather, she focuses Megan's attention on specific aspects of the leaf.

This elicits more descriptive shape vocabulary so, because of T's intervention, Megan has produced much more evidence of understanding than she did to begin with, but T's response is a leading question and, although Megan can recognize 'a point', it is not clear whether Megan knows that ovals 'don't have points'.

Helpful as ever (!), Justin demonstrates his understanding of the issue and his knowledge of the answer.

T seems to be prompted to record by Justin's intervention. She has not pressed Megan as to whether or not she can differentiate between shape and size.

Nevertheless, Justin's intervention serves to move T on around the group as his contribution is affirmed. The power to make the most of particular opportunities, explored in Chapter 6, is being exploited here by Justin.

The most significant group member names Ricky, and Ricky takes notice – he is being associated with something positive.

Once again T indicates 'OK – but not what I'm after', but also provides appropriate scaffolding through the injunction to compare and contrast.

Justin has copies of ash leaves.

T presses further, though again, T provides scaffolding by asking a focused question.

T sees an opportunity to develop the notion of curves and points, possibly for the benefit of the other children rather than for Justin.

T   they are a bit more pointed aren't they - yeah - good -

T gives Ricky back his leaf.

T   right - let's put them back again

All the children push or toss the leaves into the centre of the table.

Justin   back <u>again</u>

Megan   back again

T begins to turn them over again so that all are face upwards.

T   I wonder if there's another way - we've sorted them out by colour -

Frank stands up again.

T   we've sort them out by

Ricky   shape

T   shape - is there another way we could think to sort them out?

T looks at leaves and turns some of them over. As she speaks, Frank is standing up again and Ricky is leaning over the table. Megan throws both her arms behind the back of her head.

10:10

Frank   ummm same

Megan   size

T   good idea Megan <u>size</u>

T points to Megan but then looks back up at Frank.

T   we could sort them out according to their size - well how could we sort them what size could we decide to have?

T is now looking at Justin and Megan. Frank begins to touch the pile of leaves.

T   wait a minute Frank we're just thinking at the moment

T reaches her left hand across the table to Frank and takes one leaf from him, placing it back down on the table.

Megan   big > big <

Justin   > big <

Megan places her hands in front of her about 25 centimetres apart and then adjusts them as she speaks the other sizes.

Megan   > small <

Justin   > small <

T   yes

A teacherly intervention brings forth a teacherly evaluate.

Another marker to indicate the end of 'stage 2'.

Classic teacherly cueing draws forth a correct response from Ricky – does he understand what's going on after all, or can he (along with children everywhere!) simply fill in the gaps without understanding the concepts?

For some reason Justin is taking a more passive role and allows Ricky, then Megan, to answer. Megan again uses Frank's utterances as a cue and, perhaps having learned from earlier in the interaction that she doesn't have to bid by putting her hand up, seizes the opportunity and reveals that she can take a lead in articulating a sort criterion. T responds with a positive evaluate then scaffolds the task by specifying its parameters more closely ('what size could we decide') before asking the children to continue.

Frank is anxious to get started. T wants some thinking-through-talking.

Megan is leading as she says these words, with Justin following. Although this is almost simultaneous, they seem to have swapped roles.

Megan is demonstrating her definition of 'big' and 'small'.

'Yes' – i.e. 'go on'.

Megan	> middle size <
Justin	> middle size <
T	<u>yes</u> - we could do that like the three bears we could have big ones middle sized ones and small ones

T looks at Megan and Justin. Justin stands up and reaches for the leaves. Justin leans over the table and pulls out a big leaf. Megan stands up to start to sort out the leaves and Ricky leans over the table.

Justin	I'm having these big ones
Ricky	me too
T	well let's see if we can get a sort of pile of big ones middle sized ones small ones

T motions with her hand where she would like to see three piles of sorted leaves.

T	put them in the middle and then in the middle of the table then we can have one pile of big ones and one pile of small ones

Justin starts to climb on the table by putting his right knee on it but instead changes his mind and sits right back in his seat.

Justin	> well that's a very very good <
Frank	> I've done mine <
Justin	good - good - good - idea

Justin is looking at Megan but not touching the leaves. Megan and Ricky are still sorting through the leaves. Frank is holding up a pile of leaves.

Frank	I've done it

Frank leans across closer to T.

T	we're all going to do it make one big pile of big ones one <u>big</u> pile of middle sized ones and one big pile of - small ones =

10:11

T, who was originally looking Frank in the face, now turns to Justin. Megan climbs onto the table to reach some leaves at the other side. Justin stands up and shows a leaf to T.

Justin	= there's a fat one
T	well which one pile > will that go into then<

Justin places leaf on a pile.

'Yes' said much more emphatically, i.e. three sizes is enough. The 'three bears' is a story that the class have previously encountered and T seizes upon it to connect with past work and experience of sorting by size. (NB this is not the same school or 'three bears' story encountered in Chapter 3; the story is ubiquitous in infant schools.)

Justin isn't so passive as to pass up the chance of claiming the 'big ones'; Ricky resists.

T defuses the situation, however, by using the term 'we', rather than 'you', and naming three categories when there are four children – the task is thus defined as collaborative, though this may make distinguishing individual contributions, and therefore individual assessment, more difficult.

T is directing this sort much more actively than the previous ones. She is also associating herself with it, and with a more teacherly role, by using 'we' again. Is she tiring of the 'assessment' role? Does she need consciously to remind herself of it in some way, at the beginning of each 'stage' of the activity – she did, after all, briefly fall out of role at the beginning of stage 2. Is it perhaps that time is getting on and she needs to finish the activity – hence engendering a more teacherly, interventive style.

Interestingly, deprived of the right to accumulate a pile of 'big ones', Justin is now commentating on the work of the others – particularly, it seems, Megan – rather than being physically involved in the task. This seems to be well meant but it may or may not be well perceived by the others. Frank, meanwhile, sees the task as an individual one.

T reasserts that this is to be a collaborative enterprise, though she starts to introduce some linguistic ambiguity by talking about a 'big pile of small ones'.

Justin has spotted a problem that he deems worthy of his attention and he now re-engages physically. So far the 'big ones' have been long. The 'fat' one is a sycamore leaf.

Justin does not answer, but places the leaf on the pile of 'big ones'.

Megan	> I've don/I've done **mine** <	Megan claims an individual achievement.
T	what are those going to be then?	

T points to a pile of leaves in front of Megan.

T	what size ones are those going to be then =	
Megan	= middle sized	Why choose 'middle sized'? Has Megan uncon-
T	middle size - these are the big ones are they?	sciously taken on the 'mummy bear' identity?

T picks up some leaves from the table in front of Frank.

Frank	yeah daddy ones	Now Frank explicitly associates 'the big ones'
T	what about the rest of them what are we going to do with the rest of them =	with 'daddy ones' – perhaps introducing the three bears was not a good idea.
Megan	= these are mummies	Now Megan's 'middle sized' ones are 'mum-

Megan sits back down.   mies'.

T	> what about all the rest? <	
Justin	> those are daddies <	
T	where's the little ones - the ss/the baby ones - the little ones	And finally, no doubt against her best inten- tions, T calls the 'little ones' , 'baby ones'.

The interaction continued in this vein for another four minutes, until the category of 'size' had been worked through in similar fashion to those of colour
and shape. (The total time spent on this focus group assessment was therefore
between 13 and 14 minutes.) The third part of the task, focusing on size,
encompassed ordering, as well as sorting *per se*, as Justin and Megan started to
argue over the parameters of the smallest category and Justin suggested that
some of her 'babies' were in fact 'children'. The group then attempted to sort
and order four categories rather than the original three, with Frank, having
listened to the discussion of babies and children, actually being the one to
articulate the full ordering system as 'daddy, mummy, children and babies'.
Perhaps introducing the three bears wasn't so counterproductive in terms
of mathematics teaching, after all; though the gender issues are legion (cf.
Walkerdine 1988).

Discussion

In analysing this transcript further, there are a number of issues to which we
can attend. While set up as an opportunity for 'formative assessment', the
encounter encompasses far more than this. In interview later, the teacher
stated that she 'wanted to see how many different ways that they could do it
and make some assessment about their abilities through that'. She wanted to
do this in order to group children for future differentiated classwork. Yet in setting out to accomplish this basic purpose, the teacher also has to attend to the
social dynamics of the group, and has both a short-term pedagogic strategy for

accomplishing this (her sequencing of the task, for example) and a longer-term curriculum agenda – she knows what will come next for the class as a whole and different small groups within it. In other words, she knows what she wants to find out, and with what consequences for the future; the children do not. They, or at least some of them, are simply struggling to make sense of the present. In parallel with this, the incident also reflects, realizes in action, and further embeds, the social relationships of the children involved and the emerging power structure of the peer group. Broadly, then, we might summarize this by suggesting that the encounter has both educational and social intentions and consequences.

To begin with, a great deal can be gleaned about the children's mathematical knowledge and understanding from this extract, and so it is important to deal with it as an assessment: what can we say the teacher now knows about these children that she didn't know before the episode? In addition it is important to reflect on the way in which the teacher teased this out – to review the relatively recessive role that she played. Finally we will explore the way in which the process of the interaction was perceived and interpreted by the children concerned; i.e. how the encounter was accomplished largely by the children themselves and seemed to produce further learning as the task progressed. We will approach these issues first by reflecting on the achievements of each of the children in turn, and how these were created and elicited, before then moving on to consider further the teacher's strategy and the ways in which learning seemed to be constructed by the interaction of the group.

Assessing the children

Justin

The evidence suggests that we would be pretty safe in saying that Justin knows the vocabulary of colour, shape and size, and understands the concept of categorizing and sorting by these criteria, and probably by other criteria as well. He can also count – up to four and, again, probably well beyond. The structure of the task, and the teacher's observer role, have certainly allowed him to demonstrate a good deal about what he knows, understands and can do and, by focused questioning at particular points, probably draws more from him than otherwise might have been the case. Whether this process of 'drawing him out' can actually be said to be scaffolding new learning is more of a moot point, however. Rather, it seems as though the teacher's strategy allows him to articulate as fully as possible what he knows, but does not take him beyond this; she takes him towards the end of the continuum of what he already knows, rather than taking him into territory that he hasn't previously encountered – his zone of proximal development. In this respect, the assessment of Justin, qua assessment, could be said to fit fairly closely with the incremental models which we criticized in Chapter 2. The teacher has learned a great deal about what Justin can do in maths, and now will be able to prepare future work for him with this knowledge in mind.

In addition to the teacher's particular intentions, however, Justin also plays a central role in the group dynamics and may or may not have learned new things from this. The assessment doesn't take place in a vacuum, and will have an impact on him and carry consequences for him in other ways. Also, the teacher's questioning may have alerted him to the need in future to observe artefacts more closely and describe them more exactly. We will return to these points below. For the moment we will move on to Megan.

Megan
Megan similarly seems to understand the vocabulary of colour, shape and size, and the concept of categorizing and sorting by these criteria. And, as she reminds the teacher without being asked, she can count up to five at least. In many respects her experience of the encounter and the attainments she demonstrates are very parallel to those of Justin. Through a combination of observation and focused questioning, the teacher allows and encourages Megan to make public a great deal of her knowledge and understanding, without necessarily extending that understanding. If there is a difference between Justin and Megan it is that at times Megan has to assert her current knowledge status, in the face of Justin's interventions and potentially dominating role in the group. In this respect she perhaps gets slightly less help from the teacher than does Justin. Justin's self-assertion, combined with what appears to be a marginal tendency on the teacher's part to privilege his answers and his role in the group, seem to provide more of an 'ideal context' for him to demonstrate his knowledge, rather than Megan. He always seems to be at ease with the situation, even in control of it, whereas Megan seems slightly less secure in her understanding of the social expectations of the 'pupil role' in small group work (and possibly also the female role in a group of three boys), and has to 'push in' and hold her ground from time to time, resisting Justin's attempts to redefine the task for her. Furthermore, while Justin's answers to 'stage 1' of the task ('yeah', 'brown', 'four') are accepted by the teacher without question, Megan's first response ('pink') is modified by the teacher to 'all the pinky-red ones'. In fact some pink leaves were also on Ricky's pile, so the teacher may have been trying to narrow the definition of which leaves Megan had chosen, in order to render her answer correct as well as focus her attention on the particular shade of pink that she had chosen. Yet it may be that this particular interchange was based on a misinterpretation by the teacher. Megan seemed to be employing the criteria of both colour *and* shape to her pile, and in any case neither the teacher's original question nor Megan's answer ('Which ones did you sort out?', 'Pink') necessarily implied that she should have had *all* the pink ones (pinky-red or not), just that she had used the criterion of colour (pinkness) to sort out a small pile. Irrespective of the details of this exchange, however, the significant thing is that it occurred at all: i.e. in coming to broadly similar conclusions about Justin's and Megan's attainment, the teacher treated them in different ways. Interestingly enough, however, even if like Justin, Megan's mathematical knowledge is not extended by this particular interaction, she does seem to learn more about the particular rules of the focus group game. Towards the end of the encounter she begins to utter answers without bidding for a turn, whereas at the start she modelled the pupil role more closely by saying 'I know' and/or putting up her hand, and waiting to be asked, rather than simply announcing the answer.

With respect to an incremental model of formative assessment, however, and the practical consequences that this assessment would carry, the teacher is likely to come to a very similar judgement about Megan as she has about Justin; i.e. that Megan knows and understands a great deal, and future planning should take this into account. Indeed, in interview afterwards, the teacher confirmed that Megan and Justin would be in the 'top group' when she started differentiating classwork more explicitly.

Frank

Frank presents us with a much more ambiguous, even transitional case, and provides evidence that the very interaction which is prompted by the assessment, acts to scaffold his learning, while at the same time providing him with a significant challenge with respect to understanding the social rules of small group work. At the start of the encounter he is distracted and has to be brought back on task by a very recognizable teacher strategy – that of naming. But once involved he does seem to stick with the task, at least at the level of social ritual: he takes leaves and he puts leaves in different piles. However, he also talks about what he's doing as he's doing it, and listens to and observes Justin and Megan, and by the end of the interaction, rather than becoming bored and losing interest, he actually seems to be very engaged and keen to succeed. He demonstrates that he knows the vocabulary of colour, shape and size and can identify objects by their colour, shape and size. It is far less clear whether he understands the concepts of categorizing and sorting. At times it seems as if he does, but does not actually manage to do it. However, this may be because he is struggling to understand the nature of the task, rather than being unable to complete it. For example, he is the first in the group to articulate size as a variable, but then resists using size later when questioned by the teacher, even when pressed, perhaps because he thinks he has to be more specific about the variable at issue (shape) rather than introduce a new variable. The teacher had, after all, stressed at the start of 'stage 2' that the criterion was now going to be shape, not size. So Frank may have started to interpret the teacher's further questioning as a form of 'guessing game' – 'what is it about shape that she's after and I haven't seen yet?' – rather than as a genuine enquiry about what *else* he could say about the differences between the leaves; in other words, he misinterpreted the nature of the enquiry, rather than didn't 'know' the correct 'answer'.

There appears to be an immensely complex struggle going on here, as Frank seeks to comprehend the nature of the task and the new social rules at work in the small 'focus' group, rather than the usual IRF of the classroom. This is particularly noticeable in his constantly looking for affirmation from the teacher and perhaps being confused when he does not receive it. As she herself stated in interview afterwards: 'Frank was actually looking at me the whole time to get my approval . . . and I was trying to ignore him, really, 'cos I wanted him to do it on his own.' It may also be rather galling for him to latch on to the traditional teacherly cueing utterances which the teacher uses when moving from shape to size ('phew, at last a form of classroom interaction that I can understand'), only to see Ricky get the first one right, and then Megan jump in to appropriate his earlier use of the phrase 'big ones' to utter the word 'size', which was actually cued by Frank himself joining the sequence and saying 'ummm, same . . . '.

Overall, however, he does seem to make intellectual progress as the inter-action unfolds and, in terms of both cognitive development and social under-standing, we might speculate that of all the four children he may have benefited most from the encounter, at least in terms of his own learning. Whether or not the teacher learned anything useful in terms of an incremen-tal planning model of formative assessment is another issue. In these terms the encounter simply seemed to confirm that Frank would not be in the top group when it came to differentiated classwork.

Ricky

Ricky offers least evidence of understanding and achievement, though in some respects he is perhaps offered least opportunity to demonstrate what he knows. While Justin seizes the opportunity of the focus group structure to shape the interaction in such a way as to render it an almost ideal context in which he can succeed, Ricky seems quite unable to do so. Of all four children, he seems to struggle most with the open-ended nature of the task. This is very far from an ideal assessment context for him, though interestingly enough, when he gets a glimpse of a more familiar teacherly cue he seizes it, to demon-strate that he is on task and can utter a right answer in the right place:

Teacher: We've sorted them out by colour, we've sorted them out by
Ricky: Shape

Thus we learn that Ricky can recognize and name colours, seems to recognize different shapes but doesn't have the vocabulary to describe them very explicitly ('sort of star shape'), and can also recognize size (he disputes with Justin over who is going to collect the 'big ones'). But he seems to have little idea of the concept of categorizing and sorting, and hardly engages with the task, let alone completes it.

Yet these judgements represent both major inferences from *very* limited data – could we really be sure from this evidence? – while at one and the same time suggesting Ricky has accomplished very little. But isn't it likely that a 5-year-old would know about colours, shapes and sizes, and a great deal more besides, if only it could be teased out of him? Thus the assessment is probably least suc-cessful and least useful in Ricky's case, though this is not necessarily his fault. Indeed, in interview, the teacher reflected on the way in which she could have asked more probing questions of both him and Frank to establish more securely their level of comprehension: 'Maybe I should have gone back to Frank and Ricky and done colour again, because . . . having seen it and gone through it, I could have taken them back again and said OK you do them by colour now.' Easier said than done in a busy classroom, especially when the implicit prospective agenda in the teacher's head is to repeat the task for the group for different criteria, rather than for individuals with respect to the same criteria. Even here, however, where the evidence of cognitive engagement and achievement is so limited, there is little doubt that for the first ten minutes at least, Ricky is trying to 'keep up' with respect to the social accomplishment of the event and, perhaps, is learning something of what it is to be a pupil in this classroom, and how best to engage in a 'focus group' next time.

Teaching, assessing and learning

The contrast between this teacher's focused and purposeful questioning, and the 'guessing game' which we examined in Chapter 4, is very marked, particularly with respect to the amount of talk that the children contribute to the discussion. The juxtaposition of an initially open task with subsequent focused questioning is handled very skilfully. The task is presented not just as 'sorting out', but '*how* to sort them out'; thus no organizing criteria are provided, but the call to articulate the criteria is clear. This is more than a 'performance task' underpinned by hidden thought processes; the thought processes must be made explicit. To begin with, the pupils' responses still take a great deal for granted (as does the teacher's management of the group). But one-word answers are probed, so that the pupils' vocabulary is extended while at the same time their level of understanding is confirmed. In terms of strategy, then, the open task, the request for categorizing criteria, the observational role adopted, the focused follow-up questioning, and the sequencing and pacing of the task into different stages, all suggest that this is an extremely well designed and conducted formative assessment encounter. In addition, the teacher adapts her questioning to the children's responses, lowering the level of difficulty of the task in individual cases; though this also means that the children did not get equal treatment (perhaps especially an issue for Justin and Megan). At the same time some opportunities for further clarificatory probing were missed (e.g. the teacher's own recognition of the need to repeat the task with Frank and Ricky with respect to colour).

In addition to the explicit strategy and agenda that the teacher was pursuing, however, the whole incident was also underpinned by, and clearly had an impact on, the expectations and assumptions that the children themselves brought to the encounter. In order for the task to 'work' as planned, the children had to 'know' what was expected of them – i.e. had to understand the rules of this particular focus group game. Justin and Megan did indeed seem to know this; it is less clear that Frank and Ricky did. In many respects the teacher relied upon Justin and Megan, and perhaps particularly Justin, to orchestrate the group's work at the level of social interaction (the rules of the game) *and* with respect to the cognitive agenda – by vocalizing their own thought processes and providing the vocabulary and the concepts by which the group operated. Perhaps this explains her tendency to privilege Justin's answers and position in the group. In many respects he was filling the 'pedagogical vacuum' left by the teacher taking an observational role, and in turn she (subconsciously?) looked to him to keep the interaction going and carry it forward – to 'accomplish the lesson'.

With this, we have a further interesting example of the way in which peer group power relations can mean that different children secure different benefits from ostensibly the same teaching (and assessing) situation. The teacher's observational role leaves a power vacuum as well as a pedagogical vacuum (indeed, in terms of our earlier discussion in Chapters 5 and 6, it would be more accurate to suggest that the former is an integral component of the latter). Justin is not only best equipped to fill it, but by filling it, his role and those of the others in the group are recursively realized and compounded by the interactive process. In particular, his early appreciation that the situation did not simply call for correct answers to be cued and supplied on an individual basis, but rather that something had to be done and the doing of it talked through, simultaneously established his role as leader within the peer group, led the teacher to rely on him to facilitate the group's understanding and accomplishment of the task, and provided him with an opportunity to appropriate the power of the teacher's role to his own advantage. He also spoke individually, but on behalf of the group, when a bid for control was invited (T: 'right, are you finished, then?'; Justin: 'Yeah'). However, at least some of his contributions can also be seen as empowering of others if they could be said to articulate the thoughts of others in the group – rendering explicit what others were struggling towards. As Kreisberg notes while quoting the words of one of the teachers in his study:

> . . . the power of more powerful individuals 'frequently gives other people in the group a feeling of being empowered as well, because somebody is speaking articulately things they were thinking'. This is synergistic power. Its exercise expands the effectiveness of the individuals in the group and of the group as a whole.
>
> (Kreisberg 1992:138)

With respect to the relationship of classroom assessment to the promotion of learning, what we seem to have here is a very rich example of the possibilities inherent in peer collaboration, facilitated by the teacher setting up a structured small-group formative assessment task and adopting an observer role. This is not simply, or even largely, a mechanistic, transparent, information-gathering-by-the-teacher-for-future-planning exercise. Certainly the teacher gleans some intelligence for future curriculum planning, and in the context of a busy classroom, perhaps this is all that can be overtly and self-consciously pursued on a routine basis. (Remember how often in Chapter 3 the teachers reported that they tended to assess in groups and for group purposes; it was rare that they had the time and inclination to work in detail with individuals.) But careful planning of this maths task has also provided an exceedingly fertile environment for collaborative learning; and while the teacher cannot rely on the interaction working as well every time and producing such outcomes, they can be treated as an important and worthwhile 'parallel product' which the teacher can at least attempt to stimulate each time, as she pursues the more 'broad brush' objective of gathering evidence for curriculum planning.

Thus although the teacher is 'assessing' rather than 'teaching', learning is taking place, and indeed it is possible that the role she adopts is more facilitative of the children's learning than if she were 'teaching'. A collaborative zone of proximal development is established by the interaction, and the teacher maintains the key role in structuring the discourse based on her own prospective agenda and the kind of 'disciplinary knowing' (as opposed to knowledge of the right answer) which we encountered in Chapter 7. 'Power with' the children is established and manifest in a discourse structure which focuses the children's attention on mathematical principles and their own cognitive processes. The teacher's questions are designed to promote metacognitive reflection in the children, and the 'egocentric speech' which is elicited at various times from Justin, Megan and Frank is arguably more accessible to appropriation by the other children than a similar commentary by the teacher. Moreover, the teacher's management of the interaction, with respect to both linguistic structure and power relations, enable her (on the occasions when there is an absence of what she considers to be a suitable response from the children) to 'step in' and ask a focusing question, almost as a member of the group rather than as an overt authority figure eliciting atomized snippets from whomsoever succeeds in bidding for a turn.

To summarize, what we also seem to have here is an example of a collaborative environment in which pupils are indeed developing 'the capacity to monitor the quality of their own work during actual production' and developing 'a store of tactics . . . which can be drawn upon to modify their own work' (Sadler 1989:119). The example provides clear evidence 'that peer interaction is capable of enhancing intellectual performance because it forces individuals to recognise and coordinate conflicting perspectives on a problem' and that 'learning consists of the internalisation of social interactional processes' (Forman and Cazden 1985:330, 341). To return to our earlier discussion of appropriation, what we see embedded in this focus group assessment is, at various times, both teacher and pupils appropriating each other's words, not only to accomplish the interaction and produce a satisfactory 'event', but also to produce new learning. The event could not have taken place without teacher and pupils alike knowing enough about their roles and the social expectations of the occasion to 'launch' the interaction and then 'stick with it' in order to make sense of it and see where they took it and it took them. In turn, the pupils in particular were learning-through-talking about the nature of the task, the social rules of this particular form of schoolwork, and their role(s) within the social group. This focus group thus provides a clear example of learning processes 'which must properly be characterised as *interpsychological* – arising from the interaction between people – which play a major role in producing cognitive changes' (Newman *et al.* 1989:92–3). Furthermore, this is an example drawn from the 'natural environment' of an ordinary classroom, rather than some specially designed experiment.

Thus, even given due caution with respect to the social construction of the assessment process, it is clear that a more flexible approach to teaching and assessing, involving the design and conduct of particular small-group tasks, coupled with an overt listener/observer role for the teacher, can reveal a wealth of information about *how* children are learning as well as *what* they are learning. There is no doubt from this example that 'formative assessment' can 'work', but in ways which are perhaps not entirely anticipated by some of its proponents, and at a level of detail which it would be very hard to sustain. Formative classroom assessment is far more complex than some would suggest; in turn, and if properly operationalized, it could deliver a much richer quality teaching and learning environment; but, by the same token, it is therefore far more demanding than superficial treatments would lead us to believe. How we approach this problem will be the subject of our final chapter.

9

Formative classroom assessment: prospects for improvement

Introduction

This book has explored how classroom assessment is accomplished in and through teacher–pupil interaction. We have suggested that such assessment will always have an impact on pupil learning, but that this impact is complex, multifaceted, and is not necessarily always as positive as might be intended by teachers and as some advocates of formative assessment would have us believe. We have argued that at a theoretical level, formative assessment could be grounded in a behaviourist, mastery-learning view of how learning takes place and how instruction should be organized; or in a more social constructivist approach to learning, giving attention to the quality of teacher–pupil inter-action and the scaffolding of learning-in-action. In Chapter 4 we identified and described the complexity of classroom assessment and in particular the opaqueness of much teacher questioning, and the possibilities for misunder-standing on the part of both teachers and pupils about what a particular task involves and how the children concerned should go about engaging with it. In Chapters 5 and 6 we went on to demonstrate the way in which assessment communicates messages about behaviour as well as achievement, and begs issues of power; and how access to power can mediate apparently the same broad teaching strategy to produce different outcomes for different children. Chapter 5 in particular demonstrated the way in which a teacher's prospective pedagogic agenda mediated her interpretation of a pupil's performance.

Chapter 6 illustrated how apparently well-intended and benign feedback nevertheless still seemed to invoke a latent and inappropriate behaviourism which privileged some pupils' learning strategies at the expense of others: the same teacher assessment behaviour seemed to be positively formative in two cases but have a negative impact in two others. Chapter 7 explored different assessment contexts which provided opportunities to generate teacher–pupil dialogue that moved beyond the cueing of 'right answers'. The situations were such that the teachers' questions began to be perceived as genuine rather than ritualistic, so that what was being called forth from pupils was less of a 'competent classroom performance' and more of an authentic discussion to explore and scaffold understanding. In Chapter 8 we attempted to bring much of the theoretical and empirical discussion together and exemplify the formative potential of classroom assessment by presenting a particular example at some length. Chapter 8 demonstrated the way in which the teacher appropriated the children's words and actions to accomplish and move the activity along, in a micro-sociological sense, while at the same time communicating these practices to the children as defining small group assessment activity. In parallel with this, she also appropriated their words, and provided the opportunity for them to appropriate each other's words, in order to scaffold further learning. Here, formative classroom assessment was not simply practised as a set of discrete, information gathering procedures: set up task, observe pupils, record results. Rather, a structured task was combined with a largely, but not exclusively, observational role, and focused questioning, to provide as good an (interactive) opportunity as might reasonably be accomplished in a busy classroom, to gather evidence of achievement *and* facilitate social and cognitive development.

However, similarly well designed and conducted formative assessment incidents were relatively unusual in our study. And although extracts from other transcripts throughout the book show teachers operating with considerable skill, often under difficult classroom circumstances, whether or not they have the intended positive formative effect often appears to derive as much from contingent characteristics of the context as from particularly well planned activities. So rather than attempting to improve the procedural planning of formative assessment, and make use of the 'results' generated, particularly with respect to individual children (which, as we have suggested throughout the book, is likely to prove a logistic impossibility), teachers may be better advised to think of formative assessment as part of their pedagogy, and thus about how well-structured activities in the here-and-now can have a positive formative impact. Thus in this final chapter we will try to move beyond description, analysis and critique, and present contrasting heuristic models of formative assessment in order to provide a basis for thinking about how different approaches to teaching fit with different approaches to assessment. We see this as providing both a concise conceptual summary of our analysis and a potential tool for understanding that might enable teachers to maximize the potential of classroom assessment to improve pupils' learning. Having provided an overarching conceptual framework we will then go on to review and summarize some of the more concrete strategies by which formative assessment might be accomplished, along with some of the more obvious micro-sociological 'health warnings' that must accompany them.

A conceptual framework – convergent and divergent formative assessment

In the many assessment incidents that we observed we have identified two conceptually distinct approaches to classroom assessment, which we will term 'convergent' and 'divergent' (see Table 9.1). However, these terms are more

Table 9.1   Convergent and divergent assessment

Convergent Assessment	Divergent Assessment
Assessment which aims to discover *whether* the learner knows, understands or can do a predetermined thing. This is characterized by:	Assessment which aims to discover *what* the learner knows, understands or can do. This is characterized by:
Practical implications (a) precise planning and an intention to stick to it; (b) tick lists and can-do statements;	*Practical implications* (a) flexible planning or complex planning which incorporates alternatives; (b) open forms of recording (narrative, quotations etc.);
(c) an analysis of the interaction of the learner and the curriculum from the point of view of the curriculum;	(c) an analysis of the interaction of the learner and the curriculum from the point of view both of the learner and of the curriculum;
(d) closed or pseudo-open questioning and tasks; (e) a focus on contrasting errors with correct responses;	(d) open questioning and tasks; (e) a focus on miscues – aspects of learners' work which yield insights into their current understanding – and on prompting metacognition;
(f) judgemental or quantitative evaluation; (g) involvement of the pupil as recipient of assessments.	(f) descriptive rather than purely judgemental evaluation; (g) involvement of the pupil as initiator of assessments as well as recipient.
Theoretical implications (h) a behaviourist view of learning; (j) an intention to teach or assess the next predetermined thing in a linear progression; (k) a view of assessment as accomplished by the teacher.	*Theoretical implications* (h) a constructivist view of learning; (j) an intention to teach in the zone of proximal development; (k) a view of assessment as accomplished jointly by the teacher and the pupil.
This view of assessment might be seen less as formative assessment, than as repeated summative assessment or continuous assessment.	This view of assessment could be said to attend more closely to contemporary theories of learning and accept the complexity of formative assessment.

heuristic than descriptive – ideal types constructed from observations and which summarize tendencies. The two approaches seem to arise from teachers' differing views of learning and the relationship of assessment to the process of intervening to support learning. They are not necessarily mutually exclusive.

In *convergent assessment* the important thing is to find out *whether* the child knows, understands or can do a predetermined thing. It is characterized by: adherence to precise planning; the use of methods of recording, such as tick lists and can-do statements; and an analysis of the interaction of the child and the curriculum from the point of view of the curriculum. It is routinely accomplished by closed or pseudo-open questioning and tasks, often following the IRF pattern of standard classroom discourse, reviewed in previous chapters.

The implications of this form of assessment are essentially behaviourist, with the intention being to teach or assess the next predetermined thing in a linear or at least pre-planned progression. It is assessment *of* the child *by* the teacher. Such classroom practices seem to be grounded in a tacit view of assessment framed in behaviourist terms, even though they often seem to conflict with teachers' conscious espousal of more flexible approaches to teaching and learning. These more flexible espoused approaches might be characterized as more constructivist in orientation, albeit that teachers do not necessarily use the term 'constructivist'.

Divergent assessment emphasizes the learner's understanding rather than the agenda of the assessor. Here the important thing is to discover *what* the child knows, understands or can do. It is characterized by more flexible planning, open forms of recording (narrative, quotations etc.), and an analysis of the interaction of the child and the curriculum from the point of view of the child. This form of assessment is used more appropriately with open tasks and involves either open questioning, sometimes aimed at prompting pupils to reflect on their own thinking, or a divergence from IRF discourse, focusing on miscues – aspects of learners' work which yield insights into their current understanding. It results in more descriptive, qualitative feedback. The theoretical implications of divergent assessment are that a social constructivist view of education is adopted with an intention to teach in the zone of proximal development; as a result, assessment is seen as accomplished jointly by the teacher and the pupil. This view of assessment could be said to attend more closely to contemporary theories of learning and accept the complexity of formative assessment though, again, observed instances of such practice have not necessarily been found to be self-consciously 'constructivist'; rather they derive from more general ideological commitments to a 'child-centred approach' and are not necessarily as well structured as they could and (we would argue) should be.

In the light of our argument throughout the book, the above summary would seem to suggest that divergent assessment is the more interesting approach, and the one which seems to offer more scope for positively affecting children's learning. However, we are not claiming that teachers should adopt a divergent approach all the time, but rather that they should be aware of the problems and possibilities inherent in both approaches, and how they match with, and might be developed in the context of, their own classroom situation. When working with pupils to construct their learning paths, teachers have to balance the individual, divergent and creative thought of the pupil, generated in the dynamic context of the small group and the class, with the need to structure learning experiences and pursue the essentially convergent requirements of the curriculum. Thus it may be useful to approach some assessment tasks in a convergent manner, but we would also argue that appreciating the range of possible ways of conducting assessment and being able to move from one mode to the other in a principled way, would enhance the formative impact of classroom assessment. A judgement about which approach to adopt should therefore be based upon consideration of the nature of the knowledge and task being assessed, the availability of time and resources, and the possibilities for supplying feedback which might enhance learning. Thus, understanding the possibilities of both convergent and divergent assessment and developing the ability consciously to manipulate them would seem to be the prerequisite for teachers to make the most of formative assessment.

Accomplishing formative assessment

Our interviewing revealed that current practice in primary schools involves a highly structured day, with weekly and sometimes daily written plans scrutinized by heads and subject leaders. Because of this, and the compelling imperatives of classroom life, most instruction will involve routinized behaviour, and only infrequently will deliberate, non-routinized thinking take place, emerging from situations that are perceived as being out of the normal range of experience (e.g. the examples in Chapter 7). It appears from our data that for many teachers, convergent assessment is congruent with classroom routines and structures of discourse, and that it is only infrequently that the alternative approach emerges in a readily identifiable form. What is more often apparent is that opportunities for divergent assessment open up and may be accepted by teachers, but are hard to sustain. Three main reasons for this appear to be present. First, teachers are often deflected from a more divergent approach by the exigencies of managing the classroom (e.g. the need to complete the lesson, other children distracting attention, interruptions from outside the classroom). Second, the social and cultural context of the classroom, where individual pupils have different access to power, means that the more collaborative approach needed for divergent assessment is not always equally (and equitably) available to all pupils (e.g. the examples in Chapters 6 and 8). Third, the routine structure of classroom discourse constructed around pseudo-questions to which the teacher already knows the answer, fits closely with the closed nature of convergent assessment.

Planning at the level of the lesson or day, even if conceptualized in terms of outcomes rather than inputs, will tend to be concerned with meeting teachers' immediate goals. A divergent approach would involve thinking much more about the longer-term goals of education. Unless teachers include divergent approaches in their planning (e.g. the sorting leaves task in Chapter 8) it is only when an unusual eventuality prompts deliberation that they are likely to move from convergent to more divergent assessment (e.g. Caterina's book in Chapter 7). The sort of planning that would encourage divergent assessment would have to be flexible and enable teachers to move away from the attainment of short-term objectives (finishing the activity) towards ensuring that some element of metacognitive reflection was being consciously pursued and underlying understanding was being developed.

If planning which consists of organizing atomized objectives militates against divergent assessment, so too does a similar style of recording. We have already noted that the pedagogy of the teachers in our study was very mixed. When wanting to observe progress fairly closely, and intervene when appropriate, they often stood or sat with a focus group while the rest of the class got on with other work. Recording of non-focus group work, if any, was often in the form of a list of names with a space for a tick and possibly a short comment, whereas for focus groups, teachers would usually employ a more open format, sometimes just a blank sheet of paper, possibly supplemented by broad headings which might be related to the curricular goals of the activity. Whilst it is possible to conceive of a more detailed divergent record (see Pryor 1995 for an example), the use of a checklist would seem almost inevitably to dictate a convergent approach.

One of the problems that we have noted already in conceptualizing formative assessment is that even those who are concerned with its divergent potentialities, tend to see it from the perspective of teaching rather than learning. The important thing about divergent formative assessment is that the emphasis shifts (partly, but not wholly) from the curriculum to the learner. Thus in divergent assessment the 'feed-forward' is concerned more with the effect on current and subsequent learning than the effect on subsequent teaching. This shift of attention from teaching to learning is also important at the interpersonal level. A divergent approach by teachers would communicate to pupils that they are interested in them as people: thus children might come to understand that it is not a 'correct answer' *per se* that the teacher is anxious to elicit (i.e. a cued performance), but the child's own perception of the issue under discussion, that is, their developing understanding of knowledge under construction. This is particularly important because it suggests that paradoxically, the teachers who succeed in obtaining a more valid assessment of attainment will not be those who show interest merely in attainment, but those who also show interest in the child. Moreover, this would accord well with the professional ethic of concern for the 'whole child' which we have previously noted as predominant in primary and especially early years schooling. More problematically, such an orientation to pupils would also entail a view of the curriculum which is different from that contained in prescribed subject documentation such as that exemplified by the National Curriculum. Learning conceptualized as the construction of knowledge by the appropriation of the different perspectives of individuals within a collaborating group, has little in common with a view of the curriculum as a body of knowledge and skills that are transmitted by unidirectional instruction. The former position would see curriculum as the amalgam of texts and contexts brought forward into the arena of the classroom by both the teacher and the pupils. Of course, learning is never simply 'transmitted' or 'delivered'; pupils will always have to make sense of and internalize (or reject) the curriculum they encounter. However, we recognize the contradictory demands that teachers feel they face in such circumstances.

We have dealt with the issue of the structure of classroom speech in some detail. In examining potentially divergent assessment situations in Chapter 7, we encountered discourse structures that were likened to interviewing (the science experiment), to debate (questions on Jamaica) and to the notion of Socratic dialogue with reference to the issue of knowing what is an important question to ask, rather than the 'right answer' to elicit. Thus although we have noted that the normal structure of classroom interaction would tend to favour convergent assessment, there are models for discourse structure that might enable teachers to develop a more divergent approach. In this respect the focus of divergent assessment on *what* children know, can do and understand, requires pedagogic and linguistic opportunities for them to express and explore their ideas. An important role for the teacher, then, is to provide prompts for this and to encourage children to speculate, argue and critique. However, the teacher's response is also important. A convergent approach would focus on errors, concentrating on the way that children's performances differ from an expected and assumed norm. Divergent assessment, on the other hand, would conceptualize teacher responses as opportunities for further analysis and the self-conscious scaffolding of learning. This would require less 'recording-for-future-use' and more principled interrogative feedback, articulating the teacher's perception of what the child has just done or said in order to validate the perception and extend the child's learning by such verbal scaffolding. In turn, an important element in the developing dialogue would be for the teacher to stimulate pupils to talk about their thinking, to the teacher and to each other. There are two issues at stake here. The first is what we might term individual metacognition – the thinking about thinking which Bruner (1985) likens to the high ground from which pupils are able to get an overview of the learning activity. However, as we have seen in Chapter 8, when children in a group talk through their thinking, they are also providing a model which might be appropriated by others in the group. Secondly, therefore, collaborative interaction of this nature involves a process of group reflection which in a very real sense actually *creates* the zone of proximal development as well as allowing individuals to explore and extend it for themselves (cf. Wertsch 1985; Newman *et al.* 1989).

This interpretation of the creation of the zone of proximal development thus integrates individual learning trajectories with the social situation which calls them forth at any particular point in time. Vygotsky (1978:89) claims that 'the only "good learning" is that which is in advance of development'. Similarly one might argue that the only true formative assessment is that which looks forward to what children will understand, and therefore it must be divergent enough to accommodate this. Metacognitive reflection and discussion is obviously possible in convergent situations, and in examples of dynamic assessment such as those reported by Brown *et al.* (1992) this can be said to be happening. However, our data would lead us to question whether the social and the interpsychological conditions of convergent assessment routinely and systematically favour the kind of reflection that is necessary; it would seem rather that structures of discourse and distributions of power in divergent situations are much more likely to call forth the conditions under which metacognition is produced.

The notion that formative assessment is situated in classroom interaction and is therefore inextricably bound up with the structures of that interaction, has been central to our argument throughout this book. The implications of the changed roles of the participants in divergent assessment are therefore far-reaching. Openness to pupils' ideas and the greater emphasis put on pupil understanding mean that in successful divergent assessment, power would be shared more evenly between teacher and pupil. In the examples in previous chapters, meaning is created through dialogue. If the pupil is not active in the dialogue (e.g. Eliane in Chapter 6), either meaning is imposed or no shared meaning is accomplished. And it is this shared meaning, even if imperfectly shared, that leads to appropriation and learning (Newman *et al.* 1989). Beyond this, however, to create *power with* pupils, teachers need not only to be open to discursive negotiation with them, but also to provide direct substantive feedback, since by doing so they give them access to ideas which are culturally powerful within society. Children will create their own understanding of shared knowledge, but precisely in order for it to be shared, it needs to be talked through, interrogated by and tested against 'the authority of expertise' (Kreisberg 1992:183).

Moreover, if the process of negotiation becomes embedded in classroom practice, the process itself becomes part of the definition of the context. Teachers might amplify this effect by deliberately making the process of negotiation a subject for discussion so that a dialogue about power in the class-room is opened up. It is through such a dialogue, recursively inscribed in the social practices of the classroom, that children who find it more difficult to access classroom power at present (e.g. Bella in Chapter 6) may gain con-sciousness of their own potentiality – in effect, become empowered. This in turn may render the divergent possibilities of formative assessment more open to equitable accomplishment. Reflection on classroom processes, bringing 'metasocial' as well as 'metacognitive' reflection more fully to the fore, may help teachers as well as pupils to develop their understanding of the process of learning.

The potentially positive effects of pupils' greater sense of power on their motivation can be further enhanced by the way that it relates to success. Bron-wyn Davies describes the effects of conventional (convergent) assessment practices on pupils entering school:

> What they have formerly learned, in the process of learning to engage in discursive practices, is now subjected to authoritative teaching. The cat-egories to which they have been assigned are now potentially subsumed under educational categories of success and failure. Getting it right is not just a matter of being able to converse competently, but a matter of becoming competent in the terms that the teacher designates as compe-tent.
>
> (Davies 1993:153)

However, as our argument in Chapter 6 has made apparent, a divergent opening up of debate can transform the apparent determinism of the situ-ation: learning orientations are not fixed, nor success and failure arbitrarily produced; they are created by the effect of disempowerment. However, if they become subject to a process of negotiation which is oriented towards the reconceptualization of 'failure' – identifying school work and its outcomes as the product of learning interaction between teacher and pupil – failure could be associated less with the personal shortcomings of pupils (or indeed teachers) and more with the '[micro-]political failure' of the established dis-cursive practices of the classroom (Bloome and Willett 1991:231). Similarly, as our discussion in Chapter 6 highlighted, the issue of success is crucial when considering children's attributions. Our analysis showed that the ability of teachers to intervene in pupils' attributions in such a way as to stimulate a focus on learning goals, is hampered by a reliance on behaviourist practices associated with convergent assessment, and could be enhanced by the more constructivist approach of divergent assessment.

In seeking to establish the notion of divergent formative assessment we may too easily assume the role of advocates, and have perhaps not given sufficient attention to the problems which it raises. It should be emphasized that although both convergent and divergent assessment are categories derived from our data, they are, as we stated previously, more heuristic than descriptive; that is, they are ideal types, summarizing tendencies. So whilst convergent assessment might be seen as rather a caricature of traditional assessment practice, so, it should be acknowledged, divergent assessment might be a somewhat idealistic aspiration, which in the crowded and often tense environment of contemporary (British) primary schools would be very difficult to accomplish. Thus we run the risk of intellectual 'overreach' (Goodson 1997), exposing the complexities of formative assessment while at the same time seeking to extend its complexity still further. Divergent assessment could be even more exacting of teachers' time, and requires teachers to be both supportive and critical of pupils – a balance, as we have seen throughout the book, that is extremely difficult to strike.

The issue would be acute if we were to advocate the wholesale adoption of such an approach at the level of the individual child; however, our aspiration is rather more modest. It is to suggest that formative classroom assessment can never be reduced to a set of procedures or practices that will 'work', but rather should be conceptualized as an open, interactive process that might 'get somewhere'; we are invoking an 'intelligent systems' metaphor rather than Newtonian cause and effect. In concrete terms this would mean teachers reviewing their assessment strategies and thinking through the implications of employing a self-consciously divergent approach on key occasions. Thus the sort of activity illustrated in Chapter 8 might be designed and employed for small groups at most once a week, perhaps only once every two or three weeks – so that all children had experience of it regularly but not constantly.

So despite the complexities of the contemporary classroom and the political pressure of a prescribed curriculum coupled with accountability, we would claim that the convergent–divergent distinction does offer teachers a potentially useful conceptual framework for accomplishing formative assessment more successfully. Our intention is not to advocate the adoption of an ideal, but rather to distil elements from empirical data gathered in ordinary classroom settings, into a model which can provoke thought and lead to the development of new practice. We have demonstrated the complexities of classroom assessment, but have also encountered many interesting practices and uncovered many potential benefits. The practical issue now is to attempt to summarize and organize the positive examples from our data in order to develop our understanding of the problems and possibilities of formative classroom assessment, and attempt to improve on what is already being practised. Thus in the remainder of this concluding chapter we will lay out in more detail the constituent elements of a more positive approach to formative classroom assessment.

Table 9.2   The processes of formative assessment

Description	Possible teacher intentions	Possible positive effect for pupil
A T observes P at work (process)	Gain in understanding of why/how the pupil has approached or achieved task	Enhanced motivation due to T's attention
B T examines work done (product)	Gain in understanding of what P has done	Enhanced motivation due to T's attention
C T asks principled question (seeks to elicit evidence of what P knows, understands or can do); P responds	Insight into P's knowledge, understanding or skills	Rehearsal of knowledge, understanding or skills; articulation of understanding to realize understanding
D T asks for clarification about what has been done, is being done or will be done; P replies	Gain in understanding of what P has done and of P's understanding of the task	Re-articulation of understanding; enhanced self-awareness and skills of summary, reflection, prediction, speculation
E T questions P about how and why specific action has been taken (meta-process and metacognitive questioning); P responds	Gain in understanding of why/how the pupil has approached or achieved task. Promotion of deepened understanding and 'handover'	Articulation of thinking-about-thinking; deepened understanding and 'handover'
F T communicates task criteria (what has to be done in order to complete the task) or negotiates them with P	Communicating goals and success criteria; ensuring work is on target; adjusting pace of work	Understanding of task and principles behind it
G T communicates quality criteria or negotiates them with P	Enhancement of quality of future work; promotion of greater independence	Understanding of notions of quality to aid future self-monitoring
H T critiques a particular aspect of the work or invites P to do so	Enhancement of quality of future work; promotion of greater independence	Articulating and interrogating quality criteria; enhanced understanding of quality issues; practice in self-monitoring
J T supplies information, corrects, or makes a counter-suggestion	Communication of alternative or more acceptable product	Enhancement of knowledge and/or understanding
K T gives and/or discusses evaluative feedback on work done with respect to: task, and/or effort and/or aptitude, ability (possibly with reference to future or past achievement)	Influence on P's attributions and therefore motivation of P for further work	Enhanced motivation and self-worth when realized in a context of empowerment; development of learning goals

Table 9.2   continued

Description	Possible teacher intentions	Possible positive effect for pupil
L T suggests or negotiates with P what to do next	Insight into ways forward for immediate further teaching of individual; refocusing P on curricular goals	Insight into ways to continue working and learning. Deepening of understanding of process/ principle
M T suggests or negotiates with P what to do next time	Insight into ways forward for planning of group activities	Deepening of understanding of principle/process
N T assigns mark, grade or summary judgement on the quality of this piece of work or negotiates an agreed one with P	Information for summative assessment; communication of quality criteria; teaching/modelling skills of assessment for self-assessment	Information about present achievement with respect to longer-term goals
P T rewards or punishes pupil, or demonstrates approval/disapproval	Improvement or maintenance of relationship with pupil; enhancement of motivation	Enhanced motivation

The processes of formative assessment

Table 9.2 shows an analysis of the processes of formative assessment based around a description of what the teacher and pupils actually do. In other words it is a summary of the resources – the pedagogic strategies – that might be drawn upon to carry out formative assessment.

It should be noted that the last two columns of the table are labelled 'possible'. In other words, we have made no attempt to list all the consequences, merely the most obviously desirable ones. The focus here is mainly on cognitive intentions and outcomes, but as we have seen throughout the book, the fact that assessment is accomplished socially through interaction means that one needs to guard against giving too much credibility to a reductionist chart such as this, as an entity standing alone. Following the chart, we also therefore review each category in turn, in the light of the evidence given, and argument developed, throughout the book. The table in itself cannot and should not be used as a substitute for our previous analysis. Rather it might be an *aide-mémoire* to alert the reader to different possibilities in the classroom context. Whether any of the categories are likely to produce the desired intentions in any particular context is dependent on the many other psychological and social constituents of that context. However, we would argue that, when read in the light of the issues we have raised throughout the book, a knowledge of the range of possibilities contained in the chart would be potentially useful in the accomplishment of formative assessment.

Observing process (see Table 9.3) was very common across the whole data set. Observation of children at work enables teachers to deliberate on whether

Table 9.3   Observing process

Description	Possible teacher intentions	Possible positive effect for pupil
A T observes P at work	Gain in understanding of why/how the pupil has approached or achieved task	Enhanced motivation and focus due to T's attention

and how to intercede; thus it was often the precursor of one of our subsequent categories (B–N) discussed below. It could be associated equally with convergent and divergent assessment, depending on the type of intervention. Observation played a particularly important part in formal assessments, although some teachers organized their classrooms in ways which enabled it to become part of their everyday routine. However, without prior planning, focused observation of the sort reported in Chapter 8 proved very difficult to accomplish and often resulted in teachers being diverted onto a tangential agenda by extraneous features of the task (e.g. in Chapter 4). Also, teachers' attention was constantly sought by other children in the class, often to solve minor administrative and procedural problems. To a certain extent this was a product of the teachers' own classroom organization and management; but sometimes school policy (or lack of it) exacerbated the problem, as interruptions from outside the classroom diverted teacher attention onto relatively trivial organizational activities (e.g. passing on school dinner money, finding the owners of lost property etc.). The key point would seem to be that observation has to be sustained and accompanied by focused questioning to bring most benefit.

Table 9.4   Examining product

Description	Possible teacher intentions	Possible positive effect for pupil
B T examines work done (product)	Gain in understanding of what P has done	Enhanced motivation due to T's attention

Examining product (see Table 9.4) was an even more common procedure and, like the previous category, was often a precursor to other interaction. Similarly it is inherently neither convergent nor divergent, since its formative potential derives mainly from what accompanies or follows it. This category includes marking, which, if it is to have any formative potential with infants, must necessarily take place in the presence of the child so that feedback is oral and immediate rather than written and delayed. However, as we saw in Chapter 6 in particular, feedback also needs to focus on the quality and criteria inherent in the product, rather than just the fact of its production (i.e. effort) if accompanying feedback is to have its intended positive impact.

Questioning/eliciting (see Table 9.5) could fit easily with traditional convergent notions of assessment. It is also the category that would apply to

Table 9.5   Questioning/eliciting

Description	Possible teacher intentions	Possible positive effect for pupil
C T asks principled question (seeks to elicit evidence of what P knows, understands or can do); P responds	Insight into P's knowledge, understanding or skills	Rehearsal of knowledge, understanding or skills; articulation of understanding to realize understanding

much IRF discourse. As we have seen throughout the book, it could become ritualistic, simply cueing right answers. The issue with respect to learning is to treat the occasion of the pupil's response as a verbal articulation, and therefore a realization-in-action, of knowledge comprehended rather than simply recalled in context by a familiar pattern of interaction. For most benefit to accrue, questioning is likely to have to be focused on a particular activity (usually, though not necessarily, one which the teacher observes or has observed, cf. Chapters 7 and 8) rather than on some imagined common agenda which can simply result in the pursuit of a guessing game (cf. Chapter 4).

Table 9.6   Clarifying

Description	Possible teacher intentions	Possible positive effect for pupil
D T asks for clarification about what has been done, is being done or will be done; P replies	Gain in understanding of what P has done and of P's understanding of the task	Re-articulation of understanding; enhanced self-awareness and skills of summary, reflection, prediction, speculation

Clarifying (see Table 9.6) was important in our consideration of the notion of the genuine question, and might be characterized as the key transformative process for teachers moving questioning from a convergent to a divergent mode. This works on several levels. Asking a pupil to clarify opens up a situation by beginning the process of reflection (although specifically metacognitive elicitations have been given a separate category below). Clarifying can put the pupil in a position of relative power because the pupil is likely to know the answer in a way the teacher doesn't. However, clarifying may also challenge or even threaten pupils; thus for it to be consistently successful the pupil would have to enjoy sufficient self-confidence (*power with*) to be able to reiterate a position rather than automatically assuming it to be wrong if the teacher asks a supplementary question, and even on occasions to contradict the teacher.

Chapters 6, 7 and 8 explore metacognitive elicitation (see Table 9.7), and we have identified it as an essential divergent strategy. However, it is one which makes heavy demands on pupils and can leave them puzzled and perplexed.

Table 9.7 Metacognitive questioning

Description	Possible teacher intentions	Possible positive effect for pupil
E T questions P about how and why specific action has been taken (meta-process and metacognitive questioning); P responds	Gain in understanding of why/how the pupil has approached or achieved task. Promotion of deepened understanding and 'handover'	Articulation of thinking-about-thinking; deepened understanding and 'handover'

Its successful pursuit underlines the issue of social context and the need for pupils to be genuinely engaged with a task, rather than desperately trying to come up with the correct answer in what they perceive to be a guessing game. As we have seen in Chapter 8 in particular, metacognition may be better pursued in small groups, where the dialogue among the pupils takes on 'a life of its own' and pupils interrogate and scaffold each other's learning.

Table 9.8 Task criteria

Description	Possible teacher intentions	Possible positive effect for pupil
F T communicates task criteria (what has to be done in order to complete the task) or negotiates them with P	Communicating goals and success criteria; ensuring work is on target; adjusting pace of work	Understanding of task and principles behind it

In some respects it might be argued that task criteria (see Table 9.8) is a part of the assessment process that precedes engagement with a task, but on many occasions it was also observed while teachers were monitoring children's work. The communication of criteria was embedded in the way the task was set up, and reiterated as it was accomplished. A key issue is for the purpose of any activity to be communicated clearly. Such communication is inherently neither divergent nor convergent, but it does connect with the theme of explicitness that has occurred many times in our analysis. Children interviewed often claimed that they did not know what they were supposed to be doing.

Table 9.9 Quality criteria

Description	Possible teacher intentions	Possible positive effect for pupil
G T communicates quality criteria or negotiates them with P	Enhancement of quality of future work; promotion of greater independence	Understanding of notions of quality to aid future self-monitoring

This could be a particularly significant problem for divergent assessment, and it is important that clarity of task is not confused and conflated with divergence in its pursuit and outcomes.

Table 9.9 is similar to the previous one but is perhaps more specifically a part of formative assessment. It was not especially common in our data, and an important aspect of its successful accomplishment would be for teachers to articulate or explore such quality criteria explicitly, rather than rely on classroom management strategies to communicate when work is of an acceptable standard ('It's very good, now do something else'). The category would relate most directly to Sadler's (1989) views of formative assessment as a process of negotiation over quality criteria, which we referred to in Chapter 2, although our demonstration in Chapter 8 of the way that pupils appropriate the teacher's and each other's ideas would suggest that it might happen in a number of less obvious ways than one-to-one teacher–pupil interaction.

Table 9.10   Critique

Description	Possible teacher intentions	Possible positive effect for pupil
H T critiques a particular aspect of the work or invites P to do so	Enhancement of quality of future work; promotion of greater independence	Articulating and interrogating quality criteria; enhanced understanding of quality issues; practice in self-monitoring

The critique category (see Table 9.10) includes the provision of qualitative and interrogative feedback. It may be convergent or divergent, though divergent uses are more likely to include an invitation to the pupil to critique. Chapter 6 highlighted the problems of balancing constructive interrogative feedback, which is crucial to formative assessment, with preserving the child's feelings of self-worth. The success or not of this endeavour is liable to vary with the social and psychological factors that we indicated in Chapter 6, as well as the linguistic style of the exchange (see also K below).

On the face of it, correcting (see Table 9.11) is most likely to be enacted within a convergent approach. Indeed, pupils can also sometimes correct one another and, on occasions, the teacher, indicating a close correspondence between their understanding and the (convergent) goal of the activity. A key

Table 9.11   Correcting

Description	Possible teacher intentions	Possible positive effect for pupil
J T supplies information, corrects, or makes a countersuggestion	Communication of alternative or more acceptable product	Enhancement of knowledge and/or understanding

issue with respect to whether correcting can also enhance a divergent approach is the extent to which teacher power is grounded in the 'authority of expertise' (Kreisberg 1992) which is nevertheless still open to legitimate enquiry, and the extent to which teacher power is simply inscribed in classroom practice and therefore *not* open to clarificatory questioning.

Table 9.12   Influencing attribution

Description	Possible teacher intentions	Possible positive effect for pupil
K T gives and/or discusses evaluative feedback on work done with respect to: task, and/or effort and/or aptitude, ability (possibly with reference to future or past achievement)	Influence on P's attributions and therefore motivation of P for further work	Enhanced motivation and self-worth when realized in a context of empowerment; development of learning goals

Influencing attribution (see Table 9.12) was the particular focus of our discussion in Chapter 6. The evidence suggested that the latent 'theory of first resort' for teachers was a form of behaviourism, rather than constructivism, despite espousing views to the contrary. This is unlikely to lead to better pupil motivation according to the theory which we employed in the analysis. It would appear that where teachers intervene to influence attribution, it often has the effect of reinforcing performance goals rather than developing learning goals, which, as we have seen, can not only harm long-term motivation but also make divergent assessment approaches much harder for some children to access. Without reiterating the whole discussion of Chapter 6, the key point here must be for teachers to think about long-term as well as short-term goals and be alert to the issue of power and empowerment in the classroom.

As we have seen, much of the rhetoric of formative assessment involves an assumption that it is the teaching which 'moves on' rather than the learning: teachers are urged to plan the 'next steps' irrespective of whether or not pupils take them (see Table 9.13). And in fact in many of the shorter assessment

Table 9.13   Moving forward

Description	Possible teacher intentions	Possible positive effect for pupil
L T suggests or negotiates with P what to do next	Insight into ways forward for immediate further teaching of individual; refocusing P on curricular goals	Insight into ways to continue working and learning. Deepening of understanding of process/ principle

events that we observed, 'what to do next' was either highly convergent with respect to very short-term improvement ('full stops and capital letters') or actually comprised a 'signing off' move by the teacher ('now do something else'). To be more divergent and effectively formative, it is the pupil who must understand the nature of what it would mean to 'move on'. Our examples in Chapter 7 and Chapter 8 suggest that this can be pursued by designing a structured task and employing focused questioning which is oriented to a relatively short-term task but which nevertheless also communicates the idea that the task, and tasks in general, can be further extended and explored (e.g. Jon and the fur; Justin and Megan re. shape and size).

Table 9.14   Planning

Description	*Possible teacher intentions*	*Possible positive effect for pupil*
M T suggests or negotiates with P what to do next time	Insight into ways forward for planning of group activities	Deepening of understanding of principle/process

Planning what to do *next time* (see Table 9.14) was relatively rarely observed, and the idea of what pupils should do in a similar situation on a future occasion usually remained unsaid and, we suspect, not easily accessible to pupils. The category is relevant to the debate about the extent to which learning in one context can be transferred to another, and with respect to the developing interpretative schemas which pupils employ to 'make sense' of the classroom and the task-within-the-classroom-setting. Thus while the spelling strategies suggested in the example of Caterina's book were very specific, they also implied that resources beyond the teacher and the immediate task could be employed in the pursuit of a task. Similarly, the suggestion that the fur on the bottles in the science experiment could be reversed, indicates both that the task could be extended and that the idea of comparing and contrasting is an important one to employ on future occasions. Certainly, teachers' greater use of this category of interaction, and thereby their sharing of their prospective curricular agenda with pupils, is likely to enhance both convergent and divergent assessment.

Table 9.15   Judging

Description	*Possible teacher intentions*	*Possible positive effect for pupil*
N T assigns mark, grade or summary judgement on the quality of this piece of work or negotiates an agreed one with P	Information for summative assessment; communication of quality criteria; teaching/modelling skills of assessment for self-assessment	Information about present achievement with respect to longer-term goals

Although judgement might be part of a divergent assessment, it is all too often the only constituent element of convergent assessment (see Table 9.15). In formative terms the key point is to provide a justification for the judgement – *why* the score is high or low – along with the score itself, and in the early years in particular, to do so face-to-face.

Table 9.16   Rewarding

Description	Possible teacher intentions	Possible positive effect for pupil
P T rewards or punishes P, or demonstrates approval/disapproval	Improvement or maintenance of relationship with P; enhancement of motivation	Enhanced motivation

Rewarding (see Table 9.16) was very common, especially in schools that had established a token economy of merit marks, smiley faces and the like. The continuum might be seen to stretch from teachers' recognition of the quality of a product, often ipsatively referenced and underlining the pupil's own pride in achievement (the more intrinsic end) to the use of a reward for mere engagement with the task (extrinsic). There has been considerable debate recently about the effects of rewards, to which our discussion in Chapter 6 makes a contribution. The fact that classroom assessment is accomplished in interaction means that it would be odd if it were divorced from normal human expressions of emotion; therefore, teachers' indication of pleasure or displeasure in children's work is inevitable. However, the issue becomes much more problematic with the employment of tokens at the extrinsic end of the continuum. Even the more avid supporters of reward systems warn that negative results accrue when tangible rewards are offered 'without regard to level of performance' (Cameron and Pierce 1996:49).

Conclusions

This book has presented a fine-grained analysis of the everyday practice of classroom assessment of a small number of teachers in infant schools in England. However, the argument has highlighted many points which have a much wider application and might contribute to a better understanding of formative assessment wherever it takes place. Empirical data have enabled us to offer a critique of both assessment theory and the practice that is being advocated by policy makers and pursued by teachers. The argument put forward and the evidence assembled substantiate the central claim that all assessment practices will have an impact on pupils' learning, but that this impact can be negative as well as positive. This is because the interrelation of teaching, learning and assessment is not a set of procedures that can be unilaterally invoked by teachers, but a social interaction which takes place between them and their pupils. In order to understand the relationship, it is therefore necessary not just to take account of what is at stake in terms of cognitive processes, but also to look at other psychological and social issues. We have attempted to do this, and to investigate the positive as well as the negative effects of assessment.

The teachers featured seemed to be operating approaches to teaching and learning derived from both behaviourism and social constructivism. However, social constructivist theory has offered the more productive means of understanding those incidents that appeared to have most potential for promoting teachers' intended consequences. Formative assessment events take place in the here and now, but are both retrospective (in that they often involve reflection on what has gone before, frequently on text produced in the assessment event itself) and prospective (since the teacher has an agenda that is influenced by curricular aims and future plans for the group's learning experiences). The notion of a zone of proximal development offers an explanation of how learning in the here and now looks forward to future development. Formative assessment can then be seen as assessment where teacher and pupil collaborate in the zone to create a best performance. The text that is produced, either by the pupil or by the teacher, becomes a resource which pupils can appropriate and potentially internalize to give rise to more enduring development.

The language used in assessment interaction has a profound effect on children's present and future performance. Question and answer dialogue following the Initiation-Response-Feedback pattern is problematic, with a tendency to become ritualistic and have negative consequences for both learning and social development. When genuine questions are asked, this is less likely to happen.

The formation of an orientation towards performance goals in children, where they are more concerned with gaining favourable judgements from others, is prevalent in schools. It is linked to behaviourist notions of positive reinforcement and can have harmful effects on learning. Classroom assessment provides opportunities for teachers to attend to pupils' motivation, and in particular to foster the learning goals which enable pupils to be more intrinsically motivated.

The concept of a convergent–divergent assessment continuum may prove a useful conceptual framework for teachers in structuring classroom assessment to maximize the possibility that intended consequences are realized. Whilst it is desirable and practical for teachers to balance these approaches according to the nature of the learning task, they should always be alert to the divergent opportunities that offer most potential for learning. An analysis of the range of constituent elements of formative assessment provides the resource which teachers might draw on in accomplishing this aim. We suggest that the most promising approaches include the use of clarifying and metacognitive elicitation, focused critique involving explicit discussion of criteria, the discussion and modelling of methods of self-monitoring, and careful intervention to promote learning goals and intrinsic motivation. However, these heuristic frameworks should be seen as constructions which attempt to orchestrate the positive possibilities of classroom assessment rather than to reduce it to a formula. And in practice, as much clarifying, reflecting and scaffolding is likely to be accomplished in well-structured small group work, as in one-to-one teacher–pupil interaction.

Finally, we return to the notion that assessment is a social interaction, structuring and structured by the many forces at work in the classroom. As such it cannot be divorced from issues of power. Although power is rarely exercised in one direction, access to power in classrooms is not evenly distributed. This has an adverse effect on learning, motivation and children's social development. Although teachers will always be in a particularly powerful position, they can work towards the establishment of *power with* (Kreisberg 1992), that is, the power which is potentially empowering for all members of the class. Attention to issues of language structure, motivation and the appropriation of joint knowledge through classroom interaction seem to be fruitful ways of working towards recursively creating and utilizing *power with*.

Formative assessment has emerged from this book as a complex social and educational practice, and one that needs to be developed further. The analysis of the book has offered several ways in which the good intentions of teachers may be more systematically pursued and accomplished. In turn, it is most likely to be through groups of teachers working on these ideas at local level – testing them out and developing them *in situ* – that improvement of formative classroom assessment will come about.

Appendix

Transcription conventions for classroom interaction

(*)	inaudible (probably one word)
(**)	inaudible phrase
(***)	longer inaudible passage (e.g. sentence)
(*Tuesday)	inaudible word, 'Tuesday' suggested by transcriber
-	short pause
disapp\	incomplete word
<u>these</u>	word emphasized
Bold	word pronounced with lengthened vowel and diphthong sounds
COME HERE	words said very loudly compared to other utterances of this speaker
=	rapid change of turn of speakers (used at end of the utterance of one speaker and beginning of next speaker's utterance)
>It's mine<	simultaneous speech
Italics	non-textual material (stage directions)
the/cat/sat	word-by-word enunciation with flat intonation (e.g. emergent reader)
T	teacher
T2	second teacher
C	unidentified child
Cs	unidentified children
C1, C2	first child, second child etc.
~	rising intonation, slowing (invitation to other speaker to complete sentence)
9:42	time reading from video camera
. . . [ ] . . .	a few seconds of transcript omitted – extraneous material (e.g. interruption by another child) not relevant to point discussed in the chapter

Transcription of letters and sounds

Letter sounds are transcribed using the letter itself in lower case. Letter names are transcribed as follows:

A	=	ay	J	=	jay	S	=	ess
B	=	bee	K	=	kay	T	=	tee
C	=	see	L	=	ell	U	=	ewe
D	=	dee	M	=	emm	V	=	vee
E	=	ee	N	=	enn	W	=	double-ewe
F	=	eff	O	=	oh	X	=	exe
G	=	gee	P	=	pee	Y	=	why
H	=	aitch	Q	=	queue	Z	=	zed
I	=	aye	R	=	are			

References

Alexander, R., Rose, J. and Woodhead, C. (1992) *Curriculum Organisation and Classroom Practice in Primary Schools*. London: Department of Education and Science.

Ames, C. (1984) Competitive, co-operative and individualistic goal structures: a motivational analysis, in R. Ames and C. Ames (eds) *Research on Motivation in Education* (Volume 1). Orlando, FL: Academic Press.

Askew, M., Bliss, J. and Macrae, S. (1996) Scaffolding school knowledge through discourse: difficulties and issues, paper presented at the Annual Meeting of the American Educational Research Association, New York, April 1996.

Ball, S. (1990) *Markets, Morality and Equality in Education*. London: Tufnell Press.

Barnes, D. (1976) *From Curriculum to Communication*. Harmondsworth: Penguin.

Bennett, N., Desforges, C., Cockburn, A. and Wilkinson, B. (1984) *The Quality of Pupil Learning Experiences*. London: Lawrence Erlbaum.

Berlak, H., Newman, F., Adams, E., Archibald, D., Burgess, T., Raven, J. and Romberg, T. (1992) *Toward a New Science of Educational Testing and Assessment*. New York: State University of New York Press.

Bernstein, B. (1996) *Pedagogy, Symbolic Control and Identity: Theory, Research, Critique*. London: Taylor and Francis.

Beveridge, M. (ed.) (1982) *Children Thinking Through Language*. London: Edward Arnold.

Black, P. (1993) Formative and summative assessment by teachers. *Studies in Science Education*, 21: 49–97.

Black, P. (1994) Performance assessment and accountability: the experience in England and Wales. *Educational Evaluation and Policy Analysis*, 16(2): 191–203.

Black, P. (1995) Can teachers use assessment to improve learning? *British Journal of Curriculum and Assessment*, 5(2): 7–11.

Bloom, B. (ed.) (1965) *Taxonomy of Educational Objectives: The Classification of Educational Goals. Vol. 1: Cognitive domain*. London: Longman.

Bloom, B. (1971) Mastery Learning, in J.H. Block (ed.) *Mastery Learning: Theory and Practice*. New York: Holt, Rinehart and Winston.

Bloome, D. and Willett, J. (1991) Toward a micropolitics of classroom interaction, in J. Blase (ed.) *The Politics of Life in Schools*. Newbury Park, CA: Sage Publications.

Bourdieu, P. (1973) Cultural reproduction and social reproduction, in R. Brown (ed.) *Knowledge, Education and Cultural Change*. London: Tavistock.

Bourdieu, P. (1977) *Outline of a Theory of Practice*. Cambridge: Cambridge University Press.

Bourdieu, P. (1990) *In Other Words: Essays Towards a Reflexive Sociology*. Cambridge: Polity Press.

Bracey, G. (1987) Measurement driven instruction: catchy phrase, dangerous practice. *Phi Delta Kappan*, 68: 683–6.

Broadfoot, P. *et al.* (1988) *Records of Achievement: Report of the National Evaluation of Pilot Schemes*. London: HMSO.

Broadfoot, P. and Osborn, M. with Gilly, M. and Bücher, A. (1993) *Perceptions of Teaching: Primary School Teachers in England and France*. London: Cassell.

Brown, A. and Ferrara, R. (1985) Diagnosing zones of proximal development, in J. Wertsch (ed.) *Culture, Communication and Cognition: Vygotskian Perspectives*. Cambridge: Cambridge University Press.

Brown, A., Campione, J., Webber, L. and McGilly, K. (1992) Interactive learning environments: a new look at assessment and instruction, in B. Gifford and M. O'Connor, *Changing Assessments: Alternative Views of Aptitude, Achievement and Instruction*. Boston, MA: Kluwer.

Brown, S. and McIntyre, D. (1993) *Making Sense of Teaching*. Buckingham: Open University Press.

Browne, A. (1993) *Helping Children to Write*. London: Paul Chapman.

Bruner, J. (1985) Vygotsky: a historical and conceptual perspective, in J. Wertsch (ed.) *Culture, Communication and Cognition: Vygotskian Perspectives*. Cambridge: Cambridge University Press.

Bruner, J. (1986) *Actual Minds, Possible Worlds*. London: Harvard University Press.

Cameron, J. and Pierce, W. (1994) Reinforcement, reward and intrinsic motivation: a meta-analysis. *Review of Educational Research*, 64: 363–423.

Cameron, J. and Pierce, W.D. (1996) The debate about rewards and intrinsic motivation: protests and accusations do not alter the results. *Review of Educational Research*, 66(1): 39–51.

Central Advisory Council for Education (England) (1967) *Children and their Primary Schools*. London: HMSO.

Charlot, B., Bautier, E. and Rochex, J-Y. (1992) *Ecole et Savoir dans les banlieues . . . et aillieurs*. Paris: Armand Colin.

Cicourel, A. *et. al.* (1974) *Language Use and School Performance*. New York: Academic Press.

Clarricoates, K. (1987) Child culture at school: a clash between gendered worlds?, in A. Pollard (ed.) *Children and their Primary Schools*. Lewes: Falmer.

Cole, M. (1985) The zone of proximal development: where culture and cognition create each other, in J. Wertsch (ed.) *Culture, Communication and Cognition: Vygotskian Perspectives*. Cambridge: Cambridge University Press.

Cole, M. (1996) *Cultural Psychology: A Once and Future Discipline*. Cambridge, MA: Harvard University Press.

Collins, J. (1993) Determination and contradiction: an appreciation and critique of the work of Pierre Bourdieu on language and education, in C. Calhoun, E. LiPuma and M. Postone (eds) *Bourdieu: Critical Perspectives*. Cambridge: Polity Press.

Cooper, B. (1992) Testing National Curriculum mathematics: some critical comments on the treatment of 'real' contexts for mathematics. *The Curriculum Journal*, 3: 231–43.

Cooper, B. (1994) Authentic testing in mathematics? The boundary between everyday and mathematical knowledge in National Curriculum testing in English schools. *Assessment in Education*, 1(2): 143–66.

Cooper, B. (forthcoming) Using Bernstein and Bourdieu to understand difficulties with 'realistic' mathematics testing: an exploratory study. *International Journal of Qualitative Studies in Education*.

Cordon, R. (1992) The role of the teacher, in K. Norman, *Thinking Voices*. London: Hodder & Stoughton.

Covington, M. (1984) The motive for self-worth, in R.E. Ames and C. Ames (eds) *Research on Motivation in Education* (Volume 1). Orlando, FL: Academic Press.

Cowan, J. (1994) Stimulated video-recall. *Educational Action Research*, 2(1): 141–2.

Crooks, T. (1988) The impact of classroom evaluation on students. *Review of Educational Research*, 5(4): 438–81.

Davies, A. (1989) *The Human Element: Three Essays in Political Psychology*. Harmondsworth: Penguin.

Davies, B. (1993) Beyond dualism and towards multiple identities, in L. Christian-Smith (ed.) *Texts of Desire: Essays on Fiction, Femininity and Schooling*. London: Falmer.

Dearing, R. (1994) *The National Curriculum and its Assessment: Final Report*. London: School Curriculum and Assessment Authority.

Donaldson, M. (1978) *Children's Minds*. London: Fontana.

Dweck, C. (1989) Motivation, in A. Lesgold and R. Glaser, *Foundations for a Psychology of Education*. Hillsdale, NJ: Erlbaum.

Edwards, A. (1992) Teacher talk and pupil competence, in K. Norman, *Thinking Voices*. London: Hodder & Stoughton.

Edwards, A. and Furlong, V. (1978) *The Language of Teaching*. London: Heinemann.

Edwards, A. and Westgate, D. (1987) *Investigating Classroom Talk*. London: Falmer Press.

Edwards, D. and Mercer, N. (1987) *Common Knowledge: the Development of Understanding in the Classroom*. London: Methuen.

Elliott, E. and Dweck, C. (1988) Goals: an approach to motivation and achievement. *Journal of Personality and Social Psychology*, 54(1): 5–12.

Eraut, M. (1994) *Developing Professional Knowledge and Competence*. London: Falmer Press.

Evans, L., Packwood, S., St.J. Neill, R. and Campbell, R. (1994) *The Meaning of Infant Teachers' Work*. London: Routledge.

Feuerstein, R. (1979) *The Dynamic Assessment of Retarded Performers: The Learning Potential Assessment Device, Theory, Instruments and Techniques*. Baltimore, MD: University Park Press.

Forman, E. and Cazden, C. (1985) Exploring Vygotskian perspectives in education: the cognitive value of peer interaction, in J. Wertsch (ed.) *Culture, Communication and Cognition: Vygotskian Perspectives*. Cambridge: Cambridge University Press.

French, P. and MacLure, M. (1983) Teachers' questions, pupils' answers: an investigation of questions and answers in the infant classroom, in M. Stubbs and H. Hillier, *Readings on Language, Schools and Classrooms*. London: Methuen.

Gardner, H. (1993) *The Unschooled Mind: How Children Think and How Schools Should Teach*. London: Fontana.

Garfinkel, H. (1967) *Studies in Ethnomethodology*. Englewood Cliffs, NJ: Prentice-Hall.

Giddens, A. (1979) *Central Problems in Social Theory*. London: Macmillan.

Gifford, B. and O'Connor, M. (eds) (1992) *Future Assessments: Changing Views of Aptitude, Achievement and Instruction*. Boston, MA: Kluwer.

Gipps, C. (1994) *Beyond Testing: Towards a Theory of Educational Assessment*. London: Falmer Press.

Gipps, C., Brown, M., McCallum, B. and McAlister, S. (1995) *Intuition or Evidence? Teachers and National Assessment of Seven-Year-Olds*. Buckingham: Open University Press.

Giroux, H. (1988) Critical theory and the politics of culture and voice: rethinking the discourse of educational research, in R. Sherman and R. Webb, *Qualitative Research in Education: Focus and Methods*. Lewes: Falmer.

Goodman, K.S. (1969) Analysis of oral reading miscue: applied psycholinguistics. *Reading Research Quarterly*, Fall 1969, reprinted in K. Goodman (1982) *Language and Literacy*, Vol. 1. Boston, MA: Routledge and Kegan Paul.

Goodman, K.S. (1973) *Miscue Analysis: Applications to Reading Instruction*. Princeton, NJ: Educational Resources Information Centre (ERIC).

Goodman, K. S. (1976) Miscue analysis: theory and reality in reading, in: J.E. Merritt (ed.) *New Horizons in Reading* – Proceedings of the 5th IRA World Congress on Reading 1976; reprinted in K. Goodman (1982) *Language and Literacy, Vol. 1*. Boston, MA: Routledge and Kegan Paul.

Goodson, I. (1997) The educational researcher as public intellectual: modernist dinosaur or post-modern prospect?, paper presented at the Annual Conference of the British Educational Research Association, University of York, 11–14 September.

Graue, M.E. (1993) Integrating theory and practice through instructional assessment. *Educational Assessment*, 1(4): 283–309.

Gray, J. and Wilcox, B. (1995) *Good School, Bad School*. Buckingham: Open University Press.

Grice, H. (1989) *Studies in the Way of Words*. Cambridge, MA: Harvard University Press.

Hargreaves, A. (1994) *Changing Teachers, Changing Times: Teachers' Work and Culture in the Postmodern Age*. London: Cassell.

Harlen, W. (1996) Editorial. *The Curriculum Journal*, (7)2: 129–35.

Harlen, W. and James, M. (1996) The impact of assessment on learning, paper presented at the Annual Meeting of the American Educational Research Association, New York, April.

Harlen, W. and Qualter, A. (1991) Issues in SAT Development and the Practice of Teacher Assessment. *Cambridge Journal of Education*, 21(2): 141–52.

Harlen, W., Gipps, C., Broadfoot, P. and Nuttall, D. (1992) Assessment and the improvement of education. *The Curriculum Journal*, 3(3): 215–30.

Her Majesty's Inspectorate (1991) *Assessment, Recording and Reporting. A Report by HM Inspectorate on the First Year, 1989–90*. London: HMSO.

Kreisberg, S. (1992) *Transforming Power: Domination, Empowerment and Education*. New York: State University of New York Press.

Leont'ev, A. (1981) *Problems of the Development of the Mind*. Moscow: Progress Publishers.

Lepper, M.R. and Hodell, M. (1989) Intrinsic motivation in the classroom, in C. Ames and R. Ames, *Research on Motivation in Education* (Volume 3). San Diego, CA: Academic Press.

Licht, B. and Dweck, C. (1985) Sex differences in achievement orientations: consequences for academic choices and attainments, in English Centre, *The English Curriculum: Gender*. London: Inner London Education Authority.

Mehan, H. (1979) *Learning Lessons: Social Organisation in the Classroom*. Cambridge, MA: Harvard University Press.

Modbury County Primary School (1990) *National Curriculum Record Book*. Modbury, Devon: Modbury Marketing Ltd.

Murphy, R. and Torrance, H. (1988) *The Changing Face of Educational Assessment*. Milton Keynes: Open University Press.

Newman, D., Griffin, P. and Cole, M. (1989) *The Construction Zone: Working for Cognitive Change in School*. Cambridge: Cambridge University Press.

Nias, J. (1989) *Primary Teachers Talking: A Study of Teaching as Work*. London: Routledge.

Nicholls, J. (1989) *The Competitive Ethos and Democratic Education*. Cambridge, MA: Harvard University Press.

Nisbet, J. (1993) Introduction, in *Curriculum Reform: Assessment in Question*. Paris: OECD.

Norman, K. (ed.) (1992) *Thinking Voices*. London: Hodder & Stoughton.

Parsons, T. (1959) The school as a social system. *Harvard Educational Review*, 29: 297–318.

Pateman, T. (forthcoming 1998) Psychoanalysis and Socratic education, in S. Appel (ed.) *Psychoanalysis and Education*. New Zealand: Bergin and Garvey.

Pennycuick, D. and Murphy, R. (1988) *The Impact of Graded Tests*. London: Falmer Press.

Pole, C. (1993) *Assessing and Recording Achievement*. Buckingham: Open University Press.

Pollard, A. with Filer, A. (1996) *The Social World of Children's Learning*. London: Cassell.

Pollard, A., Broadfoot, P., Croll, P., Osborn, M. and Abbott, D. (1994) *Changing English*

Primary Schools: The Impact of the Education Reform Act at Key Stage One. London: Cassell.

Popham, J. (1978) *Criterion-referenced Measurement*. Englewood Cliffs, NJ: Prentice-Hall.

Popham, J. (1987) The merits of measurement-driven instruction. *Phi Delta Kappan*, 68: 679–82.

Pryor, J. (1995) Assessment ticksheets: don't throw out the baby! *British Journal of Curriculum and Assessment*, 5(2): 15–17.

Resnick, L. and Resnick, D. (1992) Assessing the thinking curriculum, in B. Gifford and M. O'Connor (eds) *Future Assessments: Changing Views of Aptitude, Achievement and Instruction*. Boston, MA: Kluwer.

Sadler, D.R. (1989) Formative assessment and the design of instructional systems. *Instructional Science*, 18: 119–44.

Schools Curriculum and Assessment Authority (1996) *Baseline Assessment and Value Added*. London: SCAA.

School Examinations and Assessment Council (1990) *A Guide to Teacher Assessment – Pack A – Teacher Assessment in the Classroom*. London: SEAC.

Sharp, R. and Green, A. (1975) *Education and Social Control*. London: Routledge and Kegan Paul.

Shepard, L. (1991a) Will national tests improve student learning? *Phi Delta Kappan*, 71: 232–8.

Shepard, L. (1991b) Psychometricians' beliefs about learning. *Educational Researcher*, 20(7): 2–16.

Simon, A. and Boyer, F. (eds) (1967 and 1970) Mirrors for Behaviour – Summary Volume. Research into Better Schools Inc: cited in Barnes (1976).

Sinclair, J. (1982) *The Structure of Teacher Talk*. Birmingham: English Language Research.

Sinclair, J. and Coulthard, R. (1975) *Towards an Analysis of Discourse*. London: Oxford University Press.

Stenhouse, L. (1982) The conduct, analysis and reporting of case study in educational research and evaluation, reprinted in R. Murphy and H. Torrance (eds) (1987) *Evaluating Education: Issues and Methods*. London: Paul Chapman Publishing.

Stierer, B. (1995) Making a statement: an analysis of teacher pupil talk within child conferences in the Primary Language Record. *The Curriculum Journal*, (6)3: 343–62.

Task Group on Assessment and Testing (1987) *A Report*. London: DES.

Task Group on Assessment and Testing (1988) *A Report*. London: DES.

Torrance, H. (1986) Expanding school based assessment: issues, problems and future possibilities. *Research Papers in Education*, 1(1): 48–59.

Torrance, H. (1989) Theory, practice and politics in the development of assessment. *Cambridge Journal of Education*, 19(2): 183–91.

Torrance, H. (1991) Records of achievement and formative assessment: some complexities of practice, in R. Stake,(ed.) *Advances in Program Evaluation: Using Assessment to Reform Education*. Greenwich, CT: JAI Press.

Torrance, H. (1993) Formative assessment: some theoretical problems and empirical questions. *Cambridge Journal of Education*, 23(3): 333–43.

Torrance, H. (1995) The role of assessment in educational reform, in H. Torrance (ed.) *Evaluating Authentic Assessment*. Buckingham: Open University Press.

Torrance, H. (1997) Assessment, accountability and standards: using assessment to control the reform of schooling, in A.H. Halsey, H. Lauder, P. Brown and A. Stuart-Wells (eds) *Education: Culture, Economy and Society*. Oxford: Oxford University Press.

Torrance, H. and Pryor, J. (1996) *Teacher Assessment at Key Stage 1: Accomplishing Assessment in the Classroom (The 'TASK' Project)*. Final Report to the ESRC.

Tunstall, P. and Gipps, C. (1996a) How does your teacher help you to make your work better? Children's understanding of formative assessment. *The Curriculum Journal*, (7): 2.

Tunstall, P. and Gipps, C. (1996b) Teacher feedback to young children in formative assessment: a typology. *British Educational Research Journal*, 22(4): 389–404.

Urdan, T. and Maehr, M. (1995) Beyond a two-goal theory of motivation and achievement: a case for social goals. *Review of Educational Research*, 65: 213–43.

Vispoel, W. and Austin, J. (1995) Success and failure in Junior High School: a critical incident approach to understanding students' attributional beliefs. *American Educational Research Journal*, 32(2): 377–412.

Vygotsky, L. (1978) *Mind in Society*. Cambridge, MA: Harvard University Press.

Vygotsky, L. (1986) *Thought and Language*. Cambridge, MA: MIT Press.

Walkerdine, V. (1988) *The Mastery of Reason*. London: Routledge.

Walkerdine, V. and the Girls and Mathematics Unit (1989) *Counting Girls Out*. London: Virago.

Weiner, B. (1984) Principles for a theory of motivation and their application within an attributional framework, in R.E. Ames and C. Ames, *Research on Motivation in Education*. Orlando, FL: Academic Press.

Wells, G. (1992) The centrality of talk in education, in K. Norman, *Thinking Voices*. London: Hodder & Stoughton.

Wertsch, James (ed.) (1985) *Culture, Communication and Cognition: Vygotskian Perspectives*. Cambridge: Cambridge University Press.

Weston, P. (ed.) (1990) *Assessment, progression and purposeful learning in Europe: a study for the Commissions of the European Community*. Slough: NFER.

Wiggins, G. (1989) A true test: toward more authentic and equitable assessment. *Phi Delta Kappan*, 70: 703–13.

Wiliam, D. and Black, P. (1996) Meanings and consequences: a basis for distinguishing formative and summative functions of assessment. *British Educational Research Journal*, 22(3): 537–48.

Willes, M. (1983) *Children into Pupils: A Study of Language in Early Schooling*. London: Routledge and Kegan Paul.

Willis, D. (1992) Caught in the act: using the rank scale to address problems of delicacy, in M. Coulthard, *Advances in Spoken Discourse Analysis*. London: Routledge.

Wong, E.D. (1995) Challenges confronting the researcher/teacher: conflicts of purpose and conduct. *Educational Researcher*, 24(4): 22–8.

Wood, D. (1992) Teaching talk: how modes of teacher talk affect pupil participation, in K. Norman, *Thinking Voices*. London: Hodder & Stoughton.

Wood, D., Bruner, J. and Ross, G. (1976) The role of the tutor in problem solving. *Journal of Child Psychology and Psychiatry*, 17: 89–100.

Wood, R. (1987) *Measurement and Assessment in Education and Psychology*. London: Falmer Press.

Index